THE DIGITAL FINANCIAL
REVOLUTION IN CHINA

THE DIGITAL FINANCIAL REVOLUTION IN CHINA

Edited by

DAVID DOLLAR
YIPING HUANG

BROOKINGS INSTITUTION PRESS
Washington, D.C.

Copyright © 2022
THE BROOKINGS INSTITUTION
1775 Massachusetts Avenue, N.W.
Washington, D.C. 20036
www.brookings.edu

Library of Congress Control Number: 2022933729
ISBN 9780815739555 (pbk)
ISBN 9780815739562 (ebook)

9 8 7 6 5 4 3 2 1

Typeset in Minion Pro

Composition by Westchester Publishing Services

Contents

Acknowledgments

This book is the result of the second joint research project between the National School of Development (NSD) at Peking University and The Brookings Institution. Following publication of *China 2049: Economic Challenges of a Rising Global Power* (Brookings Institution Press and Peking University Press), the two sides decided to work on a new project to document and review the exciting development of digital finance in China.

This time, the Institute of Digital Finance (IDF) of the Peking University put together a large team of Chinese experts to work with American colleagues.

We would like to acknowledge general financial support by the NSD, the Huifu, and CreditEase for this joint research project.

The IDF, established in 2015, is a leading research institution in the field of digital finance. During the past years, the Institute received generous support, including funding, data, and view exchanges from the China Finance 40 Forum, the Ant Group, CreditEase, LuFax, GLP Finance, the China National Social Science Foundation (project #18ZDA091), and many others to conduct a wide range of research, which formed the basis for some findings of this joint work. None of these organizations or their representatives, however, were involved in the research.

David Dollar and Yiping Huang

THE DIGITAL FINANCIAL
REVOLUTION IN CHINA

1

Understanding China's Digital Financial Innovation and Regulation

DAVID DOLLAR and YIPING HUANG

THE DIGITAL FINANCIAL REVOLUTION IN THE MAKING

On the evening of November 3, 2020, about thirty-six hours before the digital financial giant Ant Group's planned initial public offering (IPO), the Shanghai Stock Exchange announced its decision to suspend the listing. This immediately sent shockwaves across the global capital markets as investors struggled to comprehend the meaning of this unexpected development. Stopping an IPO just one day before is unusual, but stopping the largest IPO ever is another matter altogether. Ant also quickly suspended its dual listing in the Hong Kong Stock Exchange, citing new uncertainties in future financial performance due to forthcoming regulatory change. It became clear that the regulatory environment for the digital financial industry was about to experience a sea change, although the details had yet to be announced. This extraordinary development illustrated the awkward fact that even though China is already a global leader in several business areas of the digital financial industry, such as mobile payment, online investment, and digital lending, its regulatory framework is not yet well developed.

What are the key takeaways from the Chinese experience of digital financial innovation and regulation? To address this central question, Peking University's Institute of Digital Finance and the Brookings Institution assembled a group of Chinese and American experts to carefully analyze

China's digital financial development and draw important policy implications. First, this book depicts the current state of China's digital financial industry and explains the key factors contributing to its impressive rise. Second, it documents both business successes, such as mobile payment, and failures, such as peer-to-peer (P2P) lending. Third, it looks at the implications of some new developments, including digitization of commercial banks and issuance of the central bank digital currency (CBDC), for domestic and international financial landscapes. Finally, it assesses the role of the regulatory policy in the formation of the digital financial development trajectory in China and tries to shed some light on what is to come.

In this book, digital finance refers to the application of digital technology, such as the internet, big data, artificial intelligence (AI), and cloud computing, to financial products and processes. It covers both technology companies and financial institutions applying technology to improve financial services. These businesses are sometimes also called financial technology (fintech) or internet finance. This book prefers to use the "more balanced" term *digital finance* as, in practice, both fintech and internet finance focus more on technology companies' involvement in financial services.

The main findings of this book may be summarized as follows. During the past decade, the Chinese digital financial industry experienced an extraordinary pace of development. While most digital financial business models were initially started in the United States or the United Kingdom, China now leads in several areas, at least in terms of customer bases and transaction volumes. The People's Bank of China (PBC) will probably be the first major central bank to issue its own CBDC, e-CNY. The rapid digital financial development in China is, to a large extent, attributable to wide gaps in traditional financial markets, where most low-income households (LIHs) and small and medium-size enterprises (SMEs) were financially underserved. A central story of digital finance is the application of digital technology to assist in risk management. The most distinctive feature of many Chinese digital financial businesses is financial inclusion.

Digital technology brings a wide range of innovations to the financial sector. The "long-tail" feature, for instance, makes it possible to reach gigantic numbers of customers simultaneously at a low cost. This attribute potentially raises a question about the widely accepted assumption of "decreasing return to scale" in conventional economics. Today, each of the leading mobile payment service providers has around 1 billion users. AI and cloud computing allow the processing of financial models at a scale and speed never seen before, enabling timely individualized services. The big-data-supported credit risk assessment model, invented by large technology (big-tech) companies, not only is more reliable in predicting loan default but also supports lending to the unbanked mass. Currently, the lenders can dispatch loans to tens of millions of LIH and SME borrowers every year. The nonperforming loan ratios of such big-tech credit are generally lower than those of similar loans granted by traditional banks.

More broadly, digital finance may transform the financial and macroeconomic landscapes. The emergence of digital financial intermediation, for instance, also reduced the value of banks' physical branches. The total number of bank branches has been steadily declining since 2016. Most of the large banks have already started to lay off redundant employees. Quantitative measures show that regional gaps of digital financial services were substantially reduced. Several studies find that digital finance supports innovation, creates jobs, and improves income distribution, especially for LIHs and villagers. The big-tech credit weakens the linkage between asset price and bank loan (i.e., the so-called financial accelerator) by adopting the big-data-supported credit risk assessment approach. Monetary policy's transmission mechanism of big-tech credit is generally faster than that of bank lending. And, digital finance may also bring the regional markets closer together, such as e-commerce and logistics facilitated by mobile payment, which could improve macroeconomic stability and thus price stability. These are just some of the examples of the macroeconomic and macrofinancial implications of digital finance, although the complete picture is still being drawn.

The exact role played by financial regulation in China's digital financial development is a controversial subject. On a positive note, regulators adopted a more tolerant attitude toward digital financial innovation. It is, however, unclear whether this was because regulators saw the value of financial inclusion in such innovation or because they were not sure how to deal with this innovation. In any case, the digital financial institutions were allowed sufficient space and time to try out the new financial products and processes. Without this accommodation, it would have been difficult for big-tech companies to start and grow payment and lending businesses. Both of these are now successful models. On a negative note, the absence of regulation has led to the so-called barbaric growth and, in some cases, accumulation of significant financial and social risks. P2P lending collapsed abruptly, after a short period of dramatic rise, leaving behind significant financial and social risks.

The unexpected suspension of Ant's IPO probably marked the turning point in digital financial regulation. Regulators are now racing to construct a comprehensive regulatory framework for the digital financial industry. In 2015, ten government departments led by the PBC released a document outlining the official position on digital financial development and regulation. The regulatory authorities then issued a series of policies governing digital financial businesses, including policies on nonbank mobile payment in 2015, on P2P lending in 2016, and on internet bank loans in 2020. But a number of questions still need to be properly addressed. First, how should digital financial businesses be brought under a uniform regulatory framework that avoids excessive arbitrage behavior but leaves enough space for innovation? Second, since the traditional policy methods and tools might not be adequate for regulating the digital financial industry, how should digital technology be applied to assist regulation? Third, what is the right strategy for regulating the digital financial holding companies, especially the building of digital Chinese walls among different businesses within them? Fourth, what is the optimal data policy for ownership, rights, standards, pricing, and exchange? And finally, what are the best criteria for judging monopolies, and what are the priorities of antimonopoly policy in the digital financial industry? Answers to these questions should help shape the future digital financial regulatory framework.

The Chinese digital financial revolution is still in the making but has already generated important global implications. First, it offers an effective model for promoting financial inclusion. With the assistance of digital technology, financial institutions, for the first time in history, can provide financial services to gigantic numbers of customers in a short time frame. Second, digital technology is rapidly changing the global financial landscape. The Chinese experience offers an important case for understanding digital financial innovation and, especially, dynamic interactions between the new digital financial players and traditional financial institutions, which are also undergoing significant digital transformation. And third, the current global digital financial market may be divided into three parts: the United States, China, and the rest of the world. A big challenge is how to integrate these three markets, or at least form some kind of cooperation among them, at both the business and regulatory levels.

A NEW MODEL OF FINANCIAL INCLUSION

China's digital financial industry began in late 2004, when the e-commerce company Alibaba, of which Ant was a spin-off company, launched an online payment service called Alipay. Modeled on PayPal, Alipay was initially created to facilitate online transactions on Alibaba's e-commerce platform Taobao. The digital financial industry, however, did not see rapid growth until mid-2013, when Alibaba launched its online money market fund Yu'ebao, which allows individuals to invest small amounts of money from a mobile phone app. The company, Tianhong, which helped invest Yu'ebao's funds, quickly rose from an average-size fund to the largest in the country within one year. Later on, 2013 was widely recognized as the first year of digital financial development in China.

Today, China is one of the most vibrant digital financial markets in the world. In other active markets such as in the United States and the United Kingdom, the word *fintech* often refers to blockchain technology, cryptocurrency, cross-border payment, and CBDC. In China, the term *fintech* or *digital finance* is most likely related to providing payment, lending, insurance, and investment services to the mass market. Therefore, the Chinese digital financial industry has a distinguishing feature of financial inclusion. According to the Peking University Digital Financial Inclusion Index of China, in 2011, digital financial businesses concentrated mainly in a small number of cities on the southeast coast. In 2019, while the southeast coast still led, the gaps between east and west and between south and north were significantly reduced (Guo and Wang, chapter 2, this volume). This implies that the lagging regions were quickly catching up during those years. This is exactly what inclusion means.

Promotion of financial inclusion is a global challenge. The United Nations designated 2005 as the "year of microcredit," calling on member countries to make serious efforts to provide market-based and commercially viable financial services to disadvantaged customers. The Chinese government made various policy efforts, such as the creation of microcredit companies and the establishment of special business units within financial institutions. In general, however, little progress was made. There is a widely recognized rule in the financial industry known as the 20–80 rule, which states that, often, the top 20 percent of clients, including both the most profitable companies and the wealthiest households, contribute 80 percent of the revenues. Serving the remaining 80 percent of clients, mainly LIHs and SMEs, is practically more difficult and financially less profitable. The main difficulties of promoting financial inclusion are reaching the potential customers and assessing their financial risks.

In 2016, the Chinese government published the five-year plan for promotion of financial inclusion between 2016 and 2020. Over the next five years, China made impressive progress in this area. Much of the progress, however, occurred in the digital financial industry, which was not a priority identified by the five-year plan. The surprising success in financial inclusion was due to digital technology, which includes big-tech platforms, big data, AI, blockchain, and cloud computing. If properly applied, digital technology could multiply business scale, increase efficiency, improve user experience, reduce costs, and control risks. One important feature of digital technology is its "long tail," which means that once a big-tech platform, such as Alipay or WeChat, is constructed, the marginal cost of adding additional users is almost zero. The combination of big data, AI, and cloud computing enables digital financial institutions to provide individualized financial services to the mass market at a rapid speed. By leveraging both scale and scope economies, big-tech platforms can cover extensive markets. In fact, anyone with a smartphone with a telecom signal, no matter where one is in China, can enjoy the same kinds of financial services as those in major metropolitan cities.

In retrospect, three factors contributed to the rapid emergence of China's digital financial industry: technology, market demand, and regulation. The first contributing factor was rapid development and wide adoption of digital technology. One reason Alipay was not actively used before 2013 was that it was rather inconvenient to use Alipay on desktop computers. Smartphones changed that. Rapid development of digital technological capability in China was a result of combined efforts by both the government and the private sector. The government made massive investments in digital infrastructure across the country. The penetration rates of digital technology increased significantly. The digital infrastructure enabled individuals and enterprises to connect to the big-tech platforms from almost anywhere in the country. The private sector also played a role. In 2011, Alipay could handle only about 300 transactions per second, but in 2019 this number reached well above 300,000. New digital financial solutions are seen to be able to fill the financial inclusion gaps in emerging economies, such as the gender gap, the gap between the rich and the poor, and the gap between rural and urban.

The second contributing factor was large, unsatisfied market demand, especially that by LIHs and SMEs. Serving LIHs and SMEs is difficult owing to problems of reaching the customers and managing the risks. But it is even more difficult in China because of repressive financial policies (i.e., government interventions in the financial system). The existence of underserved LIHs and SMEs gave rise to the vibrant informal financial activities. The same is true for digital financial businesses. Since most Chinese individuals did not have any means of payment other than cash, where the mobile payment service was created, it was warmly embraced by the market. Since only about 20 percent of the SMEs were able to borrow from banks, it is not difficult to imagine the value of digital lending for those unbanked LIHs and SMEs. The same is true for many online investment products. In most cases, the digital financial products were created to fill gaps, not just to improve efficiency. This is why the mobile payment service spread rapidly in China but not in the United States (Klein, chapter 3, this volume).

The third contributing factor was the relatively accommodative regulatory environment. In fact, for quite a while, regulation was absent for many digital financial businesses. Alipay started business at the end of 2004 but did not obtain an official license until 2011. The first P2P platform, PPDai, came online in 2007, but the regulators did not announce the first regulatory policy framework until mid-2016. There were probably two reasons regulators did not rush to bring these businesses under regulation. First, many government officials saw the value of financial inclusion in digital financial businesses and so were reluctant to disrupt such activities. And second, China's financial regulatory framework is segregated by industry and focuses on financial institutions. The working rule of this system is "whoever issues the license should be responsible for regulation." In a way, digital financial companies fell into the gap area, in which no specific regulator was responsible. Regulatory "tolerance" is a double-edged sword, as it allowed the sector to grow rapidly without any constraint but, at the same time, also led to quick accumulation of financial risks.

INNOVATIVE DIGITAL FINANCIAL BUSINESSES

Development of digital financial businesses has been quite uneven across four different potential product lines. First, the most successful business is mobile payment. The two leading mobile payment service providers each have about 1 billion online users. In 2017, they rolled out the Quick Response code payment to cover close to 100 million offline shops and street vendors. Thanks to the ecosystems built around them, mobile payment services are now indispensable in most users' daily lives. Second, the other quite successful business is digital lending, although stories within this sector vary: P2P lending already failed, the big-tech credit is a huge success so far, and digital supply chain (DSC) financing is emerging and looks promising. Banks are also quickly moving their transactions online. Third, other businesses, such as insurance and investment, have yet to see a significant breakthrough, although there is wide variation within these sectors. Online investment vehicles such as Yu'ebao found immediate success by attracting numerous small-dollar transactions from retail investors. The robo-advising business, though quite promising, has not seen significant advancement. And fourth, the PBC is probably the first major central bank to issue its CBDC, e-CNY.

In addition to attracting large numbers of customers, the big-tech platforms also serve as important vehicles for collecting digital footprints left by customers when using social media, e-commerce, or search services. The ecosystems created by big-tech platforms are also important parts of the digital financial infrastructure; they not only increase customer stickiness to the platforms but also broaden the scope of data collection. Big data can then be analyzed for various digital financial businesses. Direct sale of financial products that take advantage of big-data analysis (e.g., insurance products) increases financial efficiency by better matching supply with demand. Again, the robo-advising business applies AI, cloud computing, and quantitative finance methods to big data and yields individualized investment advice to the mass market (Zhuo Huang, chapter 7, this volume). This involves an important step of satisfying the "know your client" requirement through big-data analysis, a key purpose of which is to determine investors' risk appetite, including their abilities to understand and withstand financial risks.

One of the most important innovations using big-data analysis is probably in big-tech credit, in the form of the new big-tech credit risk management framework (Yiping Huang, chapter 6, this volume). This framework contains two main elements: the big-tech platforms and associated ecosystems, and big-data-supported credit risk assessment. The big-tech platforms and associated ecosystems have at least three important roles in this framework. First, taking advantage of the long-tail feature, the big-tech lenders rapidly recruit large numbers of customers at nearly zero marginal cost. This helps overcome the common difficulty of customer acquisition. Second, the big-tech lenders collect digital footprints left by customers on the platforms. Big data may then be used for two purposes: to monitor customers' online activities and behavior in real time and to support credit risk assessment. Three, since all customers operate on the big-tech platforms and associated ecosystems, the big-tech lenders can design incentive schemes to manage loan repayment.

The big-tech credit risk assessment is a new innovation. By combining big data with machine learning models, big-tech lenders can assess credit risks without sufficient financial data or adequate collateral assets. Comparative analyses of the big-tech approach of credit risk assessment, relative to the bank approach (which relies on financial data and scorecard models), unveil two important findings. First, the big-tech approach for predicting loan default is more reliable than the traditional approach. The better performance may be attributable to both information advantage and model advantage. Compared with the scorecard model, the machine learning model is more capable of capturing interactive effects among a large number of variables. And big data include more updated real-time data and more behavior information, which are better for predicting both the ability and willingness to repay loans. Second, because they do not depend on financial data and collateral assets, the big-tech lenders can serve many unbanked customers. In fact, the big-tech approach outperforms the bank approach even more so for individuals with a shorter data history and SMEs of smaller size. These findings confirm the salient feature of financial inclusion of big-tech credit.

Another important innovation occurs in DSC financing. Supply chain financing is a regular business of commercial banks by leveraging SMEs' connections to supply and production processes. The biggest challenge of the traditional supply chain financing business is authenticity verification. Misreporting of transactions and chattels is common but is difficult to detect. DSC financing can largely overcome this problem by setting up a framework among the internet of things, blockchain technology, and big data. The internet of things links everything in the process, whether physical products and equipment or information about transactions and fund flows. All activities are under close monitoring full time. The blockchain technology ensures all information about products or transactions is accurate. Big data are also used for credit risk assessment. Compared with the big-tech credit, DSC financing is probably smaller in business scale, as different operating systems are needed for different processes. But if implemented properly, its risk management could be more reliable. And it directly supports SMEs in manufacturing and service industries with much larger loans.

The PBC's soon-to-be-released e-CNY has attracted worldwide attention, as it will probably be the first CBDC issued by a major central bank (Xu, chapter 10, this volume). The PBC started to study this issue in 2014 but apparently accelerated its pace of development after Facebook released a white paper on its digital currency, Libra, in June 2019. e-CNY is a modest first step toward CBDC, with its initial function only to replace cash in circulation. e-CNY should have a limited impact on the current financial system, particularly as it cannot be used in wholesale businesses and is not yet an international currency (Prasad, chapter 12, this volume). Its most direct effect will be on existing payment services, especially mobile payment, as e-CNY is a legal tender and charges no fee for payment. The PBC has designated nine authorized institutions, including some banks and the two mobile payment service providers, to develop their e-CNY digital wallets. These institutions may compete with each other in issuing e-CNY and handling payment transactions. So far, the most important change brought about by e-CNY, in the digital financial space, is segregation of the payment data, with only one institution, the PBC, owning the entire set of big data.

Big tech has the potential to improve international payments, a service that is currently slow and expensive. More efficient international payments would be especially beneficial to small enterprises and individuals making remittances, who currently pay an average of 6 percent to send a payment internationally. But it would take strong coordination among financial regulators to realize the potential of big-tech international payments. The major players—China, the European Union, and the United States—would have to agree on the regulation of cross-border data flows and make their emerging CBDCs or other digitized currencies interoperable (Dollar, chapter 13, this volume).

PRELIMINARY ASSESSMENT OF THE ECONOMIC IMPACT OF DIGITAL FINANCIAL INNOVATIONS

There are already a large number of studies, especially in the Chinese literature, examining the economic impacts of digital financial innovations. Most of those studies apply the Peking University Digital Financial Inclusion

Index. The findings are generally consistent with expectations of positive consequences. In fact, since digital finance is a model of financial inclusion, its economic benefits can be easily understood. For instance, the use of mobile payment is found to increase the probability of farmers becoming informal business owners with higher incomes. In this case, mobile payment serves not only as a means of payment but also as a link to the outside market. Meanwhile, there is also evidence in the literature that the use of mobile payment smooths consumption when facing shocks (Guo and Wang, chapter 2, this volume). Other studies reveal that digital financial businesses facilitate innovation, create jobs, improve income distribution, and support economic growth. The big-tech credit, in particular, is found to have a positive impact on the growth of the borrower's business.

One controversial issue concerning the economic impacts of digital finance is the data inequality problem. While the digital financial industry benefits the masses at large, it also disadvantages those who are not connected by digital technology. Most people in China use digital financial tools to organize their daily lives, and those who do not use digital equipment find it extremely inconvenient or even difficult to navigate daily life. There have been media reports of older people not able to take the subway or to pay their required contributions to social insurance because they do not use mobile payment services. On the other hand, some studies have discovered important evidence of the trickle-down effects of digital financial development (Zhang, chapter 9, this volume). Therefore, dealing with the data inequality problem requires a dual-track strategy. First, specific policies should be adopted to protect the interests of those who do not have access to digital finance. And second, more proactive policies supporting digital financial development could strengthen the trickle-down effect and reduce the negative impacts of data inequality.

Another dimension of the impact of digital finance is the transformation of the traditional financial industry. Commercial banks have rapidly stepped up efforts of digitization (Xie, chapter 8, this volume) by adopting digital transformation as an important business strategy, revamping the digital infrastructure, and establishing dedicated digital financial business units. Currently, already more than 90 percent of banks' transactions occur online. Preliminary studies find that such transformation is beneficial for both controlling risks and increasing returns.

Perhaps the least understood issue is the impact of digital finance on financial stability. On the positive side, it is evident that the fraud rates of the mobile payment services are significantly lower than those of other payment services. The big-tech lenders' average nonperforming loan ratios are also much lower than those of similar types of loans of the commercial banks. There is also evidence that big-tech credit weakens the "financial accelerator" by focusing on data, not collaterals, and thereby improves financial stability. Interestingly, volatility of the Consumer Price Index declined significantly from 2013. This was probably because of the rapid development of mobile payment, e-commerce, and logistics in recent years, which helped to more closely integrate different parts of the national market. On the negative side, the entire P2P lending industry collapsed (Shen, chapter 5, this volume). Although the overall size of the outstanding loan was modest, it involved a large number of inexperienced investors and had significant social consequences. The application of digital technology to financial transactions may affect the pattern of financial risks. However, it is not entirely clear how this will affect financial stability.

RECONSTRUCTION OF DIGITAL FINANCIAL REGULATION

Concerns about financial stability bring the discussion back to the cause of suspension of Ant's IPO: financial regulation. The regulatory framework for the digital financial industry has not yet been well developed for a number of reasons. First, the regulators initially took a friendly stand toward digital financial innovation as they saw the value of financial inclusion in these new businesses. Second, the current regulatory framework is segregated by sector; therefore, whoever issues licenses should be responsible for regulation. It was not immediately clear which regulators should regulate which digital financial institution. Third, since the digital financial industry applies advanced digital technology, the traditional regulatory methods, such as onsite and offsite inspections, are probably not sufficient for detecting risks. In addition, because the financial regulators are part of the government, making and implementing regulatory policies are often driven by political decisions. This often leads to campaign-style regulation: a violent swing between no regulatory action at all, and all actions at once.

Suspension of Ant's IPO is a good example of this unique regulatory style. At that time, Ant's digital financial businesses as a whole were not adequately and properly regulated. If the IPO went ahead as planned, the proposed regulatory changes could affect Ant's businesses and its market valuation. Suspending it in early November was good for the industry, the capital market, and Ant itself in the long run. One unanswered question is why the regulators did not take coordinated regulatory actions earlier.

Reconstruction of the new regulatory framework for the digital financial industry should follow at least two broad principles. On the one hand, the digital financial industry, like the traditional financial sector, should be fully covered by financial regulation, in order to reduce financial risks, including those resulting from excessive arbitrage. On the other hand, regarding the condition of consistent regulatory standards, regulators should also actively pursue innovation in digital financial regulation in order to balance efficiency and stability.

Detailed regulatory arrangements are still being worked out. Some of the outstanding issues can be resolved relatively quickly, while others will be difficult to settle. First, the digital financial industry, in its entirety, should be subject to the same regulatory policies, ideally with a lead regulator. Since the biggest problem for financial transactions is information asymmetry, the financial industry is the most tightly regulated economic sector. Digital finance is no exception. What is equally important is that regulations governing both the traditional financial sector and the digital finance industry should be uniform, as otherwise it could cause serious arbitrage behavior. Absence of regulation or an "appropriate degree of regulation" is harmful to the healthy development of the digital financial industry. Given the interlinks among different digital financial businesses, through shared platforms, big data, and cash flows, policy coordination is more important in the digital sector than in the traditional sector. The PBC is a natural candidate for the role of lead regulator, but its functions of making and implementing regulatory policies should be significantly enhanced and institutionalized.

Second, regulatory innovation is necessary in order to keep pace with digital financial innovation. Since digital financial transactions take place online at a massive scale and with extraordinary speed, the traditional methods of regulation would be grossly inadequate for managing financial risks, let alone resolving them. Regulators should significantly upgrade their technological capabilities by applying digital technology in performing regulatory functions. When regulators see the benefits of some new innovation but are unsure of the risk consequences, they can adopt new practices such as the "regulatory sandbox" to allow conditional experimentation under regulators' watch. The PBC already introduced the Chinese version of the sandbox, called regulatory tools for fintech innovation, at the end of 2019. Regulators should also proactively pursue regulatory innovations to support speedy and healthy development of the digital financial industry. For instance, the big-tech credit model is quite effective, judging from the large number of borrowers, very rapid speed, and good quality of loans. However, the big-tech lenders often face one important constraint: insufficient fund supply. Regulators could help ease this constraint by allowing remote opening of bank accounts, facilitating borrowing from interbank money market or capital markets by big-tech lenders, and encouraging cooperation between big-tech lenders and traditional banks.

Third, China urgently needs to make a complete set of data policies. Most of the digital financial businesses are driven by big data. In the past the government issued a number of laws or regulations on data, such as protection of individual privacy. Unfortunately, most of the regulations are either insufficient or not properly implemented. Data abuse is quite common in China, including in the digital financial industry. Recently, the Chinese government decided to treat data as a production factor—the same as labor, capital, and land. In other words, data may enter the production function to promote economic growth. In order to achieve this goal, policymakers will need to set clear rules in a number of areas. First, who owns the data—individual users or platforms? If both have some rights and inputs in the accumulation of big data, how should the decision rights and benefits be divided? Second, what are the acceptable modes of data exchange? Unlike labor or capital, data can be owned and used by multiple parties; the ideal mode of data exchange should protect the rights of owners of the original data. Third, uniform data standards are an important condition for data exchange, but who should be responsible for setting data standards—the government or the private sector? And fourth, what is the pricing mechanism for data? Without effectively resolving these issues, it will be hard for data to properly function as a new production factor. It is also difficult to expect the digital financial industry to continue to develop healthily.

Fourth, there is also an urgent need to devise a new antimonopoly policy for the digital economy, including the digital financial industry. Recently, Chinese regulators started to look into the monopoly issue, such as in the mobile payment sector. However, unlike in the traditional economy, market share might not be the most reliable indicator to determine monopoly. Since digital technology has qualities of scale and scope economies, it is natural for the big-tech platforms to become very large players in the market. In fact, this was the technological basis for the digital financial industry to realize financial inclusion. A more appropriate criterion to judge monopoly position is "contestability"—whether new players can still enter the market and compete with the incumbents. In the Chinese digital economic sector, contestability is quite obvious. In the e-commerce space, Taobao was the first leading platform. But JD.com is always around. And in recent years, the new platform Pdd.com quickly overtook Taobao. In social media, while WeChat still dominates, it faces constant competition from Weibo and is losing market share to ByteDance. Given the dynamics of the digital economy sector, especially rapid evolution of business models, it is hard to be convinced that persistent dominance and market power already exist. It might be advisable that, at this stage, regulatory policies should focus more on fair competition and consumer protection, instead of narrowly defined antimonopoly.

Finally, in the long run, the authorities need to work out an international strategy for digital financial regulation. Most of the successful digital financial businesses in China are domestic, although some leading institutions have started to "go abroad." International strategy is critical given that China is at the forefront of some digital financial innovation and that, over time, it would become increasingly costly and even impossible to enforce restrictions on digital financial transactions at the border. The international strategy could include exchange of experience and knowledge about digital financial innovation, cross-country coordination of regulatory policies, and even integration of international digital financial markets. While all such decisions are not in the hands of financial regulators, permanent segregation of the Chinese digital financial industry from the rest of the world should not be preferable. Therefore, it is important for regulators and practitioners to interact with their foreign counterparts and find effective ways to cooperate and share knowledge.

2

Quantifying Digital Financial Inclusion in China

FENG GUO and JINGYI WANG

Financial inclusion is defined as a financial system that effectively and comprehensively serves all social classes and groups. The intention of financial inclusion is to highlight the continual improvement of the financial infrastructure and the availability of more convenient financial services for people from all walks of life, especially those in underdeveloped areas or categorized as low income, at a lower cost. This concept was initially adopted by the United Nations for the International Year of Microcredit 2005 and was then vigorously promoted by the United Nations and the World Bank. As of 2014, the World Bank had joined hands with public and private partners in more than seventy countries and regions around the world on financial inclusion projects; over fifty countries and regions worldwide have established goals to improve financial inclusion (World Bank Group 2015). The concept of financial inclusion was first introduced in China in 2015 and was later recognized by the Chinese government. At the end of 2015, the State Council made more detailed arrangements for the undertaking of financial inclusion and clarified the definition of financial inclusion in the *Plan for Advancing Financial Inclusion Development (2016–2020)*: "Financial inclusion

Note: An introduction to the indicator system and index calculation methodology appears in the appendix at the end of the chapter.

17

means providing financial services to all social classes and groups with demand for appropriate and effective financial services, at an affordable cost, and based on the principle of equal opportunity and service sustainability by increasing policy guidance and support, strengthening the construction of financial systems, and improving financial infrastructure" (State Council of China 2015).

At home and abroad, the concept, theory, and practice of financial inclusion have gradually deepened: from the initial focus on the availability of banks' physical outlets and credit services to extending coverage to a variety of service areas including payments, deposits, loans, insurance, credit investigations, and securities (Jiao and others 2015). At the practical level, financial inclusion in China has gradually expanded from public welfare microfinance at the preliminary stage to integrated financial services, including payment, credit, and other services, and has undergone substantial development thanks to the extensive application of network and mobile communication technologies. China's current financial inclusion practice shows a strong correlation with innovative digital finance. The new digital financial services offered by internet companies reduce the cost of financial services products and expand access to financial services through information technology and product innovation. Therefore, innovative digital finance has become an important driving force and growth pillar for financial inclusion.[1] Specifically, in terms of coverage, traditional financial institutions need to build outlets to expand coverage, and the resulting high cost makes it difficult for them to penetrate relatively impoverished regions. However, the crossover and integration of digital technology and financial services can address such shortcomings. Even in areas without hardware facilities such as bank outlets and ATMs, customers still have access to desirable financial services through terminal devices such as computers and mobile phones. Compared with the traditional financial institutions that distribute most resources in densely inhabited and commercial areas, digital finance offers financial services that are more direct and more accessible to more customers. For the social groups covered, the innovations offered by digital financial products have lowered the access threshold for customers, weakening the "nobility" attribute of financial services, and making them increasingly available to the public. Compared with the exclusivity of traditional financial institutions, digital finance can meet the needs of small and medium-size businesses and low-income groups, who are generally un-derprivileged and unable to access financial services, thus reflecting the due meaning of financial inclusion.

Over the past few years, China has made substantial progress in the de-velopment of digital finance, which has contributed to its influence around the world (Huang and Huang 2018). However, there was no indicator sys-tem to quantify its overall development. To this end, a research team from the Institute of Digital Finance at Peking University developed an index series—the Peking University Digital Financial Inclusion Index of China (PKU-DFIIC)—in 2016, which was then updated in 2019 and 2021 (Guo and others 2020). The research team built an indicator system of digital finan-cial inclusion that is based on the traditional financial inclusion indexes pro-posed by the existing literature and international organizations and con-siders the new developments and features of digital financial services—in combination with the availability and reliability of data. The research team's indicator system considers three dimensions: the coverage breadth of digi-tal finance, the depth of use of digital finance, and the digitization level of inclusive finance. The system contains thirty-three specific indicators cate-gorized by these three dimensions. With this indicator system and an ana-lytic hierarchy process (a commonly used index compilation method in similar studies), the research team compiled the PKU-DFIIC on three geo-graphical levels: province, prefecture-level municipality, and county, covering 31 provinces (municipalities directly under the central government, and autonomous regions) and 337 cities above the prefecture level (regions, au-tonomous prefectures, leagues, etc.), and about 2,800 counties (county-level cities, banners, municipal districts, etc.) in the Chinese Mainland. The time span of the indexes at the provincial and prefectural levels is 2011–2020, and that of county-level indexes is 2014–2020. The indexes are comparable both vertically and horizontally. In addition to the overall index, the research team also compiled indexes describing the coverage breadth, depth of use, and digitization level of digital financial inclusion, as well as subindexes for payments, insurance, monetary funds, credit investigation, investment, and credit.

The purpose of compilation is to provide a set of instrumental data indi-cating the development status and evolution of digital financial inclusion without leaking the private data of financial consumers and commercial secrets of financial institutions. This report is intended to quantify China's digital financial inclusion practices in the form of indexes. Such efforts are meaningful from at least three perspectives. First, in theory, the index will provide an important reference for the study of innovative financial inclusion and the design of statistical indicator systems in China. The existing research on financial inclusion in China mainly focuses on its concept, significance, index structure, and function from the perspective of traditional financial services. A scientific and comprehensive summary of the theories and indicator systems of digital financial inclusion from the perspective of innovative digital finance is still absent for China. Based on a consolidation of the current research on indicator systems of financial inclusion and indexes worldwide and with reference to the rapid development of innovative digital finance at the current stage in China, this report has built an indicator system for digital financial inclusion to further deepen the research on financial inclusion. Second, in practice, based on the indicator system built, this report has compiled digital financial inclusion indexes at the provincial, prefecture, and county levels, which serve to display digital financial inclusion development and regional equilibrium under the current trend of innovative digital finance in China. These indexes can help policymakers and practitioners better understand the development status of digital financial inclusion in China and identify bottlenecks and obstacles to its development with the purpose of formulating corresponding policies to promote healthy and sustainable development. Third, in terms of legacy, the index has become an influential data product among researchers specializing in financial technology and financial inclusion in China after its first release in 2016 and two updates in 2019 and 2021. On the one hand, the effects of the development of digital financial inclusion have been under thorough analysis from different perspectives. On the other hand, growing numbers of themed publications, papers, and internal reports are attracting more and more scholars and doctoral students to the study of digital financial inclusion.

This chapter presents the development status of China's digital financial inclusion via the indexes generated, especially the regional and spatial structures of digital finance. The significance of digital financial inclusion to the balanced economic development across all regions in China is discussed as well.

OVERVIEW OF THE DEVELOPMENT OF DIGITAL FINANCIAL INCLUSION IN CHINA

Using the indicator system and index preparation methods discussed in the appendix, the research team obtained the digital financial inclusion index for three levels of regions: 31 provinces (municipalities and autonomous regions, collectively referred to as "provinces"), 337 cities above the prefecture level (regions, autonomous prefectures, and leagues, collectively referred to as "cities"), and around 2,800 counties (county-level cities, banners, and municipal districts, collectively referred to as "counties"). The time span of the indexes at the provincial and prefectural levels is 2011–2020, and that of county-level indexes is 2014–2020.[2] In addition to the overall index, the research team also compiled indexes describing the coverage breadth, depth of use, and digitization level of digital financial inclusion, and subindexes for payments, insurance, monetary funds, credit investigation, investment, credit, and more.

First, concerning the development of China's digital financial inclusion as a whole, the annual means and medians of the digital financial inclusion index of 31 provinces in the country from 2011 to 2020 are shown in figure 2-1. The median of the provincial index was 33.6 in 2011, grew to 214.6 in 2015, and further rose to 334.8 in 2020. The median in 2020 was ten times that of 2011, representing an average annual growth of 29.1 percent. So the leapfrog development was evident.[3] Also, a surge was observed in the digital financial inclusion index in the eastern, central, and western regions of China. From the perspective of the growth rate, China's digital financial inclusion index has been growing at a slower pace in recent years. To a certain extent, it indicates that as the Chinese digital financial market matures, it is embracing a transition from rapid growth to normalized growth. In 2020, like all other countries, China was hard-hit by the COVID-19 pandemic both economically and socially, with its annual economic growth rate dropping significantly from previous years. However, the digital financial inclusion index maintained positive growth, up 5.6 percent compared with 2019. This shows the unique advantages of digital finance amid the pandemic. In fact, digital finance and the digital economy played a crucial role in fighting the virus, including mitigating its impact on the economy (Guo 2021). For example, in early February 2020, China started rolling out the

FIGURE 2-1.   **Provincial Mean and Median of Digital Financial Inclusion Indexes, 2011–2020**

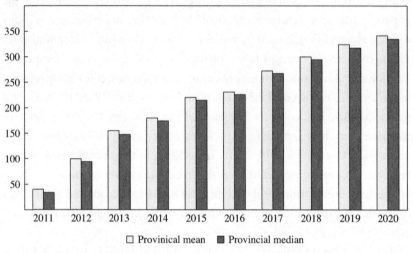

Digital financial inclusion index

☐ Provinical mean   ■ Provincial median

Source: PKU-DFIIC.

Health Code from Hangzhou, where Alipay is based. The Health Code uses three colors—red, yellow, and green—to indicate whether a citizen is a confirmed (suspected) case, has been in close contact with someone who is a confirmed case, or has traveled to a high-risk area. With it, all citizens are put under classified management. According to the research of Xiao (2021), the Health Code was a key driving factor of the economic revival in China, in addition to its unparalleled contribution to pandemic prevention. Specifically, his estimations show that this big-data technology contributed 0.5–0.75 percentage points to China's GDP growth during the pandemic.

The overall growth of the above digital financial inclusion index has masked the development gap between different dimensions. Specifically, from 2011 to 2020, the digitization-level index delivered the fastest growth, followed by the breadth of coverage index (yet quite close to the former), and then the depth of use index, which grew the slowest.[4] Moreover, each subindex showed varied growth rates in different years. As shown in figure 2-2, from 2016 to 2020, the depth of use index grew quite fast—at a speed higher than that of the breadth of coverage index in four out of the five years, mak-

FIGURE 2-2.   **Digital Financial Inclusion Indexes and Level 1
Subindexes, 2011–2020**

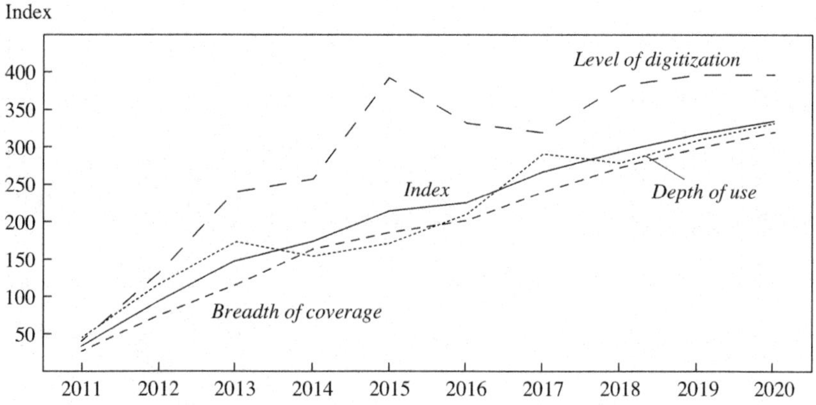

Index

Source: PKU-DFIIC.

ing it a strong driver of the growth of the digital financial inclusion index.
The reason is pretty straightforward. As the coverage and digitization of digital finance reach a certain level, the depth of use will become an increasingly important source of index growth across China. This is quite an en-
lightenment for related industry practitioners and regulators in China.

SPATIAL STRUCTURE OF DIGITAL FINANCIAL
INCLUSION IN CHINA

This section discusses the importance of analyzing the spatial structure
of digital finance inclusion, which can reveal whether the development
of digital finance inclusion in different regions is converging, and can also
inform important extended meanings for regional economic and social
development.

Rapid Convergence of the Regional Development
of Digital Financial Inclusion in China

The development of digital financial inclusion in China, like most of China's
economic characteristics, displays regional differences. As shown in figure 2-3,

FIGURE 2-3.   **Digital Financial Inclusion Index by Province in 2020**

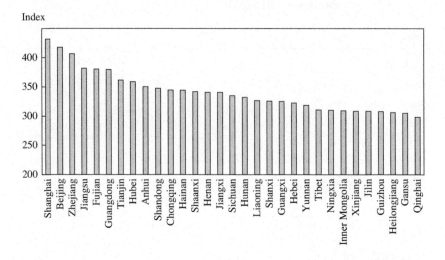

Source: PKU-DFIIC.

the highest digital financial inclusion index in 2020, which belonged to Shanghai, was 1.4 times that of the lowest, which was Qinghai Province. These results indicate that compared with traditional financial inclusion, digital financial inclusion features higher geographic penetration and has secured broader coverage (Jiao and others, 2015). Figure 2-3 also shows that Shanghai and Beijing, the two most developed cities in China, together with Zhejiang Province, where the digital economy has an active presence, delivered digital financial inclusion indexes that were significantly higher than those of other regions; thus, they were in the leading team. The provinces ranking after Xinjiang are all situated in western or northeastern China, where digital financial inclusion is far less developed. The rest of the eastern and central provinces were between the two segments.

As for specific indexes shown in figure 2-4, the smallest regional difference was in the level of digitization, followed by the breadth of coverage, and the largest regional difference lay in the depth of use. Specifically, the ratios of the highest regional indexes of coverage breadth, depth of use, and digitization level in 2020 to the lowest were 1.36, 1.89, and 1.24, respectively. Despite the large drop in the regional difference in the depth of use of digital finance from previous years, it was still the largest among the three dimensions. In terms of the depth of use, a gap remains between backward and

FIGURE 2-4.   **Digital Financial Inclusion Index by Province in 2020**

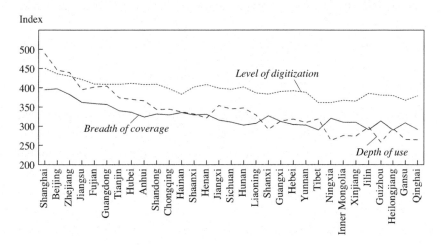

Source: PKU-DFIIC.

developed areas. Divided by business formats, the regional difference in internet investment was significantly higher than those in other business formats. This is largely attributable to the characteristics of digital finance, as it is relatively easy to allow more people to access and use digital financial services. However, there remains much space for users who have already been reached to use digital financial services more frequently, or even be highly dependent on digital finance.

More important, the gap in digital financial inclusion among provinces has greatly narrowed over time. This indicates that the less developed regions are unlikely to "lose at the starting line," which is in line with the intention of digital finance. To more rigorously demonstrate the temporal change pattern of regional gaps in the development of digital financial inclusion, we applied the classical convergence analysis approach (Barro and Sala-i-Martin 1992; Sala-i-Martin 1996). The relevant literature shows that commonly used verification methods for economic convergence are the σ convergence model and the β convergence model. In this chapter, only the results of the σ convergence model are reported.

σ convergence describes the level of stock and reflects the deviation of the regional digital financial inclusion index from the overall average and the dynamic process of such deviation. That is, if such deviation becomes smaller and smaller, then the regional digital financial inclusion index is considered to feature convergence. Specifically, the σ convergence model can be defined as follows:

$$\sigma_t = \sqrt{\frac{1}{n}\sum_{i=1}^{n}\left(lnindex_{it} - \frac{1}{n}\sum_{i=1}^{n}lnindex_{it}\right)^2}$$

wherein i represents a region (province, prefecture-level city, or county), n is the number of regions, t is the year, $lnindex_{it}$ represents the logarithmic value of the digital financial inclusion index of the region i in year t, and σ_t refers to the σ convergence test coefficient of the digital financial inclusion index in year t. If $\sigma_{t+1} < \sigma_t$, the digital financial inclusion index in year $t + 1$ is more convergent than that in year t.

Figure 2-5 reports the yearly σ convergence coefficients of the provincial and city-level digital financial inclusion indexes from 2011 to 2020, which indicate an obvious trend of convergence. Specifically, the σ convergence coefficients of provincial and city-level indexes dropped from 0.44 and 0.34 in 2011 to 0.09 and 0.09 in 2020, respectively. Figure 2-5 also shows that the

FIGURE 2-5. σ Convergence Coefficient of Provincial and City-Level Digital Financial Inclusion Index, 2011–2020

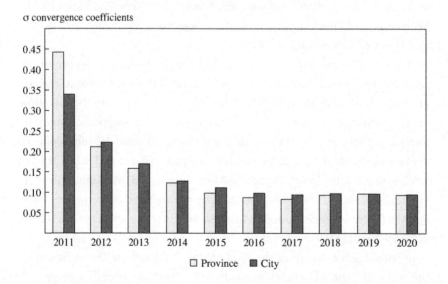

Source: PKU-DFIIC.

FIGURE 2-6.   σ Convergence Coefficient of City-Level Digital Financial
Inclusion Index, 2011–2020

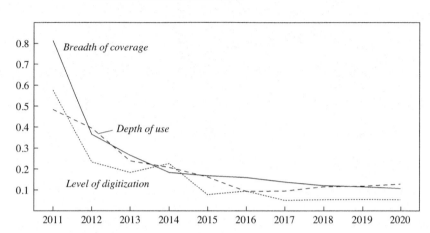

Source: PKU-DFIIC.

regional convergence rate of China's digital financial inclusion index as a
whole slowed down significantly after 2016.

To uncover the reasons for the slowdown in the regional convergence rate
over the past two years, we exported the convergence coefficients of specific
indexes, which are shown in figure 2-6. The figure indicates that the convergence coefficients of the breadth of coverage index and the level of digitization index maintained a downward trend in recent years, but the convergence coefficient of the depth of use index saw a rebound. This is the major
cause of the slowdown and even the rebound presented by the overall convergence rate of digital financial inclusion in recent years. When the index
is highly dependent on accessibility and coverage, the regional difference of
digital finance converges faster, while when digital finance comes to a new
stage driven by the depth of use, we find that a large regional variance remains in the depth of use, which can largely explain the gradual slowdown
in the regional convergence rate of the overall index.

East-West Gap in Digital Financial Inclusion

The above analysis identifies obvious regional convergence in the development of digital financial inclusion in China, which is more intuitively

FIGURE 2-7.   **Relative Rankings of Cities in Terms of Overall Index in 2011, 2015, and 2020**

2011   2015   2020

Source: PKU-DFIIC.

Note: Because of a lack of data, Taiwan, Hong Kong, Macao, and some other cities are left blank.

shown by maps. Figure 2-7 displays the rankings of cities by the digital financial inclusion index in 2011, 2015, and 2020. The echelon classification rule is as follows: using the highest index of the year as the benchmark, cities with an index higher than 80 percent of the benchmark index are classified as the first echelon, 70–80 percent are the second echelon, 60–70 percent are the third echelon, and lower than 60 percent are the fourth echelon. The higher the echelon, the darker the shade. We can see that in 2011 there was a large gap in development among cities, as the first echelon was concentrated in the Yangtze River delta, the Pearl River delta, and other large cities; the second and third echelons were few in number; and most of the cities belonged to the fourth echelon. By 2020, most of the cities were in the first and second echelons—that is, the majority of cities had a digital financial inclusion index higher than 70 percent of the highest index, implying that the gap among regions had further narrowed. This finding is highly consistent with the above convergence conclusion.

Moreover, comparing the figure with the renowned Hu Line from geo-economics, which divides China into eastern and western regions, we can see that the characteristics of the Hu Line are not obvious for the PKU-DFIIC, as the indexes for some cities west of the Hu Line also entered the first and second echelons in 2020.[5] The figure demonstrates the advantages of digital finance in accessibility and geographical penetration.

In September 2019, we drafted a research report titled "How Digital Economy Boosts the Balanced Economic Development between East and West China" (Wang and others 2019). Using the Hu Line, we calculated the difference between the two regions in terms of the accessibility and coverage of digital finance and discovered an obvious downward trend. Across the Hu Line, digital finance represented by mobile payment facilitated access to and use of advanced digital financial services by residents in remote western regions, which in turn created more opportunities for the balanced regional development of the Chinese economy. And our paper on digital financial inclusion (Guo and others 2020), which was published in *China Economic Quarterly*, also analyzed the development trend of the depth of use on both sides of the Hu Line. It was hard to obtain a clear conclusion from the total index, but when we mapped out the breadth of coverage and the depth of use separately, the result appeared to be more intuitive.

As shown in figure 2-8, the breadth of coverage index kept growing on both sides of the Hu Line from 2011 to 2020, while the development of the depth of use was concentrated in southeast China. The reason is that the breadth of coverage measures fairness in opportunity (that is, the availability of technologies and services), while the depth of use embodies the consequential equilibrium (that is, the level of final developments). Because it is free from geographic constraints and its marginal cost is almost zero, digital technology works to promote the development of underdeveloped areas and sparsely populated areas and allows residents in different areas to share the benefits of inclusion. On the other hand, the essence of digital finance is finance, after all, which cannot develop without economic activities, production, and life. As a result, eastern areas with a dense population remain more developed and active, as boosted by agglomeration and network effects. In conclusion, the technology employed by digital finance brings equal access to services, while the nature of digital finance to serve physical entities determines that it still develops in a concentrated manner.

North-South Gap in Digital Financial Inclusion

Following the discussion of the east-west gap in the development of digital financial inclusion in China, this section explores the difference between the

FIGURE 2-8.   **Relative Rankings of Cities in Terms of Breadth of Coverage (top row) and Depth of Use (bottom row) of Digital Financial Inclusion in 2011, 2015, and 2020**

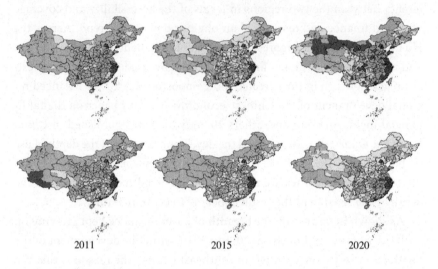

2011   2015   2020

Source: PKU-DFIIC.

Note: Because of a lack of data, Taiwan, Hong Kong, Macao, and some other county-level cities under direct administration of provinces are left blank.

southern and northern regions. The economic relations between South China and North China have been a pivotal issue in the history of the country for thousands of years. Then, during the several years since its origination, digital finance produced some interesting trends. Following traditional practices, we divided China into southern and northern regions at the prefecture-level city level using the Qinling–Huaihe Line. First, we observed the change in the ratio of the average digital financial inclusion index of northern Chinese cities to that of southern ones, as shown in figure 2-9. The following conclusions can be drawn from the figure: (1) the north-south gap in the development of digital financial inclusion in China was moderate, with the development level in the north slightly lower than that in the south; (2) northern cities had been catching up with their counterparts in the south, especially between 2011 and 2014, during which time the average index of northern cities leaped from 88 percent of the average value of southern cities to around 95 percent; and (3) starting in 2018, the gap showed a tendency

FIGURE 2-9.   **Changing Trend of Digital Financial Inclusion Index Variance between Northern and Southern Cities in China (Average of Northern Cities/Average of Southern Cities), 2011–2020**

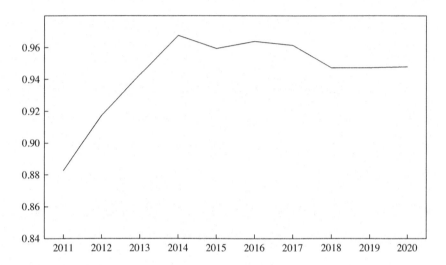

Source: PKU-DFIIC.

to expand again, but considering the short time covered and the small expansion, further observation is needed.

Figure 2-10 shows the changing trend of the gap between northern and southern cities in the three indexes: the breadth of coverage, the depth of use, and the level of digitization. We can conclude from the figure that the level of digitization in northern cities was initially higher than that in southern cities but then later lagged behind. This is the major reason the north-south gap in the overall digital financial inclusion index slightly widened over the past few years. To uncover the cause of the decline of the digitization level index in North China, we analyzed its four subindexes: mobility, affordability, credit, and convenience. It was found that, among them, the largest decline was recorded by affordability and credit; the financing interest rate environment for small and medium-size enterprises in the northern region worsened compared with that in the southern region; and the usage scenarios of credit points saw a decline as well. These findings indicate

FIGURE 2-10. **Changing Trend of Digital Financial Inclusion Index**
Variance between Northern and Southern Cities in China
(Average of Northern Cities/Average of Southern Cities),
2011–2020

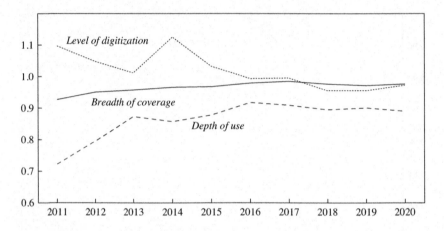

Source: PKU-DFIIC.

that digital finance requires other supporting financial and hardware infrastructure to have more room for development. With regard to the depth of
use, northern cities lagged behind at first but tried to catch up in the following years. This is also why the north-south gap in the overall digital financial inclusion index narrowed in the past few years. However, the depth of
use still had the largest variance among all three dimensions. In the future,
whether the northern region can catch up with the southern region depends
mainly on whether the gap in the depth of use can be narrowed. This is also
consistent with the conclusions obtained in the preceding paragraphs.

DIGITAL FINANCE AND DEVELOPMENT OF A
BALANCED REGIONAL ECONOMY

Such regional convergence of digital financial inclusion is of great significance, as it indicates the potential role of digital finance in alleviating the
inadequacy and imbalance of development of the regional economy. Under
traditional economic conditions, limited by geographic location and trans-

portation costs, the supply side of goods and services is often close to the demand side. Though providers of goods and services are concentrated in developed coastal cities in China, with the growth of the internet and e-commerce, many rural areas in the central and western regions and remote villages are given the opportunity to start a business. Via e-commerce platforms such as Taobao, they are able to deliver commodities and services to coastal cities, thereby sharing the benefits of economic development. Compared with the traditional economy, e-commerce has removed three barriers arising from the sparse population in the west: (1) the low infrastructure requirements of e-commerce have mitigated the disadvantage of the western region; (2) because e-commerce products are characterized mostly by customization and individualization, they do not depend on a high concentration of labor to gain advantages in cost control; and (3) well-developed e-commerce networks have expanded the distribution of products to the whole country and the world, thus mitigating the market limitation caused by low population density. Data from Alibaba's e-commerce business show that from 2013 to 2018, the gap in the number of e-commerce operators between the two sides of the Hu Line decreased by 28 percent (Wang and others 2019).

Digital finance is also equally beneficial to all regions in driving innovation and entrepreneurship. It can play the role of inclusive finance in order to provide underdeveloped regions and small and micro businesses an opportunity to catch up, thus promoting the balanced development of the economy and society. Xie and others (2018) matched the digital financial inclusion index with newly registered enterprises and other data to study the relationship between the development of digital finance and entrepreneurship. They found that the development of digital finance plays a significant role in promoting entrepreneurship. In other words, the more developed digital finance is in a region, the greater the number of new companies registered in the region each year, and the more quickly those companies will grow. Further research revealed that the lower the urbanization rate, the greater the marginal effect of the digital financial inclusion index—that is, digital finance is more effective in encouraging entrepreneurship in underdeveloped and rural regions than in developed and urban regions. Furthermore, digital finance is positively correlated to the number of new small and micro businesses each year but shows no significant positive correlation with the number of large and medium-size enterprises. This indicates that digital finance plays a greater role in promoting the establishment of small and micro businesses. Both findings demonstrate that digital finance can indeed function as inclusive finance to narrow the regional gap and help solve the financing difficulties of small and micro companies.

Another feature of the development of digital financial inclusion is that it has been shown to significantly promote household consumption, which was more obvious in rural areas, central and western regions, and middle- and lower-income groups (Yi and Zhou 2018). In their study, Yi and Zhou (2018) divided all household samples into urban and rural households, as well as households of different income classes. They found that the development of digital financial inclusion played a greater role in promoting consumption by rural residents. They attributed this to a significant gap between the two groups in the financial availability of households in China. In other words, the availability of financial services is lower for rural households than for urban households, together with more common financial repression. Thus, the development of inclusive finance is more effective in alleviating the liquidity constraints on rural residents than those on urban residents. Their research findings also show that digital financial inclusion greatly promoted consumption by low- and middle-income residents but had less of an effect on the consumption of high-income residents. This implies that the development of digital financial inclusion allows easier access to credit support for low- and middle-income classes and reduces their liquidity constraints, which ultimately results in increased consumer spending; high-income households, meanwhile, tend to experience weaker liquidity constraints, placing digital financial inclusion in a weaker role in promoting consumption. Following the same logic in their research, the role of digital financial inclusion in boosting consumption is also more evident in central and western regions. This was shown by a separate regression in which the authors divided all samples into three categories: eastern coastal area, central inland area, and western remote area. The results show that digital financial inclusion promoted consumption by residents in the central inland and western remote areas yet had no significant impact on the residents in the eastern coastal area. This is because the rapid economic and financial development in the eastern region lessens the effect of the development of digital financial inclusion on local consumption, whereas for the central and western regions, their less advantageous geographic location and the slow development of formal finance allows digital financial inclusion to boost consumption in these regions.

CONCLUSION

With reference to the existing literature, especially the literature on the compilation of traditional financial inclusion indexes, and taking into account the characteristics of digital financial inclusion, we have come up with a digital financial inclusion index for 2011–2020 for three levels of regions: 31 provinces (municipalities and autonomous regions), 337 cities above the prefecture level (regions, autonomous prefectures, leagues, etc.), and around 2,800 counties (county-level cities, banners, municipal districts, etc.). In addition to the overall index, we also compiled indexes describing the coverage breadth, depth of use, and digitization level of digital financial inclusion, as well as subindexes for payments, insurance, monetary funds, credit investigation, investment, credit, and more. Through this whole set of digital financial inclusion indexes, we discussed the development trend and spatial features of digital financial inclusion in China.

In summary, we drew several conclusions from our index. First, China's digital financial inclusion delivered leapfrog development from 2011 to 2020, with the depth of use emerging as a key driver of the growth of the digital financial inclusion index. It indicates that China's digital financial inclusion has gone beyond rough "enclosure" and reached a new stage of in-depth expansion. Second, the development of digital financial inclusion in China shows strong regional convergence, with the regional gap substantially narrowed. Digital financial inclusion has made it possible for economically underdeveloped regions to catch up with the developed regions. It has also laid a foundation for massive numbers of low- and middle-income residents and disadvantaged groups to access financial services featuring broader coverage and deeper use, thereby helping mitigate the imbalance in economic development across the country. Third, the gap between the central and western regions and the eastern coastal area has narrowed in terms of the breadth of coverage of digital finance, but there is still room for improvement in the depth of use.

The above characteristics of the digital economy can benefit the balanced development of the regional economy, which is crucial to a huge economy like China. However, it should be noted that the digital economy, as an emerging business format that is far from maturity, is only part of the synergy needed to drive the balanced development of the east and the west. To achieve this goal, concerted efforts of all parties are needed. From a macro perspective, the state-level western development plan, infrastructure investment, and other policy and economic support are fundamental factors for the growth of the western region. At the same time, the rapid economic growth since the reform and opening-up provides sufficient impetus and poses realistic requirements for the coordinated development between the eastern and western regions. Finally, advanced technologies, such as digital technology, make it possible to resolve geographic constraints. The digital economy offers more equal development opportunities for the east and the west and makes the flow of information, capital, and goods in between more frequent and smooth. As a result, recent years have seen the west catching up more quickly, which is beneficial to the balanced development of China's regional economy.

APPENDIX: INDICATOR SYSTEM AND INDEX CALCULATION METHODOLOGY

Indicator System of Digital Financial Inclusion

The prerequisite for compiling a set of scientific indexes is to design a complete and accurate indicator system. Thus, the research team referred to the indicator systems designed for traditional financial inclusion (Demirguc-Kunt and Klapper 2012; Global Partnership for Financial Inclusion 2013; Sarma 2012; Financial Consumer Protection Bureau of the People's Bank of China 2018), and considered the new developments and features of digital financial services, as well as the availability and reliability of data. As a result, an indicator system of digital financial inclusion was built based on three dimensions: the coverage breadth of digital finance, the depth of use of digital finance, and the digitization level of financial inclusion. In addition to these three dimensions, the system has 33 indicators,[6] as shown in table 2-1.

The accessibility of traditional financial institutions is shown by "number of outlets" and "number of service personnel." By contrast, under the model of internet-based new finance, because the internet by nature has no location restrictions, the reach of internet financial services is reflected by

TABLE 2-1. **Indicators for Digital Financial Inclusion**

Level 1 dimension	Level 2 dimension		Indicator
Breadth of coverage	Account coverage rate		Number of Alipay accounts per 10,000 people
			Proportion of Alipay users who have bank cards bound to their Alipay accounts
			Average number of bank cards bound to each Alipay account
Depth of use	Payment		Number of payments per capita
			Amount of payments per capita
			Proportion of number of high-frequency active users (50 times or more each year) to number of users with frequency of once or more each year
	Money funds		Number of Yu'ebao purchases per capita
			Amount of Yu'ebao purchases per capita
			Number of people who have purchased Yu'ebao per 10,000 Alipay users
	Credit	Individual user	Number of users with an internet loan for consumption per 10,000 adult Alipay users
			Number of loans per capita
			Total amount of loan per capita
		Small and micro business	Number of users with an internet loan for small and micro businesses per 10,000 adult Alipay users
			Number of loans per small and micro businesses
			Average amount of loan among small and micro businesses
	Insurance		Number of insured users per 10,000 Alipay users
			Number of insurance policies per capita
			Average insurance amount per capita

(*continued*)

TABLE 2-1. *(continued)*

Level 1 dimension	Level 2 dimension	Indicator
	Investment	Number of people engaged in internet investment and money management per 10,000 Alipay users
		Number of investments per capita
		Average investment amount per capita
	Credit investigation	Number of credit investigations by natural persons per capita
		Number of users with access to credit-based livelihood services (including finance, accommodation, mobility, social contact, etc.) per 10,000 Alipay users
Level of digitization	Mobility	Number of mobile payments
		Total amount of mobile payments
	Affordability	Average loan interest rate for small and micro businesses
		Average loan interest rate for individuals
	Credit	Number of Ant Check Later payments
		Total amount of Ant Check Later payments
		Proportion of number of "Zhima Credit as deposit" cases to number of full-deposit cases
		Proportion of total amount of "Zhima Credit as deposit" to amount of full-deposit cases
	Convenience	Number of QR code payments by users
		Proportion of "average amount" or "total amount" of QR code payment by users

the number of e-accounts. In addition, as required by financial regulatory authorities, a third-party payment account not bound with a bank card is only allowed for small-amount transfers, which greatly limits the value. Therefore, only the third-party payment accounts that are bound with bank cards are truly valid, and such account owners are deemed truly covered. With the continual expansion of third-party payment functions, third-party payment has become a crucial channel for financial management and financing. Thus, the more bank cards that are bound, the wider the coverage of financial management and transfer, and the account owner can access more financial services. Hence, the number of bank cards bound to one account has been identified as a subindex of the breadth of digital finance coverage.

In terms of the depth of digital finance usage, the research team highlighted the actual use of digital financial services, which are classified into payment services, monetary fund services, credit services, insurance services, investment services, and credit investigation services. The concept of usage is broken down into the number of actual users (number of users per 10,000 Alipay users) and the level of activeness (number of transactions per capita and average transaction amount per capita).

Regarding the level of digitization, convenience, cost, and credit are the main factors affecting the use of digital financial services, which truly reflects their low cost and low threshold. Therefore, digitization is also seen as an integral part of the indicator system. The more convenient (such as high mobility), less expensive (such as low loan interest rates), and more credit-based (such as credit-as-deposit cases) that digital financial services are, the more value digital financial inclusion will generate.

Nondimensionalization

Although all the indicators on different dimensions contain useful information for certain aspects of digital financial inclusion, the use of one indicator alone or indicators on one single dimension may lead to biased interpretations of the status quo of digital financial inclusion. Hence, it is feasible to synthesize multiple indicators into an overall index to describe digital financial inclusion, with reference to the index development methodology of traditional financial inclusion. In this regard, a number of institutions and scholars have made many efforts and attempts, which provides us with desirable references (Sarma 2012; Jiao and others 2015).

Before index synthesis, it is necessary to nondimensionalize the indicators with different properties and units. General principles for selecting a nondimensionalization function are that it be strictly monotonic, have a clear value range, provide intuitive results, offer a definite meaning, and not be heavily influenced by indicators in positive or negative forms. In this regard, efficacy functions were mostly applied in previous research (Sama 2012; Jiao and others 2015). Taking into account the rapid expansion of digital finance, and to mitigate the impact of extreme values, avoid the excessive growth of indicators, and maintain their stability, the research team adopted the logarithmic efficacy function method. Specifically, the formula is as follows:

$$d = \frac{\log x - \log x^l}{\log x^h - \log x^l} \times 100$$

Regarding the determination of the threshold value in the logarithmic efficacy function formula, if the maximum and minimum values of each indicator in different years are taken as upper and lower limits, when the maximum or minimum value is an extreme or abnormal value, the exponential value is very likely to be distorted, resulting in abnormality of the regional indicator. In addition, if the upper and lower limits of each indicator are set on an annual basis, it will lead to changes in the benchmarks of the indicator among regions in different years, resulting in vertical incomparability. Therefore, to ensure both horizontal and vertical comparability when measuring the development of digital financial inclusion in various regions in the future, the research team processed values as follows: for positive indicators, take the 95 percent quantile of the actual indicator value in each region in 2011 as the upper limit x^h, and the 5 percent quantile as the lower limit x^l; for negative indicators, take the 5 percent quantile of the actual indicator value in each region in 2011 as the upper limit x^h, and the 95 percent quantile as the lower limit x^l. Furthermore, to smooth the indicator and avoid the occurrence of extreme values, it is necessary to winsorize the values beyond the limits. For example, when the indicator value of the base year (2011) in a certain region is higher than the upper limit of indicator x^h, the indicator value of 2011 in the region will be set as the upper limit x^h. When the indicator value of 2011 in a certain region is lower than the lower limit of indicator x^l, the indicator value of 2011 in the region will be set as the lower limit x^l.

In this way, for the compilation of the digital financial inclusion index, each administrative region in 2011 (for county-level regions, 2014 is the benchmark year) is given a nondimensionalized efficacy score between 0 and 100 corresponding to each indicator. The higher the score, the higher the level of development. For data for years after 2011, the efficacy scores of the indicator may be less than 0 or more than 100.

Analytic Hierarchy Process

In nondimensionalization, the task is to determine the weights of indicators for synthesis. In this study, the research team combined subjective weighting and objective weighting to determine weights. First, the variation coefficient method was used to calculate the weights of a specific indicator on the upper-rule hierarchy; then, the analytic hierarchy process was applied to calculate the weights of the indicator of rule hierarchy on the upper-rule hierarchy targets and, finally, to obtain the total index.

The idea behind the variation coefficient method is to weight each indicator on the basis of its degree of variation in observed values. Specifically, if the variation coefficient of an indicator is large, it means that the indicator has greater explanatory power when measuring the overall difference in the assessment target and should therefore be given a greater weight. On the other hand, the analytic hierarchy process is a comprehensive evaluation method for system analysis and decisionmaking that can quantify qualitative problems in a relatively rational manner. The main feature of this process is that by building a hierarchical structure, judgments are converted into an importance comparison between two factors, thereby transforming a qualitative decision into a quantitative one that is easier to handle. The weight vectors thus generated are shown in table 2-2.[7]

After nondimensionalization and weight determination comes index synthesis. Specifically, synthesis follows a bottom-up, layer-by-layer sequence. First, calculate the indicators on each hierarchy and then weigh and consolidate the indicators to obtain the overall index. When calculating the depth of use index, since the six financial services have different start times, it is necessary to include them in the index by the time sequence. To ensure index stability, the research team used weighting normalization to ensure that the relative weights between services are consistent. Thus, the final

TABLE 2-2. **Weights of Three Dimensions of the Digital Financial Inclusion System**

Total index	Level 1 dimension	Percent	
		Level 2 dimension	
Digital financial inclusion index	Breadth of coverage (54.0)		
	Depth of use (29.7)	Payment (4.3), money funds (6.4), credit (10), insurance (16.0), investment (25.0), credit investigation (38.3)	
	Level of digitization (16.3)	Credit (9.5), convenience (16.0), affordability (24.8), mobility (49.7)	

indicator system was calculated by the layer-by-layer weighted arithmetic mean synthesis model.

NOTES

1. *Digital finance*, similar to concepts such as internet finance and financial technology, can be defined both broadly and narrowly: in a broad sense, all the financial services offered by banks and other traditional financial institutions, as well as internet companies, via digital technology are regarded as digital finance; in a narrow sense, digital finance generally refers to a new financial model employed by internet companies. *Digital financial inclusion*, then, refers to the inclusive financial services enabled by such new digital finance as defined above. The digital finance referred to in this chapter is closer to its narrow definition, but it does not deny the tendency among traditional financial institutions such as banks to embrace new digital technologies during the transformation of their financial businesses.

2. Data contained in the indexes may be obtained from the research team by e-mail: pku_dfiic@163.com (Guo Feng).

3. The growth rate of 29.1 percent cannot be seen as the average annual growth rate of China's digital financial sector. The preliminary reason is that at the time of index preparation, the logarithmic efficacy function was applied by the research team to nondimensionalize the original indicators, so the growth rate obtained based on original data should be higher than 29.1 percent.

4. One cause of the slow growth in the depth of use is that its caliber has been continually adjusted to include new services; but even if this factor is excluded, for example, as far as the payment business alone is concerned, the growth rate of the depth of use index is still relatively low.

5. The Hu Line refers to an imaginary line proposed by the famous Chinese geographer Hu Huanyong (1901–1998) in 1935 to divide China by population density. It was originally named the Aihui-Tengchong Line, and later renamed as the Heihe-Tengchong Line (Hu 1935, 1990). This line stretches from Heihe City, Heilongjiang Province, in the northeast, to Tengchong City, Yunnan Province, in the southwest; it is famous because it divides China into two contrasting parts: east and west. The majority of China's population is concentrated in the east: east of the line, 94.4 percent of Chinese people are fed by 43.7 percent of the country's territory. The land in the west accounts for 56.3 percent of the total area while the population only accounts for 5.6 percent of the total.

6. A total of twenty-six indicators were included in stage I (2011–2015) of the index.

7. Because of space limitations, the specific process has been intentionally omitted.

REFERENCES

Barro, R. J., and X. Sala-i-Martin. 1992. "Convergence." *Journal of Political Economy* 100 (2): 223–51.

Demirguc-Kunt, A., and L. Klapper. 2012. "Measuring Financial Inclusion: The Global Findex Database." Policy Research Working Paper Series 6025. Washington, DC: World Bank.

Financial Consumer Protection Bureau of the People's Bank of China. 2018. *China Financial Inclusion Index Analysis Report.* Draft research report of the People's Bank of China, Beijing, August.

Global Partnership for Financial Inclusion. 2013. "Launch of the G20 Basic Set of Financial Inclusion Indicators,"https://databank.worldbank.org/data/download/g20fidata/GPFIsummarynote.pdf.

Guo, F. 2021. "The Role and Deficiencies of Digital Economy in the COVID-19 Pandemic: A Literature Review." *Review of Industrial Economics,* (no. 1): 34–49.

Guo, F., J. Wang, F. Wang, T. Kong, X. Zhang, and Z. Cheng. 2020. "Measuring China's Digital Financial Inclusion: Index Compilation and Spatial Characteristics." *China Economic Quarterly* 19 (4): 1401–18.

Hu, H. 1935. "The Distribution of Population in China, with Statistics and Maps." *Acta Geographica Sinica* 2 (2): 33–74.

———. 1990. "The Distribution, Regionalization and Prospect of China's Population." *Acta Geographica Sinica*, 45 (2): 139–45.

Huang, Y., and Z. Huang. 2018. "The Development of Digital Finance in China: Present and Future." *China Economic Quarterly* 1 (4): 205–18.

Jiao, J., T. Huang, T. Wang, S. Zhang, and Y. Wang. 2015. "China's Financial Inclusion Development Process and Empirical Research." *Shanghai Finance*, (no. 4): 12–22.

Sala-i-Martin, X. 1996. "The Classical Approach to Convergence Analysis." *Economic Journal* 106 (437): 1019–36.

Sarma, M. 2012. "Index of Financial Inclusion—a Measure of Financial Sector Inclusiveness." Berlin Working Papers on Money, Finance, Trade and Development 07/2012. Berlin: Competence Centre on Money, Trade, Finance and Development from Hochschule fuer Technik und Wirtschaft.

State Council of China. 2015. *Plan for Advancing Financial Inclusion Development (2016–2020).* Beijing.

Wang, J., F. Guo, Z. Li, F. Wang, Z. Jiang, and Y. Li. 2019. *How Digital Economy Boosts the Balanced Economic Development between East and West China.* Draft research report of the Institute of Digital Finance, Peking University, September.

World Bank Group. 2015. *Global Financial Development Report 2014: Financial Inclusion.* Beijing: China Financial & Economic Publishing House.

Xiao, K. 2021. "Saving Lives versus Saving Livelihoods: Can Big Data Technology Solve the Pandemic Dilemma?" In *Impact of COVID-19 on Asian Economies and Policy Responses*, edited by Sumit Agarwal, Zhiguo He, and Bernard Yeung, pp. 19–24. Singapore: World Scientific.

Xie, X., Y. Shen, H. Zhang, and F. Guo. 2018. "Can Digital Finance Promote Entrepreneurship? Evidence from China." *China Economic Quarterly* 17 (4): 1557–80.

Yi, X., and L. Zhou. 2018. "Does Digital Financial Inclusion Significantly Influence Household Consumption? Evidence from Household Survey Data in China." *Journal of Financial Research* (11): 47–67.

3

China's Payment Reform and Its Implications for Other Countries

AARON KLEIN

Payment systems are critical components of an economy. The purchase and sale of goods and services require a method by which transactions can be executed. As modern economies grow more complex and transactions between buyers and sellers become more anonymous, expeditious, and reliable, the importance of payment systems grows. As Federal Reserve chairman Jerome Powell stated, "An efficient payments system provides the infrastructure needed to transfer money in low-cost and convenient ways. Efficient systems are innovative in improving the quality of services in response to changing technology and changing demand."[1]

Fifty years ago, the United States led a global revolution with the creation of magnetic striped cards linked to bank accounts and lines of credit.[2] These cards, and the corresponding terminals that read them, allowed a small piece of plastic to replace cash and checkbooks for billions of consumers and merchants and process trillions of transactions. These cards achieved such ubiquity in the developed Western world that most consumers and international travelers take their presence for granted.

The use of such cards has continued to grow, providing the backbone for e-commerce and new methods of digital payments (figure 3-1). Devices can now turn smartphones into credit card processors (Square), and transactions

FIGURE 3-1.   **Number of Non-cash Payments**

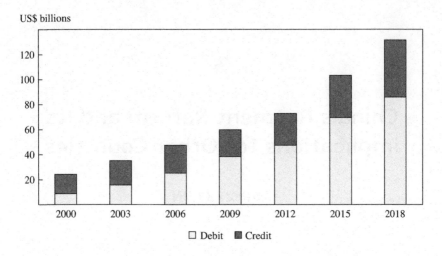

can be made securely online (PayPal). However, the underlying payment networks in the United States remain a bank-based system.

The next global revolution in payments is here. In the past decade China has experienced an internal payments revolution, leapfrogging magnetic cards and moving to a system based on smartphones and Quick Response (QR) codes. But the Chinese payment system goes far beyond just a new technological form to something revolutionary: it has largely disintermediated the banking system.

In the United States, and in most developed economies globally, the payment and banking systems have been intertwined for centuries. The connection between the two is clear: the financial institutions that hold the parties' funds are best equipped to mediate payments between the parties. Yet new financial technology and the Chinese application have created a viable alternative payments model where banks play a far less central role, and in the extreme, possibly no role at all.

This new payment form requires greater analysis to appreciate the benefits, costs, and implications of a new model. Understanding this model will help answer key questions and inform policy decisions on how the United States ought to modernize its payment system. Put more concretely, will the US-led invention of magnetic stripes and card readers be globally replaced by digital wallets using QR codes to transfer funds external to the banking system? Will banks continue to play a central role in operating payment systems, or will new tech disintermediate banks? If disintermediation occurs, what are the ramifications of combining payments with commerce instead of banking?

UNDERSTANDING THE CHINESE SYSTEM: STARTING POINTS

China seems like an unlikely candidate to develop a new payment system. The nation boasts strong banking rates for its citizens, largely as a result of the government's use of the banking system to provide benefits to citizens. Many Chinese citizens have at least two bank accounts, as the government provides subsidies for different benefits through different banks.[3] Additionally, Chinese banks worked collaboratively to create UnionPay, a Chinese-based card network.

China has the largest card network in the world with 8.2 billion cards.[4] According to the People's Bank of China, the vast majority—7.5 billion—are debit cards, while only 734 million are credit cards. Because UnionPay is protected from foreign competition by the Chinese government's refusal to allow Visa, Mastercard, or American Express into the country, it seemed plausible that UnionPay would develop into the dominant payment system within China, mimicking the card-based system in other large economies.

However, adoption of the card-based terminals among Chinese merchants ran into opposition. First, merchants did not like the fees and balked at the idea of paying even 100 basis points for processing payments. Merchants were slow to adopt card readers and reluctant to either absorb the costs or pass them along to customers. Second, card readers require either a wired telephonic system or a wireless system to communicate. Both require merchants to integrate that technology and pay the associated costs. Again, merchants showed little interest in doing so, which helps explain why there were only just over 32 million point-of-sale terminals in China at the end of 2019.[5]

Cash remained a dominant method for exchange. However, cash has its drawbacks. In China, the highest circulating note is the 100 yuan, worth roughly US$15. As the highest note in circulation, the 100 yuan is a relatively low-value note compared with the $100 bill in the United States and the €500 note. As a result, cash transactions, particularly for higher-value goods and services, are more cumbersome. It is not uncommon for Chinese stores to have a cash-counting machine to facilitate transactions and protect against counterfeit notes.

Because of merchants' resistance to cards and the challenges associated with cash, the use of an alternative system becomes more likely. The strong growth of smartphone adoption created room for an alternative system to develop. Smartphones provide a new network of communication that can compete with card readers that require landlines or wireless internet/Voice over Internet Protocol.

The second component of this revolution is the QR code. In the card-based system, the customer is not required to be online. The merchant provides the terminal and a connection, and the customer provides the payment instrument (card). The adoption of a QR code, much like the barcode before it, allows merchants who are not connected via phone or the internet to access the payment system, as only one party needs to be connected for the transaction. This feature flips the previous card system, in which merchants were responsible for providing the connection.

The QR code allows for the customer to provide the connection. All the merchant has to produce is a barcode that can be printed on a simple piece of paper (figure 3-2). The consumer can leverage the smartphone to both scan the QR code and go online to process the transaction. This lowers the merchant costs even further, particularly for those who do not have easy access to telecommunications. It even allows for person-to-person transactions for people who have codes but not smartphones. Even beggars on the street are using QR codes to receive money—in essence, tin cups have been replaced with QR codes in China.[6]

CHINA'S TRANSFORMATION

Given the starting point, the end point is quite stunning. The number of users and growth on both the Alipay and WeChat Pay platforms have been substantial and reached near ubiquity in under a decade. These two payment platforms are now the largest system in China and among the largest in the world.

Alipay has recently overtaken WeChat Pay in active users. Alipay reached 1.3 billion users in 2020, and WeChat Pay surpassed 1.2 billion users in 2020

FIGURE 3-2.   **QR Codes as Means of Payment in China**

(figure 3-3).[7] These two forms of payment dominate the Chinese market. Over 90 percent of people in China's largest cities use WeChat Pay and Alipay as their primary payment method, with cash second, and card-based debit/credit a distant third.

Mobile payments in China have reached over US$50 trillion (331 trillion yuan) annually (figure 3-4).[8] More than 94 percent of mobile payments are made over the two dominant platforms: Alipay (54.5%) and WeChat Pay (39.5%).[9] This rise is even more stunning when considering its rapidity.

How Alipay and WeChat Pay Work

Alipay and WeChat Pay rely on technologies that are widely available but not commonly used in the United States. These technologies (e.g., a digital wallet and QR codes) allow them to offer an easy, low-cost method for transmitting payment between parties nearly instantly. Understanding each technology is necessary for understanding how the system works.

FIGURE 3-3.   **Alipay versus WeChat: Number of Active Users**

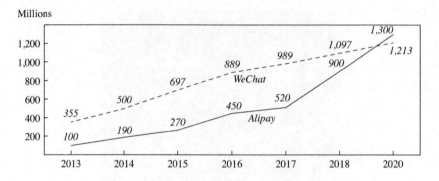

Source: Statista, China.org.cn, XinhuaNet, Technisia.

FIGURE 3-4.   **Third-Party Mobile Payment Transaction Volume**

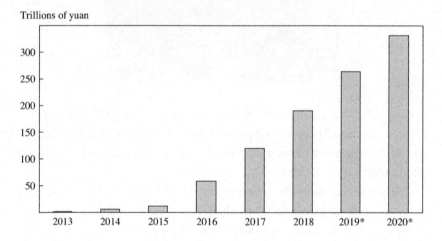

Source: IResearch Global Group.

*Projected transaction volumes

A digital wallet stores one or more of a consumer's payment credentials electronically and allows the consumer to electronically transmit funds in multiple settings.[10] The wallet is generally funded either by transferring funds from another digital wallet or by linking a bank account and transmitting funds. This concept is different from a digital representation of a credit card, as is commonly done on ApplePay.[11] A digital wallet stores money,

FIGURE 3-5.   **QR Codes Being Used as Payment Methods**

Source: Shutterstock.

whereas a digital representation of a card simply substitutes a virtual card for the physical one.

There are important distinctions between Alipay and WeChat Pay in how wallets are initially funded, which will be discussed later. For now, assume that the money is in a digital wallet and that the other side of the transaction has a corresponding digital wallet that can accept or transmit payment.

QR codes are modern two-dimensional bar codes.[12] With "QR" standing for Quick Response, QR codes are "open source," have a large data capacity, and have multiple uses, such as storing contact details or digital payments.[13] Each entity in the Alipay and WeChat ecosystems is assigned a unique QR code. Individuals have them for their accounts, merchants have them for their stores, and even specific payment points such as a parking garage have them (figure 3-5).

The payment process starts when one party, either the payer or the payee, scans the other's QR code. The scan can be done by one smartphone to another, or by a smartphone to a QR code that is digitally represented or physically printed on a piece of paper. The payer can total the amount due into the transaction for the payee to scan, or the payee can scan the code and insert the amount to be paid. This is analogous to swiping a credit or debit

The Parking Garage Metaphor

Digital wallets simply transmit the funds between the two parties directly on the platform. The funds remain in each digital wallet. Depending on the transaction, an electronic notification can be embedded that signals a transaction was completed and a bill was paid. This creates another moment of integration between the payment system and the purchase of goods and services.

Consider a parking garage. The traditional system involves taking a ticket upon entrance, paying the ticket, and presenting the paid ticket upon exit. Some newer garages have tried to improve this system by eliminating the ticket altogether. Instead, the driver uses a credit or debit card upon entry, the payment system records that unique card, and the driver presents the same card upon exit. The card is automatically charged the parking fee. Whether the traditional ticket system or the credit or debit card system, both are time-consuming, are costly, and require multiple card-reading terminals.

The Chinese system involves scanning a code upon entry, which marks the time you entered the garage. You then scan the code again upon exit, your wallet is automatically charged, and the gate opens. This requires wireless communication between smartphones and the parking garage gates. It eliminates multiple card readers, charges for card processing, and the insertion of parking tickets and/or credit cards.

The elimination of card swipe costs is particularly important for low-dollar, high-volume transactions such as those of municipal garages. If parking costs US$2, a card processing fee of 25 cents per transaction means that for every eight cars parking in the garage, one of them is paying the payment costs. Credit cards, particularly luxury platinum cards, can have fees closer to 40 or 50 cents on a US$2 transaction, further challenging the economics of the parking system.

card and either accepting the amount shown or entering the amount you want to pay.

One advantage of this system is that the card-reading terminal has been cut out completely. Instead, the Chinese system works directly from account to account via WeChat or Alipay, without a processor in between the two entities. This makes for a less costly and quicker transaction (as anyone who has waited for a credit card terminal to process can attest). It also explains why China has so few point-of-sale terminals and one of the strongest digital payment systems in the world. Cutting out the middleman saves time and money.

HOW TO FUND A CHINESE DIGITAL WALLET

The simplest and most common way to put funds in your digital wallet is to upload them from your bank account. Customers link a bank account to either platform and can upload funds instantly. In general, this service is provided at no cost to the consumer. If the sending bank charges a fee, it is usually paid by the digital wallet provider that is uploading the funds; downloading funds is a different proposition and will be discussed later.

This is similar to the method used to fund PayPal digital wallets, with an important difference in the speed of the service. With a faster payment system than that of the United States, China does not require customers to wait multiple days for funds to upload.[14]

Prefunded digital wallets in China are similar to debit and prepaid cards in the United States. The Chinese wallets generally do not function on a revolving line of credit system and should not be thought of as substitutes for credit cards. Should Ant Financial, the banking arm of the Alibaba/Alipay enterprise, wish to provide credit to fund these wallets, it can and does (as does WeChat Pay). This is an option for some, although it is not nearly as common as it is for US credit cards, nor is it provided on the same terms. Similarly, banks or other lenders could access both platforms and provide credit alternatives to prefund the digital wallets. But the terms and economics of this are less advantageous because of the lack of fee revenue generated by using the payment platforms as discussed below.

Thus, the simplest model is for users to link their bank account(s) to digital wallet(s) and then upload funds as needed. Those funds survive in the ecosystem and can be augmented by future uploads or other funds received in transfers from other persons or businesses, with consumer digital wallets more likely to be replenished by personal transfers, and business digital wallets likely to be filled by new revenue.

Digital wallets still require funds to be moved into the banking system for banking purposes. Digital wallets themselves do not pay interest, as they are not interest-bearing bank accounts. To generate interest, the user must move funds into a money market account, bank account, or other investment account. Investing requires customers to move funds out of the Alipay/WeChat Pay wallets and into the banking system. This is commonplace and can be done quite easily through both platforms. Of course, the products available and the banks able to offer services on those platforms are a function of the relationships and partnerships between the tech platform parents and other institutions.

Originally, the parent company could and did use customer funds for its own purposes to park in overnight funds and earn interest for the business. But the Chinese government started cracking down on this in 2017 with a requirement that 20 percent of customer funds had to be kept in a custodial account at a Chinese bank that did not bear interest.[15] That figure was subsequently raised to 50 percent in 2018 and then to 100 percent in 2019. The result is estimated to transfer US$1 billion in interest being earned by Alipay and WeChat back to the banking system. This move was interpreted as an attempt by the Chinese government to either rein in the use of mobile payments or support Chinese banks.[16] However, in 2020 the People's Bank of China reversed itself again to provide 35 basis points of interest to the digital wallets.[17]

Origins of WeChat Pay and Alipay

WeChat Pay and Alipay differ in how funds are spent. The difference is largely derived from the origin and purpose of each system. WeChat Pay is based on a social media platform (think Facebook) and is heavily engaged in person-to-person payments. Alipay is rooted in a digital commerce platform (think Amazon) and hence is more likely to receive business revenue or be used for business purposes.

Tencent, WeChat's parent company, wanted to incentivize purchases for online games and ecosystems (think Candy Crush) or other popular in-game purchases. Widespread credit/debit cards linked to game accounts make this easy. But in 2007, Tencent's user base lacked this system, so it created a digital coin: QQ. The QQ coin went viral both as a means of online game payment and as a speculative digital currency. Estimates were almost US$1 billion of coins traded with an appreciation of over 70 percent in value.[18]

The process of uploading QQ coins and spending them offline, coupled with speculators sharply influencing the price of the coins, made them ultimately nonviable as a medium of exchange. In this way, the QQ coin was similar to bitcoin and its inability to gain a foothold for routine payments. However, the experience certainly shaped Tencent's thinking and demonstrated the willingness of Chinese citizens to use digital currency.

WeChat Pay was rolled out around the Lunar New Year in 2014 as a service to facilitate personal funds in the form of Red Envelopes (or Red Packets).[19] It is common for individuals in China to give cash to other individuals in the new year, particularly between parents, children, and other family members. WeChat Pay proposed digitizing this exchange, which given its person-to-person social media network, was clearly synergistic.

The popularity of Red Envelope exchanges seeded many customers' WeChat Pay accounts with initial funds.[20] In its first year, 16 million Red Packets were sent. The next year, 1 billion packets were sent. In 2016, it was over 8 billion, and in 2017, 46 billion (figure 3-6). It is not clear whether WeChat still publishes separate data on Red Packets, but it has become commonplace. And as these data clearly show, the practice of digitizing this gift took off rapidly.

FIGURE 3-6.   **Total Red Packets Exchanged via WeChat**

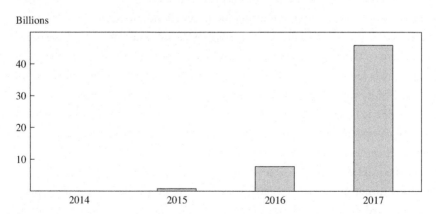

Source: The Lowdown.

With QR codes widely available and cheap for merchants to adopt, as well as a large user base funded with Red Packets, WeChat's path to creating an alternative payment platform was clear. What started with consumers then translated to merchants as merchants saw their accounts increase when customers purchased goods. Merchants can use the funds in their digital wallets to pay bills from other businesses or transfer funds for personal use. Most small businesses, after all, are closely integrated with personal accounts.

Alipay's origins differ. This platform got its start with the realization that the lack of a credit card system is a major problem. Internet commerce required electronic payment systems, which were integrated with credit and debit cards. As the Peterson Institute's Martin Chorzempa illustrated in a detailed analysis, the lack of such a system in China incentivized Alibaba to develop Alipay such that its Taobao web platform could take off.[21] With UnionPay only recently launching and not yet gaining a large number of customers, the payment market was wide open. Alibaba offers several incentives for merchants to use Alipay for purchases made on the platform: (1) a lack of any fees on such purchases for either party, (2) the potential preferential placement on digital platforms for both merchants, and (3) the ease of payment integration into business processing. Each provides substantial economic benefits that are not widely available in the bifurcated credit/debit card system. There are also potential drawbacks of this integrated model, including the lack of fees to provide services that customers want with payments—such as interest-free grace periods of credit—and anticompetitive concerns of integrating business platforms and social networks with payment platforms.

The lack of fees is a huge incentive for merchants. Consider a small business that pays over 2 percent for payment processing fees, which is the average in the United States for major cards like Visa, Mastercard, and Discover.[22] Businesses can save 2 percent of gross sales by using Alipay, provided that revenue is also spent on the platform. Payment processing fees are based on gross sales, not net revenue, and as a result, the savings potential as a share of profits is far greater. In general, business profits average only 7.9 percent of total gross revenue.[23] Saving 2 percent of gross revenue could have an impact closer to 20 percent of profit margins.

The implications differ based on business size, although it is not clear in which direction. While larger businesses are often able to negotiate lower credit card processing fees, they also typically have smaller net profit margins as a share of gross revenue. Smaller businesses generally pay more for card processing, although new entrants into the marketplace, like Square and PayPal, are driving down costs. However, small businesses also typically have larger gross margins and, depending on the nature of the business, may receive fewer payments from cards. Either way, lowering processing fees is a win for merchants.

There is also an important caveat to the zero-fee system: the funds have to be spent on the Alibaba ecosystem. This is because there is a cost to downstream funds back into the banking system, which may have a larger impact on merchants when they receive revenue through Alipay. It now creates a different final cash flow/profit structure depending on whether they received the funds through Alipay and were able to spend it elsewhere in the Ali ecosystem; had to download the funds to their bank account; received funds through an alternative digital platform (WeChat Pay); or were paid with debit cards, credit cards, or cash. It is not clear (depending on the merchant's business model and payment usage) whether the business can effectively use all of the funds on Alipay to purchase the intermediate goods and services it uses within the Ali ecosystem.

This creates incentives for the Ali ecosystem to expand in order to provide more services to businesses. It also creates a comparative advantage for pricing within the Ali ecosystem, as well as competitive disincentives for off-platform business. It is possible that Ali can recapture some (or all) of this value through alternative charges for conducting business on the platform, such as advertising fees.

This second incentive to create further avenues to expand the goods and services available on the same ecosystems as the payment networks is quite different from the American/European system. Banks do not host large platforms on which consumers and merchants may purchase goods and services. The payment processing sector of the economy—Visa, Mastercard, Square, Verifone, Venmo, PayPal, and so forth—exists to facilitate merchants accessing the payment system to complete transactions.

The movement of payment processing from the banking system to the commerce system in China raises a series of economic incentives and competitive forces that are largely absent in the US context. This is not because of the separation of banking and commerce in the United States. That separation does not place payments in the sphere of banking. Banking is generally tied to the taking of deposits or making of loans.[24] While economists appreciate the intellectual equivalency of a bank providing a revolving line of credit that allows consumers ninety days to repay with interest charged, and a service provider offering a similar window with a series of escalating late fees, the legal system defines one as banking and the other as commerce.

Payments have historically existed within banking because banks had the technology, networks, knowledge of customers, and funding structure to most easily provide these services. The Chinese payment revolution is fundamentally changing that equation. Technology—particularly interconnections on social media, the scale of digital e-commerce platforms, and adoption of modern bar codes—broadens the capability of new entrants into the system.

The final point is the converse of the earlier one: What other nonbanking services that use the payment system could potentially become integrated into a Chinese model? One possibility would be payroll processing. Rather than having employers take revenue from the digital payment system into their banks, then transfer to employee banks, only to have the employee then transfer the funds back onto the ecosystem, why not have the ecosystem handle payments directly?

The initial version of this chapter, published as a paper in 2019, noted that, at the time, services were not usually offered in a structured way through Alipay and WeChat Pay. It predicted expansion by Alipay or WeChat into payment processing as a logical extension, aided by the funds in digital wallets that retailers and employees share. (Imagine if Amazon or Facebook offered payroll processing to compete with firms like ADP.) Shortly afterward, Alipay began offering payroll services through a new application called Fabei.[25] Originally aimed at small employers, the application is capped at 250,000 yuan per day to prevent the largest employers from transitioning. Economies of scope between payment systems and payroll processing exist, and it is no surprise that Chinese payment systems would expand their services in this direction. The combination of information for workers, of both their wages and spending habits, would seem to open up additional doors for more precise targeting of advertising or allocation of credit.

How to Get Money Out of the Ecosystem (but Why Would You?)

The Chinese payment system makes it easy to continually keep funds in digital wallets. The ubiquity of acceptance, lack of fees, and ease of commerce motivate consumers. Money brought into the digital wallet system can be moved into interest-bearing accounts, like money market funds, or invested in Chinese stocks directly through broker-dealer accounts partnered with the platform.

This is particularly the case with Alipay becoming part of Ant Financial. Ant's largest mutual fund, Tianhong Yu'ebao, has almost 600 million investors, over US$178 billion in funds, and short-term interest of over 2 percent and generally provides a better return than leaving funds in a Chinese bank.[26] The growth of this fund, mirroring the growth of Alipay as a digital wallet, highlights the opportunity to merge digital wallets with broker-dealer accounts directly, further disintermediating the bank deposit relationship.

Businesses have similar motives and opportunities to keep funds in the ecosystem, but greater demands to take funds out of the ecosystem and make payments using the banking system. Both consumers and businesses need an off-ramp, and though it exists, it is not designed to be terribly attractive.

Account holders can move funds out of Alipay or WeChat Pay and back into their linked bank accounts. Alipay allows up to 20,000 yuan (roughly US$3,000) to be withdrawn, but after that withdraws are subject to a minimum of a 0.1 percent fee.[27] WeChat charges a similar fee: 10 basis points for all transfers above 1,000 yuan (roughly US$150) into bank accounts. For transfers under 1,000 yuan, there is a flat fee of 0.1 yuan.[28] While this fee is small relative to US standards—credit card transfer fees are usually in the range of 2–4 percent, and digital wallet providers like PayPal pass those fees directly on to the customer[29]—the fee appears directly to Chinese consumers. This is a stark contrast to the fee-free zone of all payments within the ecosystem. This is by design, as one analyst describes: "The transaction fees will encourage users to make fewer withdrawals and thus keep more money circulating within the WeChat Wallet ecosystem, therefore increasing the opportunities for other spending within it."[30]

CREDIT IS A BIT DIFFERENT

Fees are assessed when funds are moved out of the digital wallet and online platforms associated with each provider and back into the banking system. There is a much smaller but growing provision of credit through the Alipay and WeChat Pay system as well. As mentioned earlier, China is still a heavily debit, prefunded system with relatively little penetration of credit cards to fund purchases.

Both Ant and Tencent are entering the credit space. Unlike the well-developed and widely used credit scoring systems (the accuracy of which is another matter) in the United States and Europe, China has less in the way of credit scoring.[31] Much has been made of Ali, WeChat, and others using a social credit scoring system that incorporates factors such as how well reviewed a merchant's business is or the strength of a person's social network. It is natural for technology and social media firms to focus on data they have, especially proprietarily. Abstractly, is it any more or less accurate to predict the future cash flows of a business on past bill payments or current Yelp reviews?

The credit-based system in the United States relies heavily on interchange (swipe) fees to fund the provision of services like interest-free grace periods, rewards points, account costs, collections, and so forth. The lack of fees generated by the Chinese payment system is a significant barrier to the adoption of a similar credit-based system. As opposed to debit cards, credit cards typically offer customers interest-free grace periods between the purchase of goods and payment of the card, provided the customer is paying the bill in full and on time. This interest-free grace period provides value to the consumer and a cost to the credit provider. Rewards points are essentially (and sometimes directly) money transfers meant to entice consumers to use the card, particularly for a payment. These costs are more than offset by the charge of swipe fees, as discussed above.[32] This creates the economic environment for the provision of credit cards to consumers who never use the credit feature but are profitable customers for the bank originating the card.

The lack of fees in the Chinese payment system makes the economics of a credit-based system far more challenging and likely impossible without the creation of an alternative revenue stream (perhaps with data or selling preferred access to the platform).

Devoid of an interchange fee, the Chinese credit card system is starting to charge consumers directly, with Ant Financial imposing a 10-basis-point monthly fee on Alipay credit users who charge more than 2,000 yuan (US$300) a month.[33] Passing the cost directly on to customers decreases incentives to use credit. It is an interesting development that runs counter to the US system, where the wealthier a consumer, the lower their costs to use and access funds.

Costs of the System: Who Pays What?

A central element of this system is that transactions between parties on the same platform are free. That is, the sending and receiving of funds occur without a charge by the platform. This is not the same as the transactions being costless. All transactions involve some cost, however small, in building, maintaining, and operating the platform, a non-zero cost in digital transfers, and some cost for an error-resolution system. Most of these costs are relatively fixed; that is, marginal transactions have very little cost, and the more transactions in the system, the lower the average cost per transaction. However, the costs of operating the system are incurred by the platform; hence, from the user's perspective, both consumers and businesses can experience costless payments and instant settlement.

In addition to direct costs, there are also opportunity costs. Generally speaking, funds left in the main digital wallet on either platform are not interest bearing. Thus, the account holder is losing possible interest. Recognizing this, the platforms, particularly Alipay, have built in partner operations that provide interest-bearing accounts. Alipay has developed a robust ecosystem of financial services applications, including money market funds and stock brokerage accounts for consumers, and lending operations for small businesses.[34]

For an American consumer audience, the nearest parallel is the range of services that a combined bank and broker-dealer offers its customers: a checking account, often with no interest but immediate access; a savings account that pays interest; a money market account that pays a higher rate of interest but has either a higher minimum threshold or some limit on liquidity; and finally a brokerage account that keeps stocks, bonds, and possibly a different cash balance that itself is invested in a money market fund, sometimes on an overnight (nightly sweep) basis. In the Chinese context, Alipay and Ant Financial offer all these services. WeChat Pay and Tencent, along with affiliates, offer a similar range of services.

Importantly, in the Chinese context the payment provider has access to a broader set of information regarding a customer's financial life. For example, a regular bank probably does not know what your exact relationship is with everyone who sends you a birthday gift, but it does know the amount of the gift and the name of the sender if sent by a check. By merging its social media network with the Red Envelope funds transfer, WeChat is privy to such information. For example, if you are a younger adult who is lucky enough to receive regular or even sporadic support from your parents, grand-parents, or other extended family, WeChat is able to see into your network, both socially and financially.

This has ramifications for a host of financial services possibilities. The ability to lend against expected gift income becomes far more possible, as does a potential notification system of financial stress. Corresponding pri-vacy concerns arise, as do questions regarding liability should such future gifts not follow historical patterns. The point here is not to go into depth on the pros and cons of possible financial innovations or their resulting prob-lems; rather, it is to point out that combining information regarding social connectivity and financial flows between people and businesses opens up a range of possibilities.

For small businesses, a similar but broader set of options is available. The ability to lend against payment flows is greatly enhanced under the Chinese model. This has a direct comparison with the United States, where certain payment processors, such as Square, have begun directly lending to small businesses on the basis of cash flow conducted through payment processing.[35]

Banks and Payments: A Match Made in History?

Payment systems are network economies. Ubiquity allows consumers to be certain that sellers will accept their form of payment. Sellers similarly value ubiquity. Both parties require trust: trust that the method of payment will work, trust that the value being transacted will remain throughout the trans-action, and trust that in case of error there are steps for recourse.

There are many reasons why payments have historically been inte-grated into the banking system. Banks are chartered entities granted spe-cial authority and support by the central government to handle and create money. Banks store money for their customers, consumers, and businesses—a central role for any payment provider. Given that banks serve this role, providing payment services is a logical extension of the banking business model.

Banks are highly trusted third-party intermediaries that enjoy a strong status among counterparties, which is core to the business model of banking.[36] Consumers must trust that their deposits are available, while banks must trust their borrowers to repay funds.

Additionally, banks are ubiquitous, as most customers and businesses have a bank account. Banks are also highly networked given their requirements to interact with each other for nonretail payments. Central banks often serve as required networks, another reason why they often operate their own payment systems.

Even when payment systems form outside the banking system, they quickly integrate with the banking system. Despite some popular misconceptions, Visa is a technology and payments firm, not a bank (American Express, however, became a bank during the financial crisis). Visa issues cards and provides the technological platform, but the actual cards are sponsored by banks.

The United States has separated the business of banking from general commerce. Banks, from the top of their corporate structure (a bank or financial holding company), are generally prohibited from owning or operating a commercial enterprise. This is not the case in many other countries—notably Japan, where companies like Mitsubishi are major banks and commercial enterprises. US banks are major players in the payment space, as that is one area where they can and do operate.

Interestingly, a commercial company can provide payment services without providing banking services. The restrictions put in place by the separation of banking and commerce define banking mostly in terms of providing deposit accounts, making loans, and being a chartered bank. Historically, as banks were central in the business of payments, the US system has subtly assumed payments were on the banking side, but that does not have to be the case.

Most of the consumer protection laws protecting payments are tied to the banking system. This made sense when these laws were passed, as banks provided most payment services and were already highly regulated. Enforcement from both the government and private litigation were readily apparent, as banks are not fly-by-night operations.

Enter the Chinese system. The Chinese payment system has developed with little reliance on the Chinese banking system. This caught banks relatively flat-footed as their own payment initiatives around the traditional magnetic striped card, UnionPay, have struggled to keep up. It also caught

Chinese government officials and regulators somewhat by surprise (according to the author's conversations with various players in the ecosystem). Major reasons for adoption were the ubiquity of smartphones, ease of transactions, and distaste for fees.

The People's Bank of China and Digital Currency

China's technological leapfrog in payments provides the ability to easily move into a central bank digital currency (CBDC). CBDC is a digital form of central-bank-issued currency. While most currency is digital in nature (debit/credit cards, electronic banking), what is typically being transacted is private bank liabilities: paying for something with a debit card is spending the customer's bank's money, not the central bank's. Typically the only way a person or business can have a direct liability of the central bank is by physically holding cash. CBDC changes that by creating a new currency, digital in form, that is the liability of the central bank rather than a commercial or private bank.

The People's Bank of China has conducted four public giveaways of digital currency in four different Chinese cities since April 2020.[37] The so-called Digital Currency/Electronic Payment trials are among the first for any nation, let alone one of the largest economies on earth. In addition to stimulating spending in the wake of the COVID-19 pandemic, these giveaways allow Beijing to test out its new digital yuan. The latest and largest pilot yet was held in Shenzhen, where the government gave out 10 million yuan (about US$1.5 million).[38] Nearly 2 million individuals signed up for the lottery, and 50,000 received the 200 yuan prize. Each winner downloaded a digital wallet and used the digital currency at one of the 3,389 participating merchants, which included restaurants, gas stations, and supermarkets—including Walmart.[39] Consumer and merchant familiarity with the QR code and digital wallet infrastructure facilitated this experiment.

The innovative power of QR codes and digital wallets can be facilitated through multiple channels, including, as in this case, a CBDC. The large-scale test in Shenzhen illustrates the technological lead China gained through its experience with Alipay and WeChat Pay as well as its desire to continue innovating, potentially implementing its own CBDC. The decision to conduct this test in Shenzhen is clearly directly at WeChat, whose parent company Tencent is based in Shenzhen. Choosing this location is an assertion of governmental control over the future of China's payment system.[40] While there are potential drawbacks to a CBDC system, there are also many potential positives. As one recent paper described it, "CBDCs promise to realize a broad range of new capabilities, including direct government disbursements to citizens, frictionless consumer payment and money-transfer systems, and a range of new financial instruments and monetary policy levers."[41] China is well positioned to potentially realize some of these benefits as a direct result of earlier innovation of its payment system.

ADOPTION IN THE UNITED STATES

The natural first question is whether the Chinese system could take off in the United States, similar to how the US-led magnetic stripe system took off globally. The answer is likely no, as multiple factors make it unlikely that this system would catch on broadly in the United States. But an important corollary question is whether a payment system that disintermediates banks could take off in the United States given the country's long-standing legal separation between banking and commerce. The answer to this question is yes and has profound implications.

WeChat Pay and Alipay are accepted in the United States today. They cater mostly to Chinese travelers, including businesspeople and tourists, but also to the large number of transnational persons who work and live in both countries and continue to exist financially in both ecosystems. There are 2.5 million Chinese immigrants in the United States and 3 million persons who visit each year.[42]

WeChat Pay and Alipay are more commonly accepted, and likely to grow, in places such as New York, Los Angeles, and San Francisco, but also in areas that attract large numbers of foreign tourists, like Las Vegas and Orlando (especially Disneyland). Further, multinational companies that cater to Chinese tourism will likely add these payment forms to their existing platforms. This explains why Pier 39 in San Francisco and Guess Jeans are among the US retailers that are already accepting Alipay.[43]

Global cruise ship companies, like Royal Caribbean International (RCI), are quickly adopting Chinese mobile payment systems not only on their China-based ships but throughout their fleets. RCI began integrating Alipay on *Quantum of the Seas*, a ship "designed with our Chinese guests in mind" that sails directly out of Mainland China, but has now expanded to accept WeChat Pay and is currently piloting UnionPay mobile QuickPass.[44] Launching in 2018, RCI experienced over US$6 million in sales on the platforms in the first year and so far over US$7 million already in 2019, with an average transaction of approximately US$250.[45] As Royal Caribbean senior manager Frank Tuscano puts it: "Widespread digital wallet adoption in China was the catalyst for Royal Caribbean's latest innovation providing mobile payment services for guests that has significantly increased the velocity of commerce onboard China-based cruise ships. Guests are delighted to have a familiar, frictionless mobile payment experience at sea."[46]

The list of major US companies accepting Alipay is not confined to those whose customers are primarily Chinese tourists or have high incomes. In 2019, Walgreens partnered with Ant Financial and began allowing Alipay as a payment method at 7,000 of its US stores.[47] At first glance, Walgreens checks neither box: very few of its customers are Chinese tourists, and most transactions are small dollar. However, Walgreens is an active participant on Alibaba's online marketplace, giving it a brand presence in China and making it a likely recipient of Chinese payments. In addition to Walgreens, Boots brand, a popular beauty products and supplements company in the United Kingdom and part of the same conglomerate, is launching on the platform. Walgreens also owns 40 percent of the GuoDa pharmacy chain in China.[48]

The incentives for US companies to integrate into the Chinese payment system continue to grow as their retail and online presence in China grows. This makes sense given the economic advantages offered by the Chinese payment firms to companies that do business on their platforms. Thus, it is likely that as multinational US stores across the chain of targeted higher-income foreign tourists, or expand their businesses in China, they will also expand acceptance of Chinese payments in the United States. However, it is unlikely that American consumers will make the switch.

Why Americans Are Not Likely to Drop Their Cards for WeChat Pay and Alipay Wallets

The United States is unlikely to widely adopt these Chinese-based alternative payment forms, in large part because the current system works well for the wealthy. Ironically, what makes this platform unappealing to upper-income US consumers is the same as what makes it appealing in China: low fees.

The existing US payment system charges high fees and shares those fees with payment system providers (both banks and nonbanks) and consumers. These fees, often called swipe fees, include a minimum amount (between 20 and 40 cents) plus an average of 2 percent of the transaction. But they can range as high as 4 percent on deluxe credit cards. In total, swipe fees generate about US$100 billion a year.[49]

The system is deeply regressive.[50] Higher-income consumers are offered deluxe cards, which carry greater swipe fees and also generate more rewards. Further, because the rewards from the payment system are considered rebates and not income, they are passed to consumers tax-free. Thus, the pretax value of these rewards is even greater. For the typical high-end American who charges US$80,000 a year on a deluxe credit card that provides 1.5 percent cash back, that works out to US$1,200 of pretax income, or roughly US$2,000 of posttax income.

Given the low- to zero-fee environment offered in the Alipay/WeChat Pay system, there are simply not enough funds available to make an offer to these consumers that would entice them to give up their platinum or sapphire cards. Merchants are generally unable (because of a contract) or unwilling (because of culture) to offer differential pricing for cash versus credit.[51] There are legal prohibitions on surcharges for using cards, and while cash discounts are possible, they are not prevalent.

The recent Supreme Court decision in *Ohio* v. *American Express* restricts merchants that accept one form of a credit card from denying other versions of that card, even if those versions have higher fees.[52] The result of that decision is likely to be continued growth of high-end rewards cards, which further entice wealthier consumers, deepening the regressivity of the payment system.[53] Consumers see that growth in the continued offering of elite credit cards, with greater rewards.[54]

Further, aspects of the value proposition of Chinese payments are lost on wealthy American consumers. Rather than valuing the real-time settlement these systems provide, Americans who do not carry a balance on their credit cards enjoy thirty-day interest-free grace periods. The platform capability to integrate payments and social networking on WeChat and payments and online purchasing on Alipay is lost, as Americans are on Facebook, Instagram, Amazon, and eBay.

If wealthy consumers are a lost cause, what about competing for middle- and lower-income consumers? Even if the platform capabilities are lost,

FIGURE 3-7.   **Total Number of US Transactions, 2018**

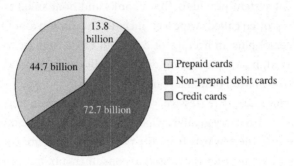

Source: The 2019 Federal Reserve Payments Study.

there is still the value of real-time settlement. One cannot suffer an over-draft on these systems, a feature of the US debit card system that costs American consumers US$35 billion a year in fees. Going down the income/payment spectrum leads to prepaid cards.

Payment forms in the United States are highly correlated with income. Growing income inequality has meant a larger group of people who rely on alternative forms of payment.[55] The explosion in prepaid cards has targeted this group and has gone largely unnoticed by wealthier Americans and policymakers for too long.

Prepaid cards, designed to look like credit and debit cards, were introduced in the 1990s and have grown substantially over the years.[56] In 2018 there were nearly 14 billion prepaid card transactions,[57] compared with just over 72 billion debit cards and just over 40 billion credit card transactions (figure 3-7). Put another way, more than one out of every ten swipes at the register in the United States is made with a prepaid card.

Consistent with the strong correlation between income and payment form, the average dollar value of a prepaid card transaction is US$25, compared with US$38 for a debit card and US$89 for a credit card (figure 3-8).[58]

Prepaid cards largely escaped regulation, as the existing system was set up under the premise of holding a bank account (debit) or a revolving loan (credit). This oversight was remedied in several steps. First, Congress passed the Credit Card Accountability, Responsibility, and Disclosure Act in 2009, designed to protect consumers from deceptive practices by credit card issuers.[59] Among other things, it included protection from rate hikes, enhanced

FIGURE 3-8. **Average Value of US Card Transactions, 2018**

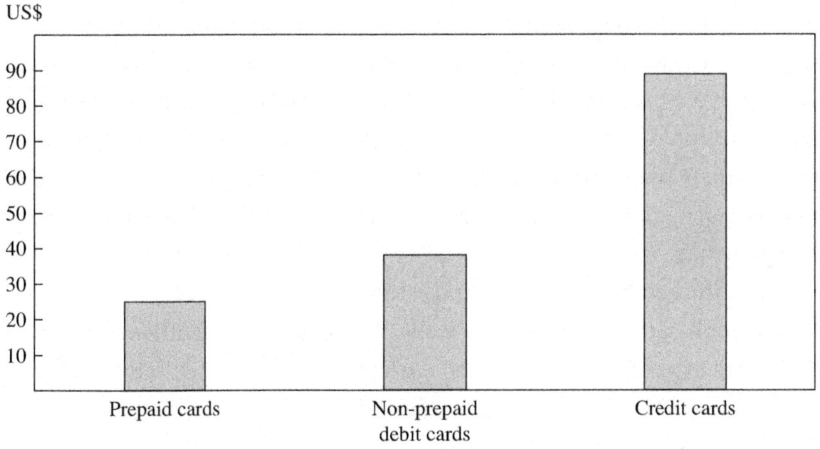

US$

Source: The 2019 Federal Reserve Payments Study.

information disclosure, strengthened protections for consumers under the age of twenty-one, and limited gift card and prepaid card provisions. Second, the Dodd-Frank Wall Street Reform and Consumer Protection Act of 2010 established the Consumer Financial Protection Bureau (CFPB) and expanded the CFPB's regulatory authority in this space. The result was a prepaid card rule by the bureau in 2017 that gave prepaid accounts important protections under the Electronic Fund Transfer Act, a system largely modeled on the regulatory regime under which debit cards operate.[60] These protections include extension of debit card fraud protections to prepaid card holders, implementation of a uniform fee to avoid hidden fees, information disclosure, and free access to basic account information.

Importantly, the bureau's original prepaid card rule also extended to digital wallets, like PayPal and Venmo.[61] If Alipay or WeChat Pay were to take off in the United States, they would likely face the same regulatory system as existing prepaid cards.

Prepaid cards are popular in the United States in part because they operate on the same payment rails as credit/debit cards, which meant that merchants did not need to add new accounts; existing payment processing companies were willing and able to integrate prepaid onto the system. If WeChat or Alipay did compete in this space, they would face some resistance from merchants if funds received through these mechanisms had to stay in that ecosystem. If combined costs to process transactions and move funds back into the banking system were higher than the existing system, they would have little incentive. But if fees were lower, which is possible given the swipe fees for prepaid and existing costs to transfer funds, then perhaps an argument could be made. Still, merchants would likely want to see some level of consumer usage before signing up. This would require both companies to make an aggressive marketing move to these markets, but so far neither company has.

Even though both WeChat and Alipay have begun accepting international credit cards to fund digital wallets, it is likely that neither company is seeking to expand to an international user base.[62] Linking with international credit cards, as opposed to debit, targets higher-income individuals, who in the United States are less interested in making the switch for their domestic purchases. It does comport with targeting international travelers. The targeting of this group appears to aim more for Chinese citizens living abroad and frequent international visitors to China, than to expand in the domestic market, which is logical for the retail payment aspect of the service. In fact, WeChat appears to have a "particular focus on those companies that specialize in high-end or designer products" as it expands into the Italian market.[63]

One final potential market to explore is person-to-person (P2P) transfers. This market in the United States has attracted substantial attention from domestic financial technology firms and social networking companies. Facebook's purchase and integration of Venmo comes to mind, but other payment processors like Square have rolled out P2P transfer functions based on moving funds between bank accounts, while PayPal has integrated digital wallets, bank accounts, and credit cards into one platform where consumers can choose P2P, person-to-business, or business-to-business transactions.

In China, WeChat Pay started with Red Packets, interfamily gifts of cash. In the United States, most families exchange gifts, not cash. This is an important cultural difference. While economists have argued that cash is a more efficient method of gifting and leads to higher utility, the practice of gifting cash has been negatively perceived, as one episode of *Seinfeld* famously demonstrated.[64]

However, the United States does have a substantially large exchange of gift cards, an interesting hybrid of cash and gift. Gift card exchanges are popular not just within families but also in broader social networks such as coworkers and volunteer groups. The most common gift card exchanged is likely the Starbucks card. It is estimated that one out of seven Americans receives a Starbucks gift card during the December holiday season.[65] Overall, gift cards in the United States were estimated at over US$193 billion in 2020, an increase of 93 percent from 2011.[66]

The impediments to using either Chinese system for gift card exchange start with the core problem that few Americans are on either system. Further, without broad acceptance, these systems seem unlikely to catch on. Put another way, the fact that so many Chinese citizens were already on both systems before WeChat and Alibaba integrated payment applications is a key reason why payments were so popular and easy to add. In this way one could imagine Amazon and Facebook being able to compete in this market, similar to Alipay and WeChat Pay. But it is very difficult to imagine people signing up for the Chinese services to give money to Americans who may not be on the system and may not know where or how they could spend it.

A final argument against US adoption is general uncertainty about the ability to access funds stored in digital wallets by Chinese companies. The ability to continually operate these systems with international cards depends on the rules put in place by these companies. Possible capital controls in China or changes in legal or regulatory structure will incentivize international travelers to more closely monitor balances. Additionally, restrictions against non-Chinese customers opening interest-bearing accounts make these digital wallets more akin to prepaid cards than to debit or credit cards. Ease and cost of use and possible uncertainty about the ability to return funds to the US financial system will likely reduce adoption.

CHINESE PAYMENTS GLOBALLY

If the US card-based system came to dominate retail payments in the developed world and in the noncash developing world, will China's new system replace it abroad, if not in the United States? In the developed world, the answer is likely no. China's system will find a place, but it will be challenging for it to supplant the US card-based system. In the developing world, the answer is not as clear and may depend on the actions taken by Chinese companies.

Starting with the developed countries, Europe, the United Kingdom, Japan, South Korea, Singapore, and other highly developed economies remain with bank-focused payment systems. While the usage of cards, in physical or digital form, varies, these countries' systems share the common structure of the US system: banks sending and receiving the funds on both ends with various payment processors in between. A widespread transition to the Chinese system by retail and merchants is unlikely for any of these countries, for reasons similar to and different from those for the United States.

The prevalence of adoption, familiarity, and sunk costs of the existing payment system serve as impediments to undergoing a large change in these developed countries. While some of these countries have different rules and structures regarding payment fees, including a higher incidence of passing along payment surcharges for card fees, by and large merchants and banks have reached an equilibrium of acceptance and partnership.

National differences in payment methods can be sticky and hard to explain. As Silva and others found in a cross-national comparison within the European Union of national check usage, "Socio-demographic characteristics of consumers can have an important role in improving the results of measures adopted by authorities or in slowing them."[67] In particular, the study found that younger and higher-educated consumers are more likely than older and less educated consumers to replace checks with other forms of payment, although legal factors and fees were also important factors.

Another key component is the prevalence, or lack, of mobile wallets. For example, Singapore, a country with a reputation for early adoption of technology (particularly financial), is reported to have one of the lowest adoption rates of mobile wallets and one of the highest loyalty rates to credit cards.[68] Countries with high mobile wallet adoption rates, or where mobile wallet providers are hoping to make that the case, will be more likely to see greater adoption. This is happening in some European countries, where a partnership was launched between six digital wallet providers in ten countries and Alipay.[69] However, these six mobile wallet providers together have only 5 million users combined, a far cry from the 1 billion on Alipay alone. Interestingly, the harmonization of this platform focuses on QR code compatibility, a reminder that the future battlefield for payment platforms may well be on QR codes, not on fees for using bank-built payment rails.[70]

Most mobile wallets have real-time payments, which improves the quality and value proposition for consumers, particularly lower-income consumers who need to more closely align their expenditures with their incomes. This important but often overlooked difference among Europe, the United Kingdom, Japan, and other nations adds to the value of their existing debit systems as compared with that of the United States, where overdraft charges cost lower-income consumers tens of billions annually.

In addition, some of the economic advantages of the Alipay and WeChat Pay systems are predicated on businesses and consumers transacting more heavily throughout those ecosystems. Without large-scale adoption of those platforms more generally, the value proposition of just their payment systems is lower for businesses and consumers.

However, the Chinese payment system revolution will still affect these countries. The impact will differ between other countries and the United States. The first difference is how quickly some merchants will begin to provide Chinese payment alternatives and how widespread this will be. The simplest prediction from this research is that where Chinese travelers and multinationals make up a large enough share of business, payment alternatives should follow. The most popular destinations for Chinese travelers are Japan, Thailand, South Korea, the United States, and Singapore (figure 3-9).[71]

FIGURE 3-9.   **Alipay and WeChat Pay Accepted as a Form of Payment in Japan**

Retail businesses with large numbers of Chinese customers should be among the first to adopt these payment forms. Indeed, this is already the case in many of these nations. One study found that "77% of Chinese tourists spent more via mobile payments on their most recent overseas trip than on previous trips over the past two years."[72]

Other differences will affect how quickly banks in these countries form partnerships with the Chinese payment providers and their affiliated banks. In South Korea, Tencent was able to execute a partnership with Woori Bank in 2015 to provide payment services for WeChat Pay.[73] The economics of this transaction relied on foreign exchange fees between the Chinese customer and the South Korean merchant, a system that is more like the credit card model previously employed.

Interestingly, when a Korean company, KakaoPay, began to implement a similar mobile wallet/QR code system for retail payments, executives from Tencent did not view it as a competitor.[74] This was because Tencent was not aiming to target Korean customers; instead, WeChat said Tencent was "targeting only Chinese people."[75]

On the other side, the South Korean government is trying to capitalize on its ability to serve the 6 million annual Chinese visitors to South Korea in order to promote its own low-cost payment network. ZeroPay, which is based on the digital wallet/QR code system, aims to help small businesses lower payment costs; it recently signed a deal to serve both Alipay and WeChat Pay.[76]

Partnerships are not limited to the developed world. WeChat has partnered with Standard Bank to allow customers to withdraw WeChat amounts at ATMs in South Africa.[77] Both Alipay and WeChat Pay are accepted in about fifty countries globally.[78]

CONCLUSION

China's payment system has evolved into a framework based on nonbank payment platforms and QR codes. It stands in sharp contrast to the Western, bank-centric, card-based model.

Absent a substantial shock, China is likely to remain on this alternative platform. Businesses serving Chinese retail customers will likely have to adopt Chinese payment platforms. Possible partnerships between Western financial institutions and Alipay and WeChat may make that transition easier. Or transaction costs and frictions may remain, creating impediments for non-Chinese firms to accept Chinese payment systems. Those developments will affect the marginal penetration of Chinese payment systems. The overall outcome seems clear: Chinese payment systems will be integrated into global payments.

However, Americans are unlikely to abandon their cards for Chinese payment platforms. First, Chinese companies and the Chinese government are not pursuing this. Policy restrictions, particularly the inability to link non-Chinese bank accounts to the payment systems, have made it increasingly difficult for foreigners to enter the payment ecosystem. Second, wealthier American consumers are economically better off with their current credit card rewards-based systems and will be difficult to lure away. To the extent that a market opportunity exists, it is with lower-income users of prepaid or debit cards. However, the economics of that business and that customer segment do not appear on the radar screens of China's payment operators.

US payment providers, both banks and nonbanks, may learn and apply lessons from the evolution of the Chinese system. The adoption of QR codes, integration of smartphone scans, and sensor/phone-based payment systems offer substantial advantages over the existing card/chip/PIN/sign device-based system. These advantages exist regardless of whether the payment is processed through the banking or nonbanking system.

Merchants eager to reduce processing costs may use some of these alternative systems to try to induce American customers to use lower-cost payment methods. The economic space to try this will grow if higher-cost payment options like ultra-reward cards grow. However, the fixed costs of adoption of new payment technology and the powerful forces of consumer habits remain as substantial barriers. Americans, after all, were a lot slower to adopt texting over phone calls compared with others around the world.[79]

NOTES

The author would like to thank the David M. Rubenstein President's Strategic Impact Fund at Brookings for its generous support of this work. Many individuals were particularly helpful in this research and deserve particular thanks: Cheng Li, Zizhu Pan, Qi Ye, Jasmine Zhao, Siddhi Doshi, Amy Hu, Martin Chorzempa, Cayli Baker, Bella Dunbar, and Mia Seymour.

1. Jerome H. Powell, "Innovation, Technology, and the Payments System." Speech at Yale Law School Center for the Study of Corporate Law, March 3, 2017.

Board of Governors of the Federal Reserve System, www.federalreserve.gov /newsevents/speech/powell20170303a.htm.

2. Jerome Svigals, "The Long Life and Imminent Death of the Mag-Stripe Card," IEE Spectrum, May 30, 2012, https://spectrum.ieee.org/computing/hardware/the -long-life-and-imminent-death-of-the-magstripe-card.

3. World Bank and the People's Bank of China, *Toward Universal Financial Inclusion in China: Models, Challenges, and Global Lessons*, February 2018, https:// openknowledge.worldbank.org/bitstream/handle/10986/29336/FinancialInclusion ChinaP158554.pdf?sequence=9&isAllowed=y.

4. Jeanne Whalen and Gerry Shih, "Beijing's Blockade of U.S. Credit Card Companies May Finally End—Now That Chinese Companies Dominate," *Washington Post*, January 21, 2019, www.washingtonpost.com/business/economy/beijings -blockade-of-us-credit-card-companies-may-finally-end--now-that-chinese -companies-dominate/2019/01/20/d52d8ad4-1354-11e9-803c-4ef28312c8b9_story .html; "Payment System Report (Q3 2019)," People's Bank of China, November 2019, www.pbc.gov.cn/en/3688259/3689026/3706133/3825642/3929683/index.html.

5. People's Bank of China, "Payment System Report (Q3 2019)."

6. Alyssa Abkowitz, "The Cashless Society Has Arrived—Only It's in China," *Wall Street Journal*, January 4, 2018, www.wsj.com/articles/chinas-mobile-payment -boom-changes-how-people-shop-borrow-even-panhandle-1515000570.

7. Rita Liao, "Jack Ma's Fintech Giant Tops 1.3 Billion Users Globally," Tech Crunch, July 15, 2020, https://techcrunch.com/2020/07/14/ant-alibaba-1-3-billion -uers/; Mansoor Iqbal, "WeChat Revenue and Usage Statistics (2020)," Business of Apps, March 2021, www.businessofapps.com/data/wechat-statistics/.

8. "China's Third-Party Mobile Payment Market Soared 58.4% in 2018," iResearch Global, May 6, 2019, www.iresearchchina.com/content/details7_54345.html.

9. Phate Zhang, "Alipay Maintains No. 1 Spot in China's Mobile Payment Market with 54.5% Share," CnTechPost, January 20, 2020, https://cntechpost.com/2020/01/20 /alipay-maintains-no-1-spot-in-chinas-mobile-payment-market-with-54-5-share/.

10. "Prepaid Accounts under the Electronic Fund Transfer Act (Regulation E) and the Truth in Lending Act (Regulation Z)," Federal Register, November 22, 2016, https://www.federalregister.gov/documents/2016/11/22/2016-24503/prepaid -accounts-under-the-electronic-fund-transfer-act-regulation-e-and-the-truth-in -lending-act.

11. Applepay homepage, https://www.apple.com/apple-pay/ (accessed December 2021).

12. "QR Codes 101: A Beginner's Guide," QR Code Generator, https://www.qr -code-generator.com/qr-code-marketing/qr-codes-basics/ (accessed December 2021).

13. "The Purpose of QR Codes," QR Code Generator, www.qr-code-generator .com/qr-code-marketing/why-should-i-use-qr-codes (accessed December 2021).

14. For a discussion of the multiple cons of the slow US payment system, see Aaron Klein, "Real-Time Payments Can Help Combat Inequality," Spotlight on

Poverty, March 5, 2019, https://spotlightonpoverty.org/spotlight-exclusives/real-time-payments-can-help-combat-inequality/; Aaron Klein, "The Fastest Way to Address Income Inequality? Implement a Real Time Payment System," Brookings Institution, January 2, 2019, www.brookings.edu/research/the-fastest-way-to-address-income-inequality-implement-a-real-time-payment-system/.

15. "Tencent and Alipay Set to Lose $1bn in Revenue from Payment Rules," *Financial Times*, July 15, 2018, www.ft.com/content/b472f73c-859e-11e8-96dd-fa565ec55929.

16. Martin Chorzempa, "Beijing's Grip on Internet Finance Is Tightening," Peterson Institute for International Economics, January 9, 2018, https://piie.com/blogs/china-economic-watch/beijings-grip-internet-finance-tightening.

17. Wu Yujian and Timmy Shen, "Exclusive: PBOC Backtracks on 'No Interest' Policy for Third-Party Payment Providers," Caixin, January 7, 2020, www.caixinglobal.com/2020-01-07/exclusive-pboc-backtracks-on-no-interest-policy-for-third-party-payment-providers-101501922.html.

18. Geoffrey A. Fowler and Juying Qin, "QQ: China's New Coin of the Realm?," *Wall Street Journal*, March 30, 2007, www.wsj.com/articles/SB117519670114653518.

19. "Chinese Embrace Digital Red Envelopes for Lunar New Year," *Financial Times*, February 21, 2018, www.ft.com/content/74e9c2a0-1792-11e8-9376-4a6390addb44.

20. Jerry Chao, "In Just 4 Years, WeChat Has Changed the Way People Give Out Red Packets," *Lowdown Momentum Asia* (blog), February 28, 2018, https://thelowdown.momentum.asia/just-4-years-wechat-changed-way-people-give-red-packets/.

21. Martin Chorzempa, "How China Leapfrogged Ahead of the United States in the Fintech Race," Peterson Institute for International Economics, April 26, 2018, https://piie.com/blogs/china-economic-watch/how-china-leapfrogged-ahead-united-states-fintech-race.

22. Chris Kissell, "How Small Businesses Can Save on Credit Card Processing Fees," *U.S. News & World Report*, October 24, 2018, https://creditcards.usnews.com/articles/how-small-businesses-can-save-on-credit-card-processing-fees.

23. Ashley Chorpenning, "How Are Profit Margins Defined and Measured?," Yahoo!Life, June 28, 2019, www.yahoo.com/lifestyle/profit-margins-defined-measured-195219788.html.

24. "What Is the Economic Function of a Bank?," Federal Reserve Bank of San Francisco, July 2001, www.frbsf.org/education/publications/doctor-econ/2001/july/bank-economic-function/.

25. Amresh Anbalagan, "Alipay Starts Doing Payroll for Companies," *Lowdown Momentum Asia* (blog), June 2, 2019, https://thelowdown.momentum.asia/alipay-does-payroll-for-companies/.

26. Stella Yifan Xie, "More Than a Third of China Is Now Invested in One Giant Mutual Fund," *Wall Street Journal*, March 27, 2019, www.wsj.com/articles

/more-than-a-third-of-china-is-now-invested-in-one-giant-mutual-fund
-11553682785; Stella Yifan Xie, "Investors Pull Cash from China's Money-Market
Behemoth as Yields Tumble," *Wall Street Journal*, June 18, 2020, www.wsj.com
/articles/investors-pull-cash-from-chinas-money-market-behemoth-as-yields
-tumble-11592481715.

27. "Alipay to Charge Bank Transfer Fee from Oct 12," *China Daily*, September 13, 2016, www.chinadaily.com.cn/bizchina/2016-09/13/content_26778445.htm.

28. Zen Soo, "Tencent to Charge Users in China for Transferring Money from WeChat Wallet to Bank Accounts," *South China Morning Post*, February 16, 2016, www.scmp.com/tech/apps-gaming/article/1913503/tencent-charge-users-china
-transferring-money-wechat-wallet-bank.

29. PayPal charges 2.9 percent plus a flat fee of 30 cents, which is not always the actual cost paid by the customer because of factors such as the type of card, negotiation between PayPal and the bank sponsoring the card, and so on. More information about PayPal fees can be found here: https://www.paypal.com/en/webapps
/mpp/paypal-fees (accessed December 2021).

30. Soo, "Tencent to Charge Users."

31. "Alipay to Charge Bank Transfer Fee from Oct 12."

32. Jennifer Surance, "Behind the $90 Billion Brawl over Credit Card Swipes," *Bloomberg Businessweek*, August 10, 2018, www.bloomberg.com/news/articles
/2018-08-10/behind-the-90-billion-brawl-over-credit-card-swipes-quicktake.

33. Nicole Jao, "Alipay to Start Charging Fees on Credit Card Repayments," Tech Node, February 21, 2019, https://technode.com/2019/02/21/alipay-charges
-credit-card-repayments/.

34. "Alipay Ramps Up Supply Chain, Lending Services to SMBs," PYMNTS
.com, October 30, 2018, www.pymnts.com/news/b2b-payments/2018/alipay-small
-business-loans-supply-chain/.

35. "Square Cash Is Open for Business," Square, March 23, 2015, https://
squareup.com/us/en/press/introducing-cashtags.

36. Aaron Klein, "Why the Wells Scandal Matters So Much," Brookings Institution, September 21, 2016, www.brookings.edu/blog/up-front/2016/09/21/why-the
-wells-scandal-matters-so-much/.

37. Rita Liao, "China's Digital Yuan Tests Leap Forward in Shenzhen," Tech Crunch, October 12, 2020, https://techcrunch.com/2020/10/11/china-digital-yuan
-shenzhen/.

38. Arjun Kharpal, "China Hands Out $1.5 Million of Its Digital Currency in One of the Country's Biggest Public Tests," CNBC, October 12, 2020, www.cnbc
.com/2020/10/12/china-digital-currency-trial-over-1-million-handed-out-in
-lottery.html.

39. Shaurya Malwa, "$1.5 Million of China's CBDC Will Be Distributed in Shenzhen," Decrypt, October 9, 2020, https://decrypt.co/44410/1-5-million
-of-chinas-cbdc-will-be-distributed-in-shenzhen; Dion Rabouin, "China's Digital

Currency Aims to Leave the Rest of the World in the Dust," Axios, October 14, 2020, www.axios.com/china-digital-currency-fca0c276-e738-471c-bb94-f93816b9864c .html.

40. Sarah Allen and others, "Design Choices for Central Bank Digital Currency: Policy and Technical Considerations," Working Paper 27634 (Cambridge, MA: National Bureau of Economic Research, August 2020), www.nber.org/system /files/working_papers/w27634/w27634.pdf.

41. Carlos Echeverria-Estrada and Jeanne Batalova, "Chinese Immigrants in the United States," Migration Policy Institute, January 15, 2020, www.migrationpolicy .org/article/chinese-immigrants-united-states-2018; "2020 U.S. Travel and Tourism Statistics," National Travel and Tourism Office, https://travel.trade.gov/outreach pages/inbound.general_information.inbound_overview.asp (accessed December 2021).

42. Suman Bhattacharyya, "American Retailers Are Using Alipay to Attract Chinese Tourists," Digiday, July 26, 2018, https://digiday.com/retail/american-retailers -using-alipay-attract-chinese-tourists/.

43. Aaron Klein, "China's Payments U-turn: Government over Technology," Brookings Institution, November 29, 2021, https://www.brookings.edu/research /chinas-payments-u-turn-government-over-technology.

44. "A New Frontier Favorite: Quantum of the Seas," Royal Caribbean International, 2021, www.royalcaribbean.com/cruise-ships/quantum-of-the-seas.

45. Data provided to the author.

46. Conversation with the author.

47. Elaine Low, "Walgreens Boots Alliance's Newest Alliance? Alibaba," Investor's Business Daily Digital, September 20, 2018, www.investors.com/news/walgreens -boots-alliances-deal-alibaba-beauty/.

48. "Swipe Fees," National Retail Federation, https://nrf.com/hill/policy-issues /swipe-fees#:~:text=Swipe%20fees%20have%20grown%20from,than%20%24100 %20billion%20a%20year (accessed December 2021).

49. Aaron Klein, "Is China's New Payment System the Future?" Center on Regulations and Markets at Brookings Institution, June 2019, https://www.brookings .edu/wp-content/uploads/2019/06/ES_20190620_Klein_ChinaPayments.pdf.

50. Aaron Klein, "America's Poor Subsidize Wealthier Consumers in a Vicious Income Inequality Cycle," NBC News, February 6, 2018, www.nbcnews.com/think /opinion/america-s-poor-subsidize-wealthier-consumers-vicious-income-inequality -cycle-ncna845091.

51. Eugene Volokh, "Restrictions on How Businesses Label Credit Card/Cash Price Differences Are Speech Restrictions," *Washington Post*, March 29, 2017, www .washingtonpost.com/news/volokh-conspiracy/wp/2017/03/29/restrictions-on -how-businesses-label-credit-cardcash-price-differences-are-speech-restrictions/.

52. "*Ohio v. American Express Co.*," Supreme Court of the United States, October 2017, www.supremecourt.gov/opinions/17pdf/16-1454_5h26.pdf.

53. Aaron Klein, "America's Poor Subsidize Wealthier Consumers in a Vicious Income Inequality Cycle."

54. Jamie Gonzalez-Garcia and Allie Johnson, "Credit Card Ownership Statistics," Credicards+com, January 2020, www.creditcards.com/credit-card-news /ownership-statistics/.

55. Carmen Reinicke, "US Income Inequality Continues to Grow," CNBC, July 19, 2018, www.cnbc.com/2018/07/19/income-inequality-continues-to-grow -in-the-united-states.html.

56. "Inside the Vault, Cards, Cards, and More Cards: The Evolution to Prepaid Cards," Fraser Federal Reserve, 2011, https://fraser.stlouisfed.org/title/inside -vault-6107/fall-2011-586640.

57. United States Federal Reserve, *The 2019 Federal Reserve Payments Study*, December 2020, www.federalreserve.gov/newsevents/pressreleases/files/2019 -payments-study-20191219.pdf.

58. United States Federal Reserve, *The 2019 Federal Reserve Payments Study*.

59. Credit Card Accountability Responsibility and Disclosure Act of 2009, Pub. L. No. 111-24 (May 22, 2009), www.ftc.gov/sites/default/files/documents/statutes /credit-card-accountability-responsibility-and-disclosure-act-2009-credit-card -act/credit-card-pub-l-111-24_0.pdf.

60. "Prepaid Accounts under the Electronic Fund Transfer Act."

61. "Executive Summary of the Prepaid Rule," Consumer Financial Protection Bureau, October 5, 2016, https://files.consumerfinance.gov/f/documents/201704 _cfpb_Prepaid_execsummary_v2.pdf.

62. "WeChat Pay Lets Users Link International Debit, Credit Cards," PYMNTS .com, January 25, 2018, www.pymnts.com/news/payment-methods/2018/wechat -pay-chinese-credit-cards/; "How to Set Up an Alipay Account as a Foreigner?," *China Daily*, January 22, 2019, www.chinadaily.com.cn/a/201901/22/WS5c46d2 a7a3106c65c34e5daa.html.

63. Michael Sandel, "The Economic Inefficiency of Gift Giving: Why You Shouldn't Buy Presents for the Holidays" *FS* (blog), https://fs.blog/2013/12/the -economic-inefficiency-of-gift-giving-why-you-shouldnt-buy-presents-for-the -holidays/ (accessed December 2021); "The Economics of Seinfeld: What's the Right Gift to Give; Cash?," YouTube, December 22, 2010, www.youtube.com/watch?v =aQlhrrqTQmU.

64. "Record Purchases of Starbucks Cards Anticipated on Christmas Eve," Starbucks, December 22, 2015, https://stories.starbucks.com/stories/2015/record-card -purchases-expected-christmas-eve/.

65. "Gift Card—Global Market Trajectory and Analytics," Global Industry Analytics, July 2020, www.researchandmarkets.com/reports/5029879/gift-card -global-market-trajectory-and-analytics?utm_source=dynamic&utm_medium =GNOM&utm_code=wg597f&utm_campaign=1410985+-+Gift+Card+Industry +Worth+%242.7+Trillion+by+2027%2c+Despite+COVID-19&utm_exec=joca220 gnomd.

66. Ibid.

67. Vania G. Silva, Esmeralda A. Ramalho, and Carlos R. Vieira, "The Use of Cheques in the European Union: A Cross-Country Analysis," March 2015, www.apdr.pt/pej2015/papers/46.pdf.

68. "Singapore Consumers Still Prefer to Pay for Online Purchases by Credit Card versus E-wallet," *Straits Times*, November 12, 2018, www.straitstimes.com/business/banking/singapore-consumers-still-prefer-to-pay-for-online-purchases-by-credit-card-versus.

69. John Detrixhe, "A Chinese-Style Payment Network to Challenge Visa and Mastercard Is Taking Shape in Europe," Quartz, June 10, 2019, https://qz.com/1639652/alipay-teams-up-with-european-smartphone-wallets-for-qr-code-payments/.

70. "EU Mobile Wallet Players, Alipay Team on QR Code Interoperability," PYMNTS.com, June 10, 2019, www.pymnts.com/news/mobile-payments/2019/europe-mobile-wallet-alipay-qr-code/.

71. Nielsen, *2017 Outbound Chinese Tourism and Consumption Trends*, 2017 www.nielsen.com/wp-content/uploads/sites/3/2019/05/outbound-chinese-tourism-and-consumption-trends.pdf.

72. Nielsen, *2017 Outbound Chinese Tourism and Consumption Trends.*

73. Jung Suk-yee, "Woori Bank Partners Tencent to Provide Fund Settlement Service, Targeting Chinese Tourists," *Business Korea*, November 26, 2015, www.businesskorea.co.kr/news/articleView.html?idxno=13116.

74. "Effortless Finance Kakao Pay," Kakao, https://www.kakaocorp.com/page/service/service/KakaoPay?lang=en (accessed December 2021). Hong Kong and Macao are excluded because they are special administrative regions.

75. Eva Yoo, "WeChat Pay's Global Expansion 'Going Well': Q&A with Grace Yin, Director of WeChat Pay Cross-Border Operation," Tech Node, January 16, 2018, https://technode.com/2018/01/16/wechat-grace-yin/.

76. Yoon Young-sis, "Seoul City to Introduce 'Zero Pay' for Small Business Owners," *Business Korea*, July 27, 2018, www.businesskorea.co.kr/news/articleView.html?idxno=23970.

77. "Welcome to Virtual Banking," Standard Bank, www.standardbank.co.za/southafrica/personal/products-and-services/bank-with-us/digital-wallets (accessed December 2021).

78. Tingyi Ghen, "The Cross-Border Payment War of WeChat Pay and Alipay," WalktheChat, February 25, 2019, https://walkthechat.com/the-cross-border-payment-war-of-wechat-pay-and-alipay/.

79. "No Text Please, We're American," *The Economist*, April 3, 2003, https://www.economist.com/business/2003/04/03/no-text-please-were-american.

4

Digital Financial Infrastructure in China

XUN WANG

Financial infrastructure has long been viewed as the underlying foundation of the financial system and has played a critical role in financial and economic development. While digital finance has experienced rapid growth in China in recent years, sustainable and healthy development and innovation in digital finance depend on appropriate hard and soft digital financial infrastructure. Hard infrastructure includes information infrastructure, mobile payment architecture, and a credit reference system; soft infrastructure includes a regulatory framework, codes of conduct, and mechanisms for enhancing financial innovation.

In the past decade, digital technological advances including big data, cloud computing, blockchain, and artificial intelligence fostered the new industry of digital finance in China and allowed ordinary households, street vendors, and small and medium-size enterprises to access financial services. Big techs such as Alibaba, Tencent, JD, and Baidu have provided infrastructure, capital, and know-how to support these trends, contributing to China's leading position in digital finance. These hard infrastructures help promote household consumption, risk sharing, entrepreneurship, and capital allocation.

However, the surge of digital financial infrastructure provided mainly by private financial technology (fintech) companies in China carries risks.

Digital financial services provided by fintech companies are characterized as cross-product, cross-industry, and cross-regional, which result in large network effects. Person-to-person (P2P) platforms aim to provide online lending by using online big data and have the potential to provide new investment channels for ordinary people (the so-called long-tail customers). However, at the very beginning, P2P platforms were oriented as information intermediation, which was commercially unsustainable. These platforms generally lacked the capability of risk controls since they were incapable of reducing (and were not incentivized to reduce) information asymmetry between the online lenders and borrowers, but operated for a very long period without financial supervision. The result was that P2P lending without financial supervision generated severe problems of adverse selection and moral hazard, and a large number of customers suffered losses.

As a consequence, soft infrastructure is essential to support healthier and more sustainable development in digital finance. The development of digital financial infrastructure in China is associated with a significant reduction in transaction costs and enhancement of financial inclusion. The digital financial infrastructure is mainly initiated by private big techs in China and thus is viewed to be complementary to traditional financial infrastructure in the less developed financial system. Since new financial risk might emerge without proper financial supervision, reforms in the regulatory framework and adoption of "suptech" are needed to maintain financial stability.

In this chapter, we carry out a detailed analysis by focusing on some key dimensions of China's digital financial infrastructure, including mobile payments and digital credit reference. Reviewing its development; understanding the benefits, costs, and implications; and discussing the remaining issues will help inform policy decisions. We address the following questions: How does China's digital financial infrastructure evolve? What contributes to its revolutionary development? What are the potential effects of the digital financial infrastructure on financial services and the economy? What are the prospects of China's digital financial infrastructure in the coming years? Are there any implications for financial supervision?

BACKGROUND OF DIGITAL FINANCIAL INFRASTRUCTURE IN CHINA

The rapid development of digital financial infrastructure in China is largely attributed to the quick spread of mobile internet, rapid development of digital technology, and an underdeveloped traditional financial system.

The Quick Spread of the Internet and Smartphones

Technological development provided the necessary conditions for both the spreading of digital payment coverage and improvement in other digital financial infrastructure. The number of internet users in China has surged from 140 million in 2006 to around 1 billion in 2020. The internet penetration rate has risen from 10.5 percent in 2006 to 70.4 percent in 2020. In urban areas the rate has increased from 26 percent in 2007 to 80 percent in 2020; in rural areas it has increased from 7.4 to 56 percent (figure 4-1), with the three most recent years exhibiting an acceleration.

The advent of the smartphone has led to a combination of the mobile phone and the internet. Among China's internet users, the ratio of accessing the internet through a smartphone has surged from 12 percent in 2006 to 99.7 percent in 2020. Hence, as shown in figure 4-2, the smartphone penetration rate has risen from 1.3 percent in 2006 to 70.2 percent in 2020. According to a Nielsen survey, the smartphone penetration rate in China was 66 percent, which was in the same range as most developed countries but significantly higher than Brazil (36 percent), Turkey (19 percent), and India (10 percent).[1] Compared with the payment system built on desktop computers, mobile terminals offered tremendous flexibility in terms of time, location, and ease of using mobile payment. Service providers also made massive investments to improve both user experience and service reliability. The number of transactions that Alipay can handle per second increased from about 200 in 2011 to 210,000 in 2017, and the fund-loss rate was reduced to less than one in a million. The adoption of the Quick Response (QR) code also brought about revolutionary changes to the extension of the mobile payment service.

FIGURE 4-1.   Internet Penetration in China, 2006–2020

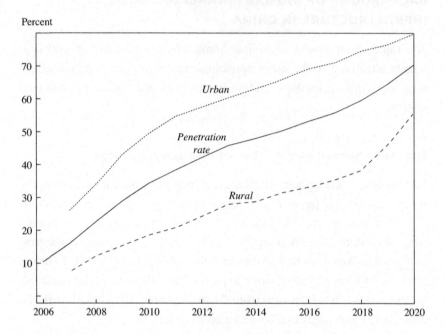

Source: China Economic Information Center (CEIC) Global Database, https://www
.ceicdata.com/.

Rapid Development of Digital Technology

Finance is an industry of dealing with risks. The key component of financial risk evaluation, asset pricing, and monitoring is the processing of
information. Evidence shows that advances in information-processing
technology, including information recording, analytical algorithms, and
computing power, will promote financial development (Huang and others
2020). In the 1980s, the development of digital technology in the finance industry allowed computers to replace manual work and paperwork, and the
internet has further enhanced the digitization of financial operations since
the 1990s. Since the 2008 global financial crisis, emerging digital technologies represented by mobile internet, big data, cloud computing, blockchain,
and artificial intelligence have been booming and are reshaping the finance
industry in terms of a business model, risk pricing and market structure, and
the regulatory environment.

FIGURE 4-2.   **Smartphone Penetration in China, 2006–2020**

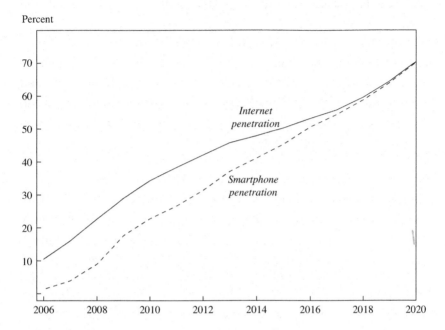

Percent

Source: China Economic Information Center (CEIC) Global Database, https://www
.ceicdata.com/.

The buzzword *fintech* refers to innovative financial products or services delivered via the emerging digital technology. Fintech can be classified into the following categories according to the application: (1) digital identification, smart contract, big data, and cloud computing in financial infrastructure; (2) mobile payment, digital currency, and distributed ledgers application in a payment and clearing system; (3) equity crowdfunding, online lending, and distributed ledgers application in external financing; (4) robo-advisor in wealth management; and (5) internet insurance.

Advocates of fintech note how it will significantly enhance the efficiency of financial services. Financial services will be more inclusive, increasing the empowerment of people and better connecting them. Consumers will have more choices and receive more favorable pricing. Households will build up their risk-sharing capabilities with lower transaction costs. Small and medium-size enterprises (SMEs) will have better access to external finance. Financial institutions, including traditional banks and fintech companies, will become more productive with greater capital efficiency and stronger operational resilience. Moreover, regulatory authorities' adoption of digital technology may help enhance regulatory efficiency.

While the concept of fintech was initially introduced in the United States, its development has been much faster in China than in most other countries in terms of breadth and depth. In the field of mobile payment, Alipay and WeChat Pay in China, with market shares of 53.8 percent and 38.9 percent, respectively, in 2018, have been providing payment and transfer services to hundreds of millions of customers. Alipay alone had 870 million active users by the end of 2018, over three times that of PayPal globally (Huang and others 2020). Chinese payment providers not only cover more customers but also depend much more on mobile technology. The annual growth rate of mobile payment by banks and third-party providers reached 36.7 percent in 2018 (PBOC 2018), which is far beyond the growth rate of payment transactions by PayPal. In the field of wealth management, more than 600 million accounts invested in the online money market product Yu'ebao in 2018, which has more than US$160 billion in assets, while the famous Wealth front has only US$11.3 billion in assets under management. In the field of financing, according to Alibaba's 2018 financial report (Alibaba 2019), Ant Financial issued more than RMB 2,000 billion (or more than US$290 billion) to over 15 million SMEs by the end of 2018, with an average nonperforming loan ratio of 1.3 percent.

An Underdeveloped Traditional Financial System

While the initial motivation of developing Alipay was to solve the problem of lack of trust among counterparties, there was also a significant gap in the supply of payment services. Compared with the financial systems in other countries, the Chinese system exhibits two unique features: a very high proportion of banks in the financial sector and a very high degree of financial repression (Lardy 2008; Huang and Wang 2011). Following Rajan and Zingales (1998) and Hsu and others (2014), among others, we use the ratio of banking assets to the sum of banking assets and stock market capitalization as a proxy for financial structure. As shown in figure 4-3, the upward-sloping correlation line indicates that greater financial repression is associated with a greater bank-based financial system. The United States and Hong Kong, often viewed as market-based financial systems, are located in the

FIGURE 4-3.   **International Comparison of Financial Systems, 2015**

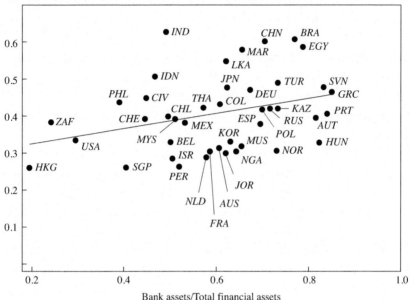

Source: Huang and Ge (2019).

Note: The horizontal axis indicates share of banks in total financial assets, and the vertical axis represents degree of financial repression.

AUS: Australia; AUT: Austria; Bel: Belgium; BRA: Brazil; CHE: Switzerland; CHL: Chile; CHN: China; CIV: Cote d'Ivoire; COL: Colombia; DEU: Germany; EGY: Egypt; ESP: Spain; FRA: France; GRC: Greece; HKG: Hong Kong; HUN: Hungary; IDN: Indonesia; IND: India; ISR: Israel; JOR: Jorden; JPN: Japan; KAZ: Kazakhstan; KOR: Korea, Rep.; LKA: Sri Lanka; MAR: Morocco; MEX: Mexico; MUS: Mauritius; MYS: Malaysia; NGA: Nigeria; NLD: Netherlands; NOR: Norway; PER: Peru; PHL: Philippines; POL: Poland; PRT: Portugal; RUS: Russia; SGP: Singapore; SVN: Slovenia; THA: Thailand; TUR: Turkey; USA: United States of America; ZAF: South Africa.

lower left corner. Japan and Germany, often viewed as bank-based financial systems, are located in the middle of the figure. China is located in the upper-right corner, indicating a greater level of financial repression and a bank-dominated financial system.

Improving financial inclusion is an especially challenging task in China. For example, owing to the underdeveloped social credit system, the average penetration rate of credit cards was 0.47 cards/person in China in 2018, compared with 2.9 in the United States. And the traditional card payment services, such as the point-of-sale machine, are often slow, inefficient, and expensive. Most of the SMEs and low-income individuals had to rely on cash for financial transactions. When the mobile payment services came online, they were immediately embraced by the market. Nowadays, withdrawals of RMB 20,000 or less are free, and the excess amount is charged a fee of 0.1 percent. For these reasons, some experts argue that other countries such as the United States would not be able to replicate the Chinese experience of the mobile payment service (Klein 2019).

The favorable regulatory environment also offered room for China's digital finance, especially its mobile payment system, to experiment and grow. In 2004, China enacted the law of electronic signature, which makes it possible to legally sign contracts electronically. After 2005, the State Council released a series of policy documents to support e-commerce development. However, there was no strict regulatory restriction on mobile payment until the People's Bank of China (PBC) released "Measure for the Administration of Payment Services for Non-financial Institutions" in June 2010. Since then, the PBC has issued nearly 270 third-party payment licenses. While granting third-party payment licenses was considered an innovative policy step, in many other countries some controversial issues may need to be resolved before these licenses can be granted. For instance, should these virtual accounts be regulated as payment accounts or deposit accounts? At the start of 2019, the PBC became the new custodian of all customer funds deposited by third-party payment groups, tightening control of mobile payment transactions and clearing. The central bank pays no interest on the reserved money, the amount of which reached RMB 1.24 trillion in November 2018.

DEVELOPMENT OF DIGITAL FINANCIAL INFRASTRUCTURE

The development of digital financial infrastructure depends on hard infrastructure, as well as soft infrastructures, especially regulatory effectiveness and efficiency.

Hard Infrastructure

The features of hard infrastructure include information and information processing, the system of payments, clearing and settlement, and the digital credit reference.

Information and Information-Processing Infrastructure. The basic function of information infrastructure is to record and collect customer big data. Since the beginning of the new century, the smartphone has been ubiquitous, the hardware of sensor equipment has largely improved, and the internet of things (IOT) has developed quickly. With these advancements, more and more information could be recorded. In digital society, human activities generally rely on financial accounts, social network accounts, e-commerce accounts, and other application accounts. These accounts are directly associated with one's personal identity. The widespread application of biometric recognition techniques will further strengthen the links between accounts and personal identities, enabling accounts to effectively record the behavior of account owners in various scenarios.

Big-tech companies such as Alibaba, Tencent, JD, and Baidu have developed their own digital customer authentication systems to provide remote account-opening services for customers based on biometric recognition techniques. Through an analysis of this recorded behavioral information, the account owner can be profiled; and important characteristics such as preferences, credit scores, and income level can be inferred, laying the foundation for precision marketing and online loan extending. For example, e-commerce data can be used to evaluate the credit of merchants and consumers. And data collected by social media and search engines can help evaluate consumer preferences and precision marketing.

Owing to the extreme importance of customer data, big-tech companies attach much attention to the setup of internet data centers (IDCs). Alibaba Cloud already has IDCs in Hangzhou, Qingdao, Shenzhen, Hong Kong, Southeast Asia, Europe, and the United States. In May 2020, Ali Cloud announced that it was investing RMB 200 billion (US$30.1 billion) in IDC construction over the following three years. Tencent has built up its IDCs all over China and has extended its cloud service and AI business to the United States, Germany, Russia, Korea, and India. The new-generation internet companies such as ByteDance, the parent company of TikTok, are also eager to build cloud platforms and IDCs.

One problem with these private big-tech IDCs is that they are basically independent and provide relevant information support for their own business models. The main reason is the competition between the different big techs—for example, Alibaba and Tencent. However, cooperation between new internet banks and new internet companies is possible when they are complementary. XW Bank, founded in 2016, has cooperated with ByteDance and other internet companies to evaluate customers' credit scores based on compiled big data. Although the PBC launched the construction of a financial data center in Guizhou Province in 2020 and traditional commercial banks have established their own fintech companies, connectivity of information infrastructure in digital finance among the central bank, government, traditional banking sector, and private big techs still has a long way to go.

System of Payment, Clearing, and Settlement. China's mobile payment system experienced revolutionary development over the past decade, and the market is now mainly dominated by two platforms: Alipay and WeChat Pay. To a large extent, the new payment system has replaced bank cards and cash in several areas—for example, the way families send "red packets" and remittances, small vendors and market stalls collect bills, and even how homeless people ask for money, with QR codes replacing the tin cup. China seemed an unlikely candidate to develop a new payment system. The leapfrogging of China's mobile payment system partly reflects the underdeveloped social credit system in China. While at the end of 2020 China had the largest card system in the world with close to 9 billion cards and 6.4 cards per capita, according to the PBOC, 91 percent of them are debit cards rather credit cards, indicating an underdeveloped social credit system (PBOC 2021). Additionally, UnionPay, a bank-card-based network that connects accounts of different banks in China, has been functioning since 2002. To access the card-based payment system, merchants need to be equipped with card readers that connect to the internet (which incurs costs); additionally, they must pay a processing fee for each transaction, which has resulted in a slow adoption of this system.

Alibaba started Taobao in 1999 as an e-commerce platform that required users to pay for purchases via their bank accounts. The biggest challenge then was the lack of trust due to information asymmetry between the buyer and the seller. In 2004 the company introduced Alipay to solve the problem of mutual trust on Taobao by providing a secure transaction. Alipay is an online digital payments solution based on escrow, where Alibaba holds the money until the buyer signs off on receiving the goods. In 2008 Alipay officially introduced its mobile e-wallet, which launched its meteoric growth. While it took Alipay five years to reach 100 million customers before 2008, it added 20 million new users in the first two months of 2009. Today, it has 1.2 billion users around the world.

Tencent, a leading social network platform in China, entered the payments industry a different way. Based on the online chatting product QQ, the company pivoted into online gaming. To meet the needs of individuals topping up their online gaming accounts, it introduced the online payment tool Tenpay in 2005. In 2011, Tencent launched a smartphone-based social messaging application, WeChat, which has 1.2 billion users. In 2013, Tencent created a new payment product, WeChat Pay, by integrating Tenpay into WeChat. The payment tool is embedded in WeChat and enables users to send each other money directly through the messaging window (CGAP, 2019).

Alipay and WeChat Pay are now the two dominant payment platforms in the Chinese market. The number of active users of Alipay and WeChat Pay increased from a little over 100 million and 350 million, respectively, in 2013 to around 1.2 billion each in 2019. A number of events marked the development of China's mobile payment system. First, the release of the first smartphone, the iPhone by Apple, in January 2007 made it possible to use mobile payment services anywhere, anytime. Second, the success of Ant Group's money market fund Yu'ebao significantly boosted awareness of, and enthusiasm for, the fintech industry, including mobile payment. Third, the distribution of red envelopes (cash) on WeChat Pay during the Chinese New Year holiday in 2014 became widespread and attracted hundreds of millions of new users. And finally, the adoption of QR codes for mobile payment made it possible for any business, formal and informal, to access the payment system without being connected via phone or the internet.

The total transaction value of mobile payment jumped from RMB 14.5 trillion in 2013 to RMB 347.1 trillion in 2019, recording an annual growth rate of around 70 percent. The number of mobile payment transactions reached 101.4 billion in 2019, rising by 67.6 percent from the previous year. The share of mobile payment in total noncash payment value rose from less than 1 percent in 2013 to 9.2 percent in 2019, and the share of mobile payment in the total number of noncash payment transactions increased from 3.3 percent to 30.6 percent during the same period, reflecting a low-value but high-frequency feature of mobile payment transaction.

NetsUnion Clearing Corporation and Online Payment Interbank Settlement System are two important infrastructures for facilitating mobile payment transactions. NetsUnion, approved by the PBC and founded in August 2017, is the national online payment clearing platform for nonbank payment institutions and mainly handles online payment services involving bank accounts initiated by a nonbank institution. Online Payment Interbank Settlement System, founded in August 2010, is the RMB interbank payment settlement infrastructure of the PBC.

In order to support the transfer and liquidation of transactions in the world's largest network payment market, the NetsUnion platform[2] adopted a distributed cloud computing architecture and established six centers in three cities (Beijing, Shanghai, and Shenzhen) to ensure the smooth functioning of the payment system in processing massive and highly concurrent online transactions. In 2019 on China's Singles Day, online payments hit RMB 1.48 trillion, and NetsUnion processed 1.54 billion transactions valued at about RMB 1.16 trillion during the shopping frenzy, including all the transactions via Ant's Alipay and Tencent's WeChat Pay.[3] Traffic peaked in three minutes past 00:00 when the platform settled 71,500 transactions per second. The number of transactions handled by the platform has grown by 32.2 percent year over year, and the transaction value has increased by 147.25 percent year over year.[4]

Digital Credit Reference. A credit reporting system is a critical element of a country's financial infrastructure and is essential to facilitating access to financial services. Inadequate access to finance and credit represents one of the most critical constraints to economic development. Lenders often lack necessary information to assess the creditworthiness of potential customers, including a lack of reliable and unique identification for individuals and businesses, particularly for rural and self-employed households and for micro, small, and medium enterprises (MSMEs). The credit reporting system plays an important role in gathering and distributing reliable credit information, improving creditor protection, and strengthening credit markets. The Credit Reference Center of the PBC (PBCCRC) is the core of China's personal credit reporting system. Founded in 2004, the PBCCRC established a unified national personal credit information database in 2006. The core of its credit information is provided by commercial banks and financial institutions and is supplemented by information from other public bodies.

With the rise of digital finance, combining machine learning, artificial intelligence, and big-data analytics can help locate valuable personal behavioral laws in the mass of information and efficiently evaluate the borrower's risk. The cloud computing platform can establish a big-data credit reporting system and provide infrastructure for risk prevention in financial activities. In this context, the Baihang Credit Information Company was formally registered in Shenzhen on March 19, 2018. Baihang Credit is the first and only market-oriented company in China that has obtained a personal credit reporting business license. It is organized by the market self-regulatory organization, National Internet Finance Association of China, and eight market institutes: Zhima Credit, Tencent Credit, Qianhai Credit, Kaola Credit, Pengyuan Credit, Zhongchengxin Credit, Zhongzhicheng Credit Report, and Huadao Credit. On July 17, 2020, the PBCCRC and Baihang Credit signed a strategic cooperation agreement to jointly promote the development of China's credit reporting market. China established a "government + market two-wheel-drive" credit reporting framework with the government-dominated PBCCRC and market-led Baihang Credit complementing each other.

Since 2006 the personal credit reporting system has included an increasing number of respected institutions and gathered a large amount of high-quality information. The PBCCRC has become the world's largest credit system in terms of population and data coverage, providing standardized credit files for every single person and company in China that engages in credit-related activities. As of June 2019, the PBCCRC had collected information on 1 billion natural persons and 27.57 million enterprises and other institutions. The credit system played a vital role with regard to the prevention of financial risk, the preservation of financial stability, and expediting the growth of the financial sector. In the first half of 2019, twenty-one nationwide Chinese banking institutions made use of the credit system to refuse RMB 393.7 billion in loan applications from high-risk customers, as well as issue advance warnings on RMB 780.3 billion in outstanding high-risk loans and clear up RMB 95.7 billion in nonperforming loans (Luo, 2019).

Nonetheless, the PBCCRC system, which in theory is supposed to be comprehensive, has serious limitations. It is limited to mostly commercial banks' credit and loan records, so it does not reflect the new world of digital finance, which is beyond the reach of traditional banks. In this context, market-oriented credit registries could make good use of the enormous amount of nonfinancial information on the internet alongside collecting information from big-tech platforms, making it possible to evaluate credit risks for borrowers who have little or no credit history. As a critical complement to the PBCCRC, Baihang Credit can effectively help credit risk management in nonbanking financial institutions and the fintech industry, alleviating information asymmetry problems, lessening credit risks, and improving the efficiency of credit services in the long-tail market. As of September 2019, Baihang Credit had signed cooperation and sharing agreements with 1,071 institutions and supplemented its database by including data from UnionPay, Telecom, and the public sector. The credit system has collected information on more than 71.4 million borrowers and 112 million credit accounts. In terms of market services, Baihang Credit launched the online verification test of three products: the personal credit information system, special attention list platform, and information verification platform. From May to September 2019, the total inquiry volume of personal credit exceeded 23 million, and the daily inquiry volume exceeded 400,000 and has been steadily increasing.[5]

Baihang Credit was formed with government support, took advantage of the development of digital finance, and grew with the cooperation with digital finance institutions. It has had a significant impact on the prevention of financial dishonesty and fraudulent activity due to a lack of information in the nonbanking industries in the digital economy era. It fills in the gaps of legal personal credit reporting on digital platforms and microfinance, which is conducive to improving risk prevention and control of the digital financial services and preventing systemic financial risks. A "government + market two-wheel-drive" credit reporting system better meets the needs of long-tail customers and promotes financial inclusion.

Soft Infrastructure

Soft infrastructure refers to the institutions and mechanisms through which digital finance can achieve healthy and smooth development.

Regulatory Framework. China's current regulatory framework for the financial sector took shape in 2003 with the establishment of the China Banking Regulatory Commission, which is responsible for regulating commercial banks, financial asset management companies, and trust companies. The PBC, the China Banking Regulatory Commission, the China Insurance Regulatory Commission, and the China Securities Regulatory Commission constitute the main body of the financial regulatory framework. The PBC is responsible for monetary and macro-prudential policies; and the other three authorities are in charge of regulating the banking, insurance, and securities industries, respectively.

What is unique about China's financial supervision framework is its institutional approach. On the contrary, universal financial operations have been developed in short order to meet the diversified financial demands of clients. The mismatch between the institution-based financial regulation and the comprehensive operating of financial intermediaries is weakening the effectiveness of financial regulation owing to the regulatory loopholes in the framework and regulatory arbitrage from the institutions.

The effectiveness of financial regulation in China has been declining since 2013 (figure 4-4). There are likely two reasons for this decline: (1) the current regulatory framework did not fully cover the rapid growth of non-traditional financial operations, and (2) regulatory arbitrage by financial institutions led to a strengthening of supervision and tightening of the monetary supply. Therefore, under organization-based supervision, a strengthening in macro-prudential supervision might be associated with an increase in credit growth and asset prices due to regulatory arbitrage.

Another weakness in China's financial supervision is the protection of consumers. To ensure consumers get a fair deal, financial markets need to be honest, fair, and effective. Without proper financial conduct regulation, financial service firms could harm the consumers' interests by increasing the complexity of the products and impair the integrity of the financial system through unfair competition. However, these issues can be mitigated with the right regulatory framework. The well-functioning financial systems of Australia and the Netherlands employ a so-called Twin Peaks regulatory framework. On one side of this framework, prudential regulation closely watches the systemic risks; on the other side, financial conduct regulation independently aims to censor the conduct of financial institutions and protect consumers' interests.

FIGURE 4-4.   **Index of Effectiveness of Financial Supervision of China,**
2005–2015

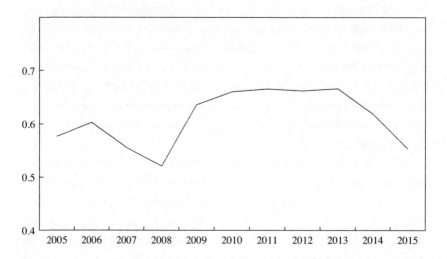

Source: Huang and Wang (2017).

Note: This index has been normalized to the [0,1] interval. 1 stands for the highest effectiveness, and 0 indicates the poorest financial supervision.

The Chinese government has recognized the importance of reforming the regulatory framework and conduct regulation. The Financial Stability and Development Committee of the State Council was set up in July 2017 to coordinate the regulatory policies and authorities. The central government decided to merge the China Banking Regulatory Commission and the China Insurance Regulatory Commission, forming the China Banking and Insurance Regulatory Commission in March 2018. Reform of the regulatory framework will continue to address systemic risk and promote financial stability.

The Mechanism of Promoting Financial Innovation. Although digital financial innovations in China have been at the forefront, financial supervision has failed to keep pace. The in-depth integration of digital technology and financial operations has increased the network and social effects of financial operations, and at the same time, it has made the monitoring and supervision of financial risk more difficult. The occasional risk events that emerge not only damage the legitimate rights and interests of consumers but also challenge the stability of the financial system.

To balance stability and innovation, the PBC introduced a regulatory "sandbox"[6] in January 2020 and then approved the first six regulatory pilots for fintech innovation applications, four of which are applications for banking credit and two of which are applications for payment. Later in April, the PBC supported the expansion of pilot projects in six cities (district)—Shanghai, Chongqing, Shenzhen, Xiong'an New District, Hangzhou, and Suzhou—and guided licensed financial institutions and fintech companies to apply for innovation testing, suggesting a shift to active, dynamic, and principled supervision.

At present, the regulatory sandbox mainly focuses on the application of frontier technologies such as big data, blockchain, and artificial intelligence in the financial system. All qualifying institutions, including state-owned banks, joint-equity banks, city commercial banks, payment institutions, clearing organizations, and technology companies, are allowed to apply for financial innovation testing in the framework of the regulatory sandbox.

EFFECTS OF DIGITAL FINANCIAL INFRASTRUCTURE

Digital financial infrastructure in China has helped to reshape the financial landscape, improve households' risk sharing, and promote entrepreneurship. These effects are important for China's sustainable development in the coming decades.

Reshaping Financial Markets

Payment for goods and services that is made through a consumer's mobile terminal is called mobile payment. Mobile payment is now the primary payment method in third-party payments. Correspondingly, cash payment is called first-party payment, and payment made through a banking system is called second-party payment.

If digital finance is viewed as a financial revolution in China, mobile payment can be considered the most revolutionary part of digital finance. China's mobile payment system has been the world's leader in terms of the number of users, technology, and the growth of payment amount. The main

FIGURE 4-5.   **Primary Payment Methods in China, 2009–2018**

Trillion won

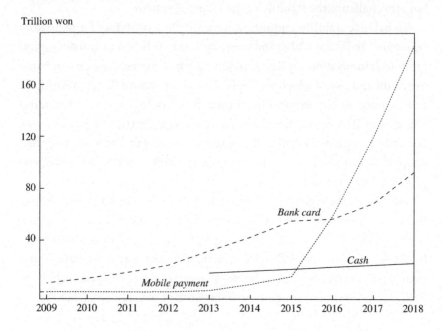

Source: Wind Economic Database, https://www.wind.com.cn/NewSite/edb.html.

mobile payment platforms in China are Alipay, WeChat Pay, UnionPay, Lakala, JD Pay, Apple Pay, and Huawei Pay.

In 2013 and early 2014, Yu'ebao and WeChat Pay, respectively, were launched in China. Since then, mobile payment has become immensely popular and has achieved fast development. Over 90 percent of residents in large cities in China use mobile payment as their primary payment method, with debit/credit card second and cash third, as shown in figure 4-5. Measured by the amount of household consumption, mobile payment overtook cash in 2015 and then overtook bank cards in 2016. Mobile payment has changed households' payment habits, saved transaction time, reduced transaction costs, promoted consumption, and shaped the pattern of the financial market, especially the payment market.

Improving Household Risk Sharing

Informal social networks in China provide an important means by which households and individuals share risks, while the insurance they provide is often incomplete. This incompleteness may have several causes, including moral hazard and limited commitment, both of which result in positive correlations between consumption and realized income.

Transaction costs—the cost of transferring money or other forms of resources between individuals—are another complementary source of the incompleteness. Rapid development and acceptance of mobile payment is a recent phenomenon in China, which has allowed individuals to transfer purchasing power within the ecosystems of Alipay or WeChat Pay and has dramatically reduced the cost of sending money across large distances and to other bank accounts.

Since China's entry into the World Trade Organization in 2001, families and social networks in China have become dispersed over large distances owing to internal migration mainly from the west to the east coastal areas. This migration is largely motivated by employment and other opportunities. By the end of 2018 there were 288 million migrant workers in China, among which over 60 percent left their home cities to find work. Furthermore, the families of over 70 percent of the leaving-home migrant workers stayed behind. In this context, lowering transaction costs could have significant impacts on the frequency and size of the internal remittances, and hence smooth risk.

The predominant use of Alipay or WeChat Pay is for P2P remittances. Before the mobile payment system was available, most households delivered remittances though China Post or bank transfer. This traditional process was relatively costly and time-consuming. With mobile payment, individuals perform a few simple steps on the payment system app. Not only are the costs of the transfers lower, but the convenience and efficiency of the process mean substantial reductions in the costs of sending and receiving money (Wang and others 2019).

Promoting Entrepreneurship

Although SMEs, most of which are privately owned, play an important role in supporting innovation, creating jobs, and promoting local and national economic growth in China, they still suffer from significant credit constraints. In the state-owned bank-based financial system, MSMEs rely heavily on their own retained earnings for investments and operational costs.

The mobile payment system in China not only facilitates payments and transfers but also promotes entrepreneurship and innovation. Lower-cost transfers and real-time payments motivate the start-up and operation of small business activities. Before the advent of mobile payments, it was quite inconvenient for small vendors to break large-denomination bills. The rapid scaling up and widespread acceptance of mobile payments based on QR and Near Field Communication (NFC) codes technology have made them a very efficient form of payment. A vendor can simply post a QR code on the door or somewhere conspicuous, the customer scans the QR code, and the money is transferred, with the payment directly deposited in the vendor's bank account or electronic wallet, after being settled by NetsUnion.

In addition, lower transaction fees encourage small businesses to accept the mobile payment solution, further benefiting from the network externalities of the payment system. Formally, shop owners can open merchant accounts that charge much lower payment fees than what China UnionPay has traditionally offered (0.6 percent for Alipay and 0.1–2.0 percent for WeChat Pay versus 0.5–4 percent for UnionPay) (CGAP 2017). Also, a point-of-sale terminal is not required, which is critically important for small businesses because of their low-value, high-volume transactions. Informally, shop owners who are not willing, or for whom it is not necessary, to register a merchant account can facilitate a simple P2P transfer between buyer and seller by displaying their personal account wallet QR code. Account holders can transfer funds from Alipay or WeChat Pay into their linked bank accounts. Alipay charges a 0.1 percent service fee to account holders who exceed the free transfer limit (RMB 20,000). WeChat Pay charges 0.1 percent for all amounts above RMB 1,000 transferred into bank accounts.

Mobile payments eliminate the need to fumble for cash, write a check, or wait for an invoice, which greatly improves the settlement efficiency (Jack and Suri 2011). The reduction in transaction frictions may facilitate trade from two aspects: on the one hand, by improving the efficiency of existing trade; and on the other, by enabling new transactions that would not have happened without mobile money. The reductions in transaction costs, along with the strengthening of informal insurance networks and the increasing financial inclusion, may help households make more efficient decisions by relaxing the trade-off between risk and return that households would otherwise face (Jakiela and Ozier 2016; Di Falco and Bulte 2013). Some empirical studies have shown that adoption of mobile payment significantly boosts the number of newly registered businesses and improves business performance (Xie and others 2018; Yin, Gong, and Guo 2019; Huang, Wang, and Wang 2020). Mobile payment users are more likely than non-mobile payment users to operate small-scale and self-employed informal businesses. The impact of using mobile payment primarily derives from the transition of families from agricultural workers to business owners and the development of informal businesses (Wang 2020). The impact on entrepreneurial activities is associated with significant increases in employment and in income for family members, with more pronounced effects on low-income and rural households.

A favorable credit reference environment has also helped in promoting financial inclusion. Fintech and big-tech companies have access to massive real-time data that can be critical inputs to credit risk evaluation—for example, payment transactions, consumption patterns, social connections, and digital footprints. Combining big data, machine learning technology, and other complex artificial intelligence algorithms, fintech and big-tech platforms can also develop a more accurate picture of people's financial lives and creditworthiness from both the extensive (exclusion) and intensive (default and price) margins (Gambacorta and others 2019; Jagtiani and Lemieux 2019; Huang and others 2020). In China, each of the three leading virtual banks—MYbank (affiliated with Alibaba), WeBank (affiliated with Tencent), and XW Bank (affiliated with tech giant Xiaomi)—provides loans to millions of small firms annually, more than 80 percent of which have no credit history, while keeping a very low default rate. Borrowers apply with a few taps on a smartphone and, if approved, receive loans within several minutes. For example, MYbank's lending business operates on the so-called 3-1-0 model, which promises user registration and application within 3 minutes, money transferred to an Alipay account within 1 second, and 0 human intervention. It has kept its average nonperforming loan ratio at around 1 percent, which to some extent may reflect the smaller size and shorter duration of its loans. MSMEs have been severely affected during the COVID-19 pandemic, and as a result, MYbank's average nonperforming loan ratio has increased but has remained contained at 2 percent. A high-quality digital infrastructure system is changing the way financial services providers interact with smaller companies that were previously underserved by state-owned banking giants.

EVOLUTION OF CHINA'S DIGITAL
FINANCIAL ECOSYSTEM

On October 18, 2003, at Alibaba's office in Hangzhou, a young staffer dashed into the office of the newly established Department of Guaranteed Transactions and announced cheerfully, "The first transaction came in! Please confirm it!" The whole room brightened. Unfortunately, two minutes later, she came back and sadly stated that "the buyer changed his mind and wanted to withdraw the fund." Later, following the employee's patient persuasion, the buyer, Zhenzhong Jiao, a university student in Xi'an, bought the second-hand Fuji camera for RMB 700 from Weiping Cui, a Chinese student studying in Yokohoma in Japan (Lian and others 2017).

This was Alibaba's and probably also China's first online (peer-to-peer) payment transaction. Alibaba had set up the online shopping platform Tao-bao five months before this deal. But transactions were rare owing to the lack of trust between buyers and sellers. Alibaba had to intermediate by providing a guarantee of payment: The buyer would first wire the money to Tao-bao, then Taobao would notify the seller to ship the product. Once the buyer confirmed receipt of the product, Taobao would pay the seller. This process worked but was quite inefficient—it normally took about two weeks to complete a transaction. Matching buyers and sellers also became a big burden for both Taobao and the cooperating bank, the Industrial and Commercial Bank, as the number of transactions began to grow. In the second half of 2004, the bank notified Alibaba that it wanted to terminate the partnership.

This served as a wake-up call for Alibaba: in addition to the payment guarantee, it also needed effective infrastructure to manage cash flows. After some unsuccessful explorations with potential partners, such as UnionPay, Alibaba's then chairman Jack Ma decided to create the company's own payment system. At a foot spa in Guangzhou in August 2004, Ma asked his colleague Zhaoxi Lu, "Have you heard about Paypal?" "No," Lu replied. Ma continued, "That's great. We are going to create a new product called Alipay. And you will be the CEO of this new adventure." On December 29, 2004, a rare heavy-snow day in Hangzhou, the Alipay system came online, with its own website, members, and virtual accounts. The rest, as they say, is history (Lian and others 2017).

Mobile payment service, which is dominated by leading players Ant Financial Services' (part of Alibaba) Alipay and Tencent's WeChat Pay, has become a fixture of daily life in China. Both players have built ecosystems around their mobile payment tools. People use Alipay or WeChat Pay to purchase goods, order coffee delivery, pay utility bills, book a taxi, buy airline tickets, make donations, transfer money, and even invest in financial products. Almost all commercial outlets in China, including street vendors, use mobile payment services' QR codes to conduct business. Chinese tourists also use mobile payment services to purchase souvenirs and luxury goods at international airports and major department stores around the world. In 2020, a total of 123 billion transactions were conducted using mobile payment services, an increase of 21.5 percent from a year ago, according to the PBC's report on payment systems.

China did not invent the mobile payment business, as both M-PESA in Kenya and PayPal in the United States are older. But Alipay and WeChat Pay took the mobile payment service to a new level of global phenomenon. It attracted massive interest from business practitioners, academics, and policymakers around the world who asked such questions as "Why did it grow? Is it possible to replicate it in other countries? What are the major economic and financial consequences? How should it be regulated?" There is already a growing literature looking at the effects of mobile money adoption on household welfare (Aker and others 2016; Munyegera and Matsumoto 2016; Beck and others 2018), saving behavior (Mbiti and Weil 2013), informal insurance network and risk sharing (Jack and Suri 2014; Klapper and Singer 2014; Riley 2018), and financial inclusion (Demirguc-Kunt and others 2018).

In China, a few big-tech companies have established comprehensive multilicensed digital financial ecosystems. For example, as one of the largest e-commerce companies globally, Alibaba used its e-commerce business as a foundation of the digital financial ecosystem, first entering into the payments sector before expanding into financing and wealth management, with an emphasis on the hundreds of millions of previously underbanked individuals and MSMEs. Mobile payment is an irreplaceable gateway of this ecosystem, through which the platforms deepen engagement across their massive user bases. As customers start using digital wallets as their payment instrument of choice for day-to-day purchases, they will become much more likely to buy the massive numbers of products and services embedded in the wallet, such as wealth management and insurance products, e-commerce services, credit services, and convenient solutions for bill pay. The payment apps are integrated into vast offline and online consumption and bill payment scenarios from taxi hailing and takeout delivery to utilities and credit card payments. For instance, around 80 percent of customers use more than three categories of products in Ant's ecosystem, and 40 percent use five or more.

The business opportunities from the ecosystem can be significant. Ant's Yu'ebao (or Leftover Treasure), China's first-ever online monetary fund specially designed for Alipay, was the largest money market fund in the world in 2017. It benefited from the platform synergy created when Alipay added the money market fund to its app. Users can directly transfer money from their balances in Alipay or linked debit cards into Yu'ebao, where the money can be used to purchase money market funds, as well as for mobile payment in all consumption scenarios. The user can also withdraw money from Yu'ebao without paying a transaction fee. Tencent's LingQianTong (or Mini Fund), similar to Yu'ebao, was released in 2018 and allows users to earn interest from their balances as well as transfer payments to pay bills, send virtual red packets, and pay off credit card balances. By embedding investment funds into payment apps, Ant and Tencent have reshaped China's mutual-fund industry in recent years. The funds they sell made up nearly a fifth of the industry's assets under management in 2018 at its peak of scale, up from just 6 percent five years earlier.

The cross-selling strategy allows money and data to stay within the digital financial ecosystem and thus creates a data-network-activities (DNA) feedback loop. Financial services embedded in the platform both benefit from and fuel the DNA loop (Bank for International Settlements 2019). The network externalities of payment platforms attract more users and exert more value for existing users, which generates more data detailing the network of links between fund senders and recipients. Big-data analytics enhance existing services and allow the provision of a wider range of financial services, such as insurance and lending, which in turn attracts more users, yields even more data, and enhances the feedback loop. The source and type of data and the related DNA synergies vary across big-tech platforms. They differ from each other in core businesses or target groups. For example, as an e-commerce platform, Alibaba collects data on sales and profits from vendors, combining financial and consumer habit information from Alipay. Tencent took another route, expanding beyond the powerful social nature of its WeChat platform to build a consumer-oriented financial network that taps into its huge user base. Combining advanced technology with big-data analytics, China's big-tech companies have established comprehensive financial ecosystems.

CONCLUSIONS AND IMPLICATIONS

Digital financial infrastructure plays a fundamental role in supporting new digital technologies that empower the financial system. Motivated by market opportunities, digital financial infrastructure such as big-data centers, computing centers, mobile payment systems, and credit references for long-tail customers including households and SMEs was mainly set up and maintained by private big-tech companies in China. While the government attaches much importance to digital financial infrastructure, both hard and soft digital infrastructure fail to keep pace. Specifically, the government should take policy actions in several areas.

First, the government should collaborate with industry to help coordinate advances in hard and soft infrastructure. New technologies, distributed ledger technology in particular, could generate significant gains in the security, accuracy, and efficiency of processes such as wholesale payment and clearing and settlement, thus improving the resilience of the system and significantly saving bank capital. However, it is still not clear that the only risk is technological. The regulatory authorities in China should help distinguish between the new technology's potential and its hype—for example, through providing proof of concept. It is also necessary for regulatory authorities to think about joining big-tech firms and private market participants in becoming members of global collaborations like Hyperledger.

Second, the government should consolidate digital infrastructure by integrating data from different sources; and it should initiate the integration of credit reference, industry and commerce, and taxation data from relevant government agencies. On the basis of ensuring the protection of customer privacy and other legitimate rights, the government should consider promoting the integration and sharing of data from government agencies, traditional financial institutions, and big techs.

Third, the government should strengthen the rule of law in digital finance. Data associated with identity are important, but the financial value of other types of data (including desensitized personal data) should not be underestimated. Privacy protection does not aim to exclude the sharing of personal information, but to effectively manage the sharing process to avoid the abuse of private information. Regulatory authorities should establish or improve relevant codes of conduct, set up industry standards, and promote legislation on consumer protection.

Fourth, the government should reform the institutional approach of financial supervision. Regulatory agencies should set clear policy objectives and seek accountability of regulatory policy. The government should consider granting regulatory autonomy and authority. While different supervision approaches have different advantages, China's institutional approach has experienced a loss of efficiency owing to the weakness of the approach when facing universal operations of financial institutions. The government should consider further reforming the regulatory framework and changing from the institutional approach to a functional approach, and at the same time, strengthening the conduct-of-business regulation.

Finally, the government should employ new technology to empower financial supervision and balance innovation and stability. In recent years, dynamic financial innovations have created new sources of financial risks, such as shadow banking and the network effect in digital finance. The outmoded mechanisms for detecting financial risks are no longer appropriate. Sup-techs (Fintech for financial supervisors) should be empowered by new digital technology. Some of the innovative transactions have positive business value, by motivating effective interest rate liberalization and supporting the real economy. For those activities, the regulatory authorities could probably find ways to facilitate innovation. The employment of sandboxes, popularly used in fintech, is a good example. For financial innovations proposed by financial institutions and big techs, the regulatory authority can extend the sandbox experiment to allow innovative businesses to operate in the specified fields or locations in order to verify the authenticity of the innovation and, at the same time, lock in risks. In this way, real financial innovations are encouraged while financial risks are effectively controlled.

NOTES

1. Nielsen, *The Global Consumer: A Global Snapshot*, February 2013, https://www.nielsen.com/wp-content/uploads/sites/3/2019/04/Mobile-Consumer-Report-2013-1.pdf.

2. NetsUnion Clearing Corporation is the operator of China's nationwide centralized platform for the processing of online transactions undertaken by the

country's third-party payment providers involving bank accounts. NetsUnion was established by the Payment and Clearing Association of China and is subject to the supervision and regulation of the PBC.

3. "Singles Day" is for the celebration of being unattached. Started by students in the mid-1990s, the data was selected in observation of its four solitary digits: 11/11.

4. Guohui Li, "On the Day of 'Double Eleven,' the Network Platform Had 1.54 Billion Transactions, and the Transaction Amount Exceeded 1.16 Trillion Yuan, All Reaching New Highs," Financialnews.com.cn, November 12, https://www .financialnews.com.cn/if/hydt/201911/t20191112_171238.html.

5. Hao Xinyao, "Baixing's Credit Stalemate, the Competition between Tencent and Alibaba," Sina Tech, September 30, https://tech.sina.com.cn/i/2019-09-30 /doc-iicezueu9262910.shtml.

6. A "regulatory sandbox" allows financial institutions and fintech companies to experiment with innovative financial products or services in a real commercial environment, but within a well-defined space and duration.

REFERENCES

Aker, Jenny C., Rachid Boumnijel, Amanda McClelland, and Niall Tierney. 2016. "How Do Electronic Transfers Compare? Evidence from a Mobile Money Cash Transfer Experiment in Niger." *Economic Development and Cultural Change* 65 (1): 1-37.

Alibaba. 2019. *The 2018 Fiscal Year Report,* https://www.alibabagroup.com/cn/ir /reports.

Bank for International Settlements. 2019. *BIS Annual Economic Report 2019.* Basel: Bank for International Settlements, https://www.bis.org/publ/arpdf/ar2019e3 .pdf.

Beck, Thorstan, Haki Pamuk, Ravindra Ramrattan, and Burak R. Uras. 2018. "Payment Instruments, Finance and Development." *Journal of Development Economics* 133 (7): 162–86.

CGAP (Consultative Group to Assist the Poor). 2017. "China's Alipay and WeChat Pay: Reaching Rural Users," December, https://www.cgap.org/research/publica tion/chinas-alipay-and-wechat-pay-reaching-rural-users.

———. 2019. "China: A Digital Payment Revolution," September, https://www .cgap.org/research/publication/china-digital-payments-revolution.

Demirguc-Kunt, Asli, Leora Klapper, Dorothe Singer, Saniya Ansar, and Jake Hess. 2018. *The Global Findex Database 2017: Measuring Financial Inclusion and the Fintech Revolution.* Washington: World Bank.

Di Falco, Salvatore, and Erwin. Bulte. 2013. "The Impact of Kinship Networks on the Adoption of Risk-Mitigating Strategies in Ethiopia." *World Development* 43 (3): 100–110.

Gambacorta, Leonardo, Yiping Huang, Han Qiu, and Jingyi Wang. 2019. "How Do Machine Learning and Non-traditional Data Affect Credit Scoring? New Evidence from a Chinese Fintech Firm." BIS Working Paper 834. Basel: Bank for International Settlements.

Hsu, Po-Hsuan, Xuan Tian, and Yan Xu. 2014. "Financial Development and Innovation: Cross-Country Evidence." *Journal of Financial Economics* 112:116–35.

Huang, Yiping, and Tingting Ge. 2019. "Assessing China's Financial Reform: Changing Roles of Repressive Financial Policies." *Cato Journal* 39 (1): 65–85.

Huang, Yiping, Zhang Longmei, Li Zhenhua, Qiu Han, Sun Tao, and Xue Wang. 2020. "Fintech Credit Risk Assessment for SMEs: Evidence from China." IMF Working Paper 20/193. Washington: International Monetary Fund, https://www.elibrary.imf.org/view/journals/001/2020/193/001.2020.issue-193-en.xml.

Huang, Yiping, and Xun Wang. 2011. "Does Financial Repression Inhibit and Facilitate Economic Growth: A Case Study of China's Reform Experience." *Oxford Bulletin of Economics and Statistics* 73 (6): 833–55.

———. 2017. "Reforming China's Financial Supervision System." National School of Development, Peking University, unpublished working paper.

Huang, Yiping, Xue Wang, and Xun Wang. 2020. "Mobile Payment in China: Practice and Its Effects." *Asian Economic Papers* 19 (3): 1–18.

Jack, William, and Tavneet Suri. 2011. "Mobile Money: The Economics of M-PESA." NBER Working Paper No. 16721.Cambridge, MA: National Bureau of Economic Research.

———. 2014. "Risk Sharing and Transactions Costs: Evidence from Kenya's Mobile Money Revolution." *American Economic Review* 104 (1): 183–223.

Jagtiani, Julapa, and Catharine Lemieux. 2019. "The Roles of Alternative Data and Machine Learning in Fintech Lending: Evidence from the LendingClub Consumer Platform." *Financial Management* 48 (4): 1009–29.

Jakiela, Pamela, and Owen Ozier. 2016. "Does Africa Need a Rotten Kin Theorem? Experimental Evidence from Village Economies." *Review of Economic Studies* 83 (1): 231–68.

Klapper, Leora, and Dorothe Singer. 2014. "The Opportunities of Digitizing Payments." Working Paper. Washington: World Bank, https://openknowledge.worldbank.org/handle/10986/19917.

Klein, Aaron. 2019. "Is China's New Payment System the Future?" June. Brookings Institution, https://www.brookings.edu/wp-content/uploads/2019/05/ES_20190617_Klein_ChinaPayments.pdf.

Lardy, Nicholas. 2008. "Financial Repression in China." Working Paper PB08-8. Washington: Peterson Institute for International Economics.

Lian, Wei., Hui Bian, Xianghui Su, and Pengcheng Cao. 2017. *Ant Financial: From Alipay to New Financial Ecosystem.* Beijing: China Renmin University Press.

Luo, Yubing. 2019. "The Credit Reference Service Empowers Financial Development." [In Chinese.] *China Finance,* 9: 146–48.

Mbiti, Isaac, and David N. Weil. 2013. "The Home Economics of E-Money: Velocity, Cash Management, and Discount Rates of M-Pesa Users." *American Economic Review* 103 (3): 369–74.

Munyegera, Ggombe Kasim, and Tomoya Matsumoto. 2016. "Mobile Money, Remittances, and Household Welfare: Panel Evidence from Rural Uganda." *World Development* 79 (3):127–37.

PBOC (People's Bank of China). 2018. "Report on the Overall Operation of the Payment System in 2018." [In Chinese.] Beijing: Author.

PBOC. 2021. "Report on the Overall Operation of the Payment System in 2020." [In Chinese.] Beijing: Author.

Rajan, Raghuram G., and Luigi Zingales. 1998. "Financial Dependence and Growth." *American Economic Review* 88: 559–86.

Riley, Emma. 2018. "Mobile Money and Risk Sharing against Village Shocks." *Journal of Development Economics* 135 (11): 43–58.

Wang, Xue. 2020. "Mobile Payment and Informal Business: Evidence from China's Household Panel Data." *China & World Economy* 28 (3): 90–115.

Wang, Xun, Xue Wang, Yiping Huang, and Shilin Zheng. 2019. "Digital Finance and Risk Sharing: Household Level Evidence from China." Working Paper No.1. Institute of Digital Finance, Peking University.

Xie, Xuanli, Yan Shen, Haoxing Zhang, and Feng Guo. 2018. "Can Digital Finance Promote Entrepreneurship? Evidence from China." [In Chinese.] *China Economic Quarterly* 17 (4): 1557–80.

Yin, Zhichao, Xue Gong and Peiyao Guo. 2019. "The Impact of Mobile Payment on Entrepreneurship—Micro Evidence from China Household Finance Survey." [In Chinese.] *China Industrial Economics* (3): 119–37.

5

The Rise and Fall of the Peer-to-Peer Lending Industry

YAN SHEN

Various financial innovations have appeared over the course of history. Some are good, some are bad, and some switch between good and bad. Generally speaking, a good financial innovation should meet at least two conditions: it should respond to the reasonable demand for financial services, and it should ensure that financial risks are generally transparent and controllable. So-called reasonable demand means that borrowers not only have real financing needs for production and consumption but also have the ability to repay. The challenge of risk transparency and control is that the biggest difficulty in financial transactions is information asymmetry, and the adverse selection and moral hazard problems caused by this can easily lead to the failure of financial transactions.

Peer-to-peer (P2P) online lending was originally considered a financial innovation to meet the needs of the real economy, when the first P2P platform, Zopa, started operating in the United Kingdom in 2005. China embraced this new business model with great enthusiasm. The country's first P2P platform, PPDai, was launched in 2007. In 2014, China's total P2P transaction value (RMB 253 billion, or US $38 billion) exceeded that of both the US market (US $6.6 billion) and the European market (US $3.9 billion). In 2017, China's total P2P transaction value reached the prime value of RMB 2.8 trillion, compared with RMB 21.2 billion in 2012 according to the website

WDZJ.com. However, the sharp rise of the P2P industry was followed by a sharp decline. By October 2020, all P2P platforms had gone bankrupt or were required to start the bankruptcy liquidation process. In a short span of ten years, China's P2P industry experienced the whole process of germination, development, expansion, crisis, and extinction.

As a lending practice based on the internet, P2P in China raises at least four unanswered questions: What were the development stages of P2P lending in China? How did P2P rise and fall? Why did P2P rise and then fall? What are the implications for financial inclusion and regulation? The answers to these questions may help explain some basic laws for cultivating immature financial markets in the digital age. This chapter aims to sort out such a process and shed light on future financial innovation and development.

THE RISE AND FALL OF P2P

P2P lending was a major component of China's financial technology (fintech) market, which started in 2004, the year that the first third-party payment service, Alipay, came online. The P2P lending platform debuted three years later when PPDai went online. Of all the fintech products, P2P was among those embraced most readily by the Chinese government. However, a high proportion of "problematic" or "bankrupted" platforms accompanied the fast growth of the industry. Figure 5-1 compares the numbers of annual operating platforms and the cumulative numbers of operating and bankrupted platforms. The annual number of platforms in operation peaked at 3,433 in 2015, then steadily dropped to 2,448 in 2016, 1,931 in 2017, 1,021 in 2018, 344 in 2019, and 3 in November 2020. The cumulative number of platforms increased sharply in 2014 and 2015, and there were more than 6,000 platforms by 2019. The difference between the two categories is the cumulative number of "bankrupted" platforms. Figure 5-1 shows that the market practically disappeared in 2020.

Accompanying the sharp increase and drop in the number of operating platforms were the variations in transaction value and loan balance. As displayed in figure 5-2, the annual transaction value increased over ten times between 2014 and 2017 and then shrank by two-thirds of its size in over two years, to RMB 965 billion in 2019. The variation in total loan balance was smaller, but by 2019 a total loan balance of RMB 492 billion remained unpaid to lenders. By 2020, the platform that had been collecting P2P loan data,

FIGURE 5-1. **Number of Operating Platforms and Cumulative Number of Operating Plus Bankrupted Platforms, 2013–2020**

Number of platforms

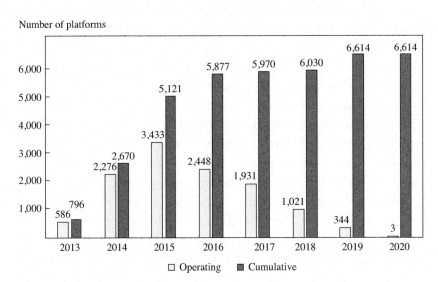

Data source: www.WDZJ.com (Home of Online Lending).

FIGURE 5-2. **Annual Transaction Value and Loan Balance (2012–2019)**

100 million yuan

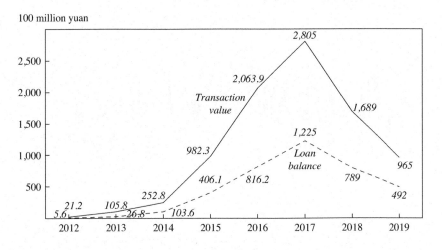

Source: WDZJ.com.

WDZJ (short for Home of Online Lending), stopped updating the transaction value and loan balance data.

Another perspective for examining the rise and fall of P2P is to consider the changes in fintech-related media news sentiment, where discussions about P2P were a dominant component until 2019. Huang and Wang (2018) constructed a sentiment index for the fintech industry using 18 million economic and financial news items since 2013. They used the potential Dirichlet distribution and hierarchical Dirichlet process to evaluate media attention and media sentiment. Figure 5-3 presents the net news sentiment index. If the index is greater than 1, the proportion of positive news items is higher than that of negative news items; if the index equals 1, the two are equal; and if the index is less than 1, negative news items prevail.

Figure 5-3 depicts the changes in the mood of news texts from January 2013 to December 2019. The figure shows that starting in the second half of 2014, the media's sentiment toward internet finance is favorable and moving in an upward trend. After December 2015, enthusiasm begins to

FIGURE 5-3.   **News Sentiment toward the Fintech Market, 2013–2019**

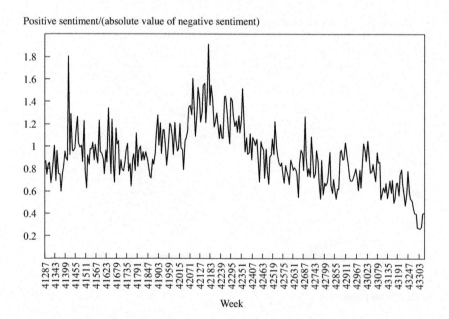

Positive sentiment/(absolute value of negative sentiment)

Week

Source: Huang and Wang (2018).

fade. Up until "The Interim Measures for the Management of Business Activities of Online Lending Information Intermediaries" was released in August 2016, the news text sentiment index was dominated by negative reports. When a large number of platforms went bankrupt in June 2018, the net sentiment index dropped to 0.29, reflecting the very pessimistic attitude of the media toward the development of internet finance.

HOW P2P ROSE AND FELL

To understand why P2P lending rose and fell in China, this section digs deeper into the background of the development of this market. At the beginning of the twenty-first century, there was a large gap between the supply and demand of credit services in China. On the one hand, formal financial services tended to favor large enterprises and clients with high net worth. Over 70 percent of small and medium-size enterprises (SMEs), farmers, and urban low-income families could not obtain adequate and appropriate financial services. Owing to the small scale and dispersed geographical distribution of most SMEs, enterprise management information was presented mostly in the form of "soft information," making it difficult for banks to implement market-oriented risk pricing for SMEs at a low cost.

On the other hand, after more than thirty years of rapid economic growth, the size of China's middle class approached the size of the total population of Europe, and residents' demands for diversified investment and financial management channels had increased. Although China's formal financial system had a high penetration rate, it targeted a small number of high-networth customers rather than mostly ordinary customers. In sum, the majority of SMEs and individuals were still underserved by formal financial institutions around 2000 (Wang, Huang, and Shen 2016).

P2P lending may harbor great potential by promoting financial inclusion through two mechanisms: using internet technology to make direct lending possible and establishing risk-sharing agreements. The first P2P platform, Zopa, was launched in 2005 in the United Kingdom. Zopa stands for "zone of possible agreement," reflecting the idea of setting up an area where lenders and borrowers can meet directly and agree on interest rates, terms, and risk sharing. The first online lending platform in the United States, Prosper, was launched in 2006 as an "eBay model for loans," akin to an online auction. In 2007, LendingClub emerged as the first platform to register online loans as bonds. Zopa, Prosper, and LendingClub have two characteristics in common. First, all the transactions are completed online and there are no offline elements; second, the arrangements for risk sharing are decided by lenders and borrowers through direct negotiation. This business model directly challenges the role of banks as intermediaries in financial activities, reflecting the hope of eliminating their exploitation. The idea is that lending to the poor can also be profitable. For example, in 2006, Muhammad Yunus of Bangladesh won the Nobel Peace Prize for founding the Grameen Bank. As Grameen Bank's customers are poor, providing unsecured loans to them has created a model where poor people can obtain loans without collateral.

These two mechanisms brought a new perspective to China's goal of developing financial inclusion. Meanwhile, the conditions for fostering the online lending market seemed to be mature based on the following five elements. The first element is technology. There have been many advances in data collection and related technologies since 2000. For example, in China the internet penetration rate jumped from 37.7 percent in the first half of 2011 to 46.9 percent half a year later, and it climbed steadily after that. The second element is internet accessibility. In December 2013, the number of internet users in China reached 600 million, with an internet penetration rate of 45.8 percent. The popularity of mobile terminals greatly reduced the cost of internet lending equipment. The third element is the source of funds. The new middle-income class was eager for more instruments for wealth management, and they also generated demand for new loan products. At the same time, venture capital institutions were optimistic about the development of individual online lending platforms. In 2014, the average individual online lending platform received about US $20 million of venture capital, and PPDai received US $50 million of venture capital that year. The fourth element is talent. Thanks to China's rapid progress in expanding higher education, there were sufficient reserves of talent in the field of financial digital transformation. The fifth element is the scene for online lending. China had joined the global industrial chain, and the industrial structure and services were constantly upgraded.

Founded in 2007, PPDai started the direct online lending business model and acted as a pure information intermediary: all transactions were completed online, and the platform did not share risks in borrowing and lending. In 2009, Hongling Venture Capital was founded in Shenzhen and started the model of promising lenders the safety of their funds. In 2010, Renren-Dai was founded by two students from Peking University and Tsinghua University. IDts business focused on high-growth people. By 2012, platforms of various ownership systems and backgrounds had emerged, including Yiren-Dai by CreditEase, Lufax by the PingAn Group, and Kaixindai with the support of the National Development Bank.

Gradually, these new platforms brought hope for the promotion and expansion of financial inclusion. New technology seemed to provide access to funds to those who originally could not borrow and at a lower interest rate. Further, it was hoped that P2P lending would contribute to China's interest rate liberalization. The enthusiasm for P2P had grown tremendously by 2013, which is often called the first year of internet finance. That year, the phenomenal event was that the total number of lenders in Alibaba's online market fund Yu'ebao exceeded 1 million within merely six days of operation, showing the power of the internet for financial services.

Starting in 2013, the development of the fintech industry switched to the fast lane. The landmark event of 2014—namely, "internet finance"—was written into the Government Work Report, which delivered the signal that the regulatory authority had adopted an encouraging attitude toward internet finance. In 2015, the reform of the commercial register system took place. From this year on, new enterprises no longer needed to pay the registered capital in full; instead, they were required to provide the capital they promised to pay. Furthermore, the requirement of a minimum of registered capital was abolished, allowing more platforms to enter the niche market of individual online lending. After 2014, growth of the P2P lending market exploded.

According to data from the Wind Economic Database, digital payments in China increased more than tenfold between 2013 and 2016, from RMB 6.6 trillion to RMB 78.7 trillion. The market size of all other fintech products (online market funds, P2P lending, online consumer financing, and online insurance) also increased more than tenfold, from RMB 1.4 trillion to RMB 15.5 trillion. At the end of 2016, P2P lending was approximately 8 percent of short-term personal loans.

After ten years of development, the P2P industry exhibited three characteristics: large size, many problematic platforms, and a large number of borrowers and lenders. By 2014, the size of China's P2P market surpassed that of the United States (US $10.4 billion) and the United Kingdom (US $2.4

billion), becoming the world's largest P2P market. Meanwhile, the cumulative proportion of problematic platforms climbed from 33 percent in 2015 to 85 percent by the end of 2016. The total number of lenders and borrowers was fewer than 2 million at the end of 2014 but exceeded 20 million by the end of 2016. In 2017, there were about 17.13 million lenders and 22.43 million borrowers, increases of 24.58 and 156.05 percent, respectively, compared with 2016, far surpassing developed countries such as the United Kingdom and the United States (Li and Shen 2018).

Until 2015, the regulatory authority had adopted a very tolerant regulatory attitude, but the increasing number of bankrupted platforms called for stricter regulation. In July 2015, the document "Guidance on Promoting the Healthy Development of Internet Finance" was issued by ten ministries and departments, followed by "Interim Measures for the Management of Business Activities of Online Lending Information Intermediaries" in August 2016. In 2017, the regulators accelerated the pace of establishing compliance requirements for online lending. That year, the documents "Guidelines on the Depository of Online Lending Funds" and "Guidelines on the Information Disclosure of the Business Activities of Online Lending Information Intermediaries" were released, one after the other. The two documents, together with "Interim Measures on the Management of Business Activities of Online Lending Information Intermediaries" and "Guidelines on the Management of Archival Registration of Online Lending Information Intermediaries," issued in 2016, constitute the institutional framework of "one measure and three guidelines" (1 + 3 framework) for the online lending industry.

At the end of 2017, the significant number of bankrupted P2P platforms and the rampage of "payday loans" created complaints that forced the regulatory authority to take a firm attitude toward regulating the P2P market. The documents "Notice on Standardizing and Rectifying the 'Payday Loan' Business" and "Notice on Special Rectification and Check of P2P Lending Risk" had been released, signifying the start of rectifying P2P lending risks as the prime task on the regulatory agenda. Since then, the market expectation has become pessimistic, and the trust of lenders has been greatly reduced. A new round of online loan risks appeared in the middle of 2018 when the regulatory authority again announced a delay in providing legal status to P2P platforms. More than 900 platforms went bankrupt in 2018.

In August 2018, the regulator issued "Notice on Carrying Out Compliance Inspection of P2P Online Lending Institutions" and attached "List of Compliance Inspection Problems of Online Lending Information Intermediaries (article 108)," which officially launched the compliance inspection of the industry. According to the regulatory requirements, online lending institutions would conduct three rounds of institutional self-inspection, self-regulatory inspection, and administrative inspection, in accordance with the 1 + 3 framework; and carry out key inspections on capital pools, self-financing, and payment and information disclosure. Article 108 covers thirty-six cases, including violation of prohibitions; violation of statutory obligations and risk management requirements; failure to fulfill the obligations of protection for lenders and borrowers; violation of information disclosure requirements; violation of regulatory requirements in key areas; and other violations of relevant laws, regulations, and regulatory provisions. Article 108 revealed that compliance checks were the focus of the regulatory work.

In January 2019, the Office of the Leading Group for the Rectification of P2P Online Lending Risks issued the "Notice on Further Implementing the Compliance Inspection and Follow-Up Work of P2P Online Lending" (referred to as document 175) to the offices of the Inter-financial Rectification Group in all provinces and municipalities. This document required speeding up the clearing of risks in the online lending industry. The basic principle was that existing institutions should be the main direction of work; and the core requirement was active promotion of administrative verification, data submission, rectification, and acceptance. P2P platforms that failed to comply with the complete administrative verification process were to be gradually removed.

The hope that some platforms would successfully complete the archival filing process diminished over time. In July 2019, at the symposium "Online Lending Risk Rectification Work," regulators sent a clear signal that the "three decreasing" requirements (i.e., to reduce the number of platforms, industry scale, and numbers of lenders and borrowers) would be strictly implemented. The regulatory authorities would encourage efforts toward benign exit through methods like compliance inspection, monitoring, and carrying out penetrative verification. The regulatory authorities considered reducing the number of P2P platforms as the main direction of work. By

November 2020, the China Banking Regulatory Commission announced that the risks embodied in internet finance were under control, as only three P2P platforms were still operating; lending and participation had fallen for twenty-eight consecutive months. This announcement indicated the de facto extinction of the P2P lending market in China.

WHY P2P LENDING FAILED IN CHINA

This section attempts to identify the reasons for the failure of the P2P industry. While the rise of P2P lending was under the goodwill of promoting financial inclusion, exploring the driving forces of the tragic fall of this industry can help shed light on how to foster and regulate new financial innovations in the future.

To start, the section takes a closer look at the cost of lending to SMEs and low-income individuals. Such costs include the ex ante risk of adverse selection (borrowers have higher probabilities of default) and the ex post risk of moral hazard (borrowers are reluctant to pay back their loans). In traditional financial systems, adverse selection is managed mainly through prior due diligence and appropriate approvals. Moral hazard can be dealt with in four ways: judicial guarantee, implicit or explicit guarantee, collateral, and risk margin. Lending without appropriate control of these risks may produce a high level of nonperforming loans or diminish the reputations of lenders owing to improper debt collection.

With the rapid development of the internet, new technologies such as artificial intelligence and big data have brought new hope and new countermeasures for dealing with credit risks. For example, online lending with a car as collateral is such an arrangement. The borrower can drive away in the car after putting it up for collateral for a loan, and the platform will use GPS to track the car. If the owner does not pay back the loan, the platform can find the car. In this way, the platform saves the cost of storing the car, and the owner can continue to use the car even though it has been used as collateral. Therefore, digital technologies have the potential to reduce information asymmetry and connect borrowers and lenders at a lower cost.

However, such financial innovations require some preconditions to be fully functional. The failure of P2P can be attributed to the lack of these preconditions. To start, China's digital infrastructure was immature compared with those of more developed countries. Failing to tackle the weakness in the business environment, the P2P business model of the majority of the platforms was unsustainable. Further, the regulators' initial lax tolerance and subsequent harsher stance resulted in regulatory uncertainty that affected the smooth operation of the market. Finally, there was insufficient understanding of the role of the media in the development of a mature financial market. Shen and Wang (2021) show that the media played an "amplifier" role in the expansion and decline of the P2P market.

Immature Digital Infrastructure

Compared with platforms operating in developed countries such as the United States and the United Kingdom, the Chinese P2P platforms operated in an environment with fragile digital infrastructure. China's P2P market was developed when China was still a developing country, with large numbers of borrowers who lacked credit reports, and vulnerable lenders who were used to guarantee benefits from investments. The lack of a mature regulatory scheme as well as data reporting procedures made it difficult to monitor the performance of the platforms.

As financial repression remained severe, China's online lending was expanding more rapidly than that in developed countries. In 2015, China's per capita gross domestic product was about 15 percent of that of the United States, yet the amount raised online in China was as high as US $30,000 per capita. However, in 2016 and 2017, the per capita amount of borrowing decreased because the growth of the number of borrowing projects exceeded the growth rate of the size of the industry, which was still similar to the per capita level of consumer loans in many developed countries.

The Chinese lender and borrower profiles were also different from those in the United States and the United Kingdom. The lenders in the US online lending market were mainly institutional lenders and qualified lenders with abundant funds. Although the proportion of institutions and qualified lenders varied in different market segments in the United States, the lowest proportion was 53 percent and the highest proportion was over 90 percent in 2016. In the US market, borrowers were mainly individuals, whose main purpose was to repay the turnover of credit cards or other existing debts. In the United Kingdom, 70 percent of the funds in the UK online lending market came from individual lenders, and the rest came from institutional lenders. From the perspective of borrowers, the P2P market in the United Kingdom provided 149 million pounds in loans to micro-, small-, and medium-size enterprises and 91 million pounds in consumer loans in 2015. Therefore, corporate loans accounted for 62 percent of the funds, including 609 million pounds in real estate loans. By contrast, in China, a large number of individual lenders provided funds to individual borrowers, with the total number of borrowers approaching 40 million in 2017. According to data collected by WDZJ, the leading information-sharing platform for online lending in China, at least 40 percent of online lenders in 2017 were younger than age forty. The monthly incomes of 80 percent of the lenders was less than RMB 10,000. From the lending side, the WDZJ data indicate that more than 80 percent of the borrowers were between the ages of twenty and forty, and more than 50 percent had a monthly income of less than RMB 4,000. In general, much of the lending involved young lenders who were vulnerable to the financial risks and low-income, young borrowers with dubious ability to repay.

If China had mature instruments to assess borrowers' ability to repay, lending to a large number of individual lenders may not have been an issue. However, China lacked the credit reporting systems established in the United States and the United Kingdom when P2P debuted. In the United States, FICO scores are built by Experian, Equifax, and TransUnion. Similar credit scores are built in the United Kingdom by Callcredit, Equifax, and Experian. Among Prosper's borrowers, for example, 80 percent of their FICO scores are above 680, and LendingClub's loans are concentrated among prime individual borrowers. By comparison, China's credit system was underdeveloped. The number of people with credit records in the central bank's credit reporting system was only 380 million in 2015, and the online lending platforms were not connected to the central bank's credit system. Therefore, it was costly for online lending platforms to judge borrowers' qualifications.

China was also backward in terms of online lending statistics. The United Kingdom and the United States have detailed statistics year by year on the proportion of natural persons and institutional lenders among lenders, proportion of corporate loans and consumer loans among borrowers, qualification of borrowers, purpose of borrowing, and so forth under the existing legal framework. China did not have unified official statistics for all the P2P platforms, let alone statistical indicators in line with international statistics.

Unsustainable Business Model

In 2007, PPDai adopted a business model of P2P direct lending in which it did not participate in the transactions between borrowers and lenders and did not bear the risk of default. The bottleneck of this business model was the low willingness of lenders to lend and the slow growth of market size. Most lenders believed that P2P projects were similar to deposits and wealth management products in banks. The lenders were used to guaranteed principal and interest but found that identifying qualified borrowers was difficult, and so they were reluctant to lend large amounts in this market.

To solve the problem of funding sources, online lending platforms evolved into two new models. The first was the "full-guarantee" model represented by Hongling Venture Capital, and the second was the "half-guarantee" model represented by RenrenDai. Under the full-guarantee model, VIP members were promised the full amounts of principal and interest. That is, if the borrower fails to repay on schedule, the platform guarantees that it will make the payment to the lender. In the half-guarantee model, the platform sets up provisions for risk funds, and at the same time forms portfolios of loans with different returns and risks, with the goal of diversifying risk for lenders. If the risk pricing can cover the default losses on the whole, then most lenders can recover the principal and interest on schedule. In the case that asset allocation fails to accomplish complete risk diversification, the platform allocates part of the risk reserve to repay the lenders once losses occur. The half-guarantee model was popular for helping to grow market size, but at the expense of switching credit risk from the lenders to the platforms.

But the diversification practice under the half-guarantee model brought three new problems. First, the requirements on the lenders' professionalism in investment, time, and energy were high. As the term of the loan was often twenty-four to thirty-six months, paying back equal amounts of principal and interest each month was the most common repayment method. Under this arrangement, lenders not only had to decide whether to lend to countless borrowers but also needed to make many decisions about the repayments they received each month. Second, a small loan of US $100, for example, could lead to hundreds or even thousands of small payments, if broken down into smaller scales and installments. P2P platforms were mostly internet-based enterprises without payment licenses; hence, arranging a massive number of small payments was costly. Third, lenders tend to favor loans with shorter maturities, while borrowers prefer longer maturities, so there was a maturity mismatch between the demands of lenders and borrowers.

To solve these problems, automatic bidding, capital pools, and rolling fundraising were gradually brought into the practice of P2P lending. To improve the efficiency of capital use and investment income and facilitate lenders' ability to manage payment collection within the lending period, the platform provided lenders automatic bidding. To reduce the payment cost, the platform combined several payments made by the same lender or borrower within a period of time into one, and then paid the lender or borrower separately, thus forming a capital pool. Then the borrower needed only to pay his or her loan to the platform, which then collected the funds and paid them to the lender, greatly reducing the number of payments. The platform solved the maturity mismatch problem through the following intermediary services: when the original lender needed liquidity, the platform provided a secondary market where the lender could transfer the lender's rights. The new lender received the credit rights of the original lender through match-making of platforms. If the transfer were successful, the original lender could exit or hold the debt until maturity, which formed a rolling fundraising mechanism.

The emergence of automatic bidding, capital pools, and rolling fundraising transformed the direct lending relationship between individuals into a payment relationship between borrowers and the platform. The platform's business model was therefore gradually transformed from P2P direct lending to a model in which the platform provided fixed income for lenders and a guarantee for the related risks. Such arrangements would likely comply with the requirements of P2P platforms being information intermediaries, rendering the business model unsustainable.

Regulatory Attitudes

Compared with the regulatory authorities in the United States and the United Kingdom, China's regulatory authorities reacted slowly on whether and how to regulate the P2P market. The United States adopted very strict regulation of online lending platforms after the 2008 financial crisis. P2P platforms had to obtain a license to operate in any state and comply with various laws related to lending in that state, or they were subject to the supervision of the Securities and Exchange Commission. In the United Kingdom, the Financial Conduct Authority has been the main regulator since April 2014, and platforms need to acquire licenses from this agency before beginning formal operations.

As described in the section on how P2P rose and fell, however, China did not have a regulatory framework for P2P until 2015, so the P2P market developed without appropriate regulations for nearly ten years. Then a series of regulatory measures were announced and implemented in July 2015, but they created controversial issues on at least three major aspects. The first issue was that the platforms should position themselves as information intermediaries. To operate legally in the country, the platforms needed to go through an "archival filing" process acknowledging them as information intermediaries. As P2P platforms had already become credit intermediaries, the vast majority of the platforms would have had to shut down immediately if these regulatory policies were strictly implemented. The second issue was the supervisory responsibility of local governments. P2P platforms were a nationwide business; therefore, if local governments were responsible for regulating them, serious regulatory arbitrage problems would emerge. Later, the interim administrative measures made a proper compromise, and the China Banking Regulatory Commission and local governments shared the responsibility for supervision. The third issue had to do with the archival filing process. Even if online lending platforms were positioned as information intermediaries, the regulators should have set unified entry thresholds and issued licenses to eligible institutions. Allowing institutions to engage in financial transactions without explicitly setting thresholds and licenses made it difficult to avoid the situation of "mixing good and evil." In short, after eight or nine years of growth of the P2P industry, the regulators suddenly came up with very strict regulatory standards that were impossible for most platforms to meet. Such regulatory uncertainty may have expedited the speed of the failure of the P2P lending market.

The Media's Role

The media also played a role in the rise and fall of P2P lending in China. Using text data composed of 18 million news articles published from March 2013 to July 2018, Shen and Wang (2019) constructed a lender decision model and a weekly digital financial media attention and news text sentiment index. They evaluated the impact of media reports on the transaction volume of 275 online lending platforms during the period. Their analysis has three main findings. First, as lenders had limited access to information in this nascent market, media reports mattered for the size of P2P lending. Transaction volume increased when the media paid attention to this market with optimistic attitudes, and decreased when the media tone was pessimistic. Second, the impacts of media reports on platforms of different sizes were different. Among them, the transaction volume of large platforms was more affected by the sentiment of news texts; the transaction volume of small platforms was more affected by whether the media were concerned. Third, further analysis of the mechanism shows that media reports had an asymmetrical impact on the supply and demand of funds in the online lending market and were mainly concentrated on the supply side. The ups and downs of media attention and sentiment had a significant ability to predict the increase or decrease in the number of lenders and the per capita amount of the loans. The number of lenders on small platforms was more sensitive to media reports. These findings provide empirical evidence that media attention and sentiment affected the supply and demand of funds and likely acted as an amplifier of the rise and the fall of P2P.

LESSONS FOR THE FUTURE

In this recounting of the what, why, and how of the rise and fall of China's P2P industry, there is probably no doubt that it was a failed and misguided financial venture. The industry had a very good financial inclusion gene, but it went off the rails. The fundamental cause was inadequate risk control, rooted in the immature digital infrastructure, nonsustainable business model, inadequate regulatory strategy, and media reporting. The question is whether the collapse would have been avoidable if history had taken different routes at different stages of P2P development. This section considers a few thought experiments for alternative scenarios.

The first consideration is what might have happened if PPDai had been incorporated into the regulatory framework when it went online in 2007. In this case, anyone who wanted to participate in the P2P business would have had to meet certain qualifications, especially the ability to control risks. It is likely that the total number of platforms would have been smaller and would not have developed so fast. Likewise, the quality of the platforms would have been relatively better, and the business model would have been more standardized, compared with the "good and evil mixed" situation that appeared.

The second thought experiment considers what might have happened if the regulatory authorities had seen the value of P2P for inclusive finance and were willing to support its healthy development. In this scenario, the regulatory authorities would have actively promoted the creation of favorable conditions for P2P, such as constructing a credit culture, combating borrower debt evasion, and so on. These steps would have had the potential to help reduce the extreme behaviors of some borrowers and platforms.

The third thought experiment is that if after the interim measures were announced in 2016, the regulatory authorities had decided to provide "archival filing" to some excellent platforms and adjustment periods for those platforms that failed to meet the information intermediary positioning. At the same time, the regulatory authorities would have taken measures to strengthen the credit reporting system, stabilize the mood of the market, and safeguard the legitimate rights and interests of lenders so that even if the platform went down, the debts of the borrowers would not perish.

From an outsider's point of view, the attitudes of the regulatory authorities are understandable. Financial regulations for traditional financial institutions are built on the model of institutional regulation—that is, the China Securities Regulatory Commission regulates the securities industry, the China Banking Regulatory Commission regulates the banking industry, and the China Insurance Regulatory Commission regulates the insurance industry. When the P2P industry began to grow rapidly in 2013, different regulatory authorities attempted to shift the regulation responsibilities to others, given that no one had rich experience in how to regulate this new industry and that there was no clear standard on who should do so.

The rise and fall of P2P lending still leaves several questions unanswered for the emergence of similar new business/industry in the future. First, who should regulate the new business/industry? Second, how can the sustainability of a business model be identified before it generates large losses for the general public? Third, what long-term measures are needed to prevent risks when the new business/industry is in its initial stage? If regulatory authorities do not learn from past failures, they may face a similar dilemma when a new business model appears.

The first lesson is that functional regulation may be more appropriate for regulating fintech enterprises. Under functional regulation, financial activities are regulated according to their nature, and financial products with the same function and legal relationship are subject to consistent regulation according to the same rules, regardless of the type of financial institution. For example, any institution engaged in the credit business—providing funds, risk analysis models, or channels—is subject to supervision under a unified framework. This provides an idea for the regulation of fintech platforms. First, the target of functional supervision is not limited to financial licensees. As long as nonlicensees are engaged in a part of the credit business, they are all within the scope of supervision. For nonlicensed institutions in the financial business chain, timely regulatory intervention can be carried out according to their market influence and degree of systemic importance. Second, functional supervision is managed from the product dimension rather than the balance sheet dimension of institutions, and it has unique regulatory effectiveness for off-balance-sheet businesses.

Meanwhile, conduct regulation should also be strengthened, focusing on legal compliance and consumer protection, in response to fintech platforms. The key issues are related party transactions, platform monopoly, data property rights, and personal privacy, which is a larger and more fundamental proposition.

The decline of the online lending market also shows the urgency of strengthening the digital infrastructure. Because of the lack of access to the central bank's credit system, the risk of borrowers cannot be effectively identified. It is necessary to speed up the construction of an online credit reporting system. It is imperative to set up standards for what personal information can be collected, how to collect it, how to audit algorithms for analyzing data, and how to identify the authenticity, timeliness, and appropriateness of data sources, as well as promote real information sharing and protect data privacy.

On how to identify a sustainable business model, the regulatory authority may borrow heavily from the UK regulatory sandbox. Since 2019, the People's Bank of China has been implementing the so-called Pilot Projects for Fintech Innovation. Such pilot projects are built in the spirit of a regulatory sandbox and are different from traditional financial pilots in at least three dimensions. First, the fintech pilots focus on innovation testing. This testing is suitable for businesses that have been at the forefront of financial innovation and need to discover whether it is true innovation and guard against corresponding risks. Traditional pilots focus on testing whether mature businesses in developed countries also work in the Chinese market. Second, the fintech pilots provide a lenient innovation environment. Traditional financial pilots focus on providing a lenient market environment, mainly by selecting certain regions or specific individuals and granting preferential policies on tax and business registration to pilot units or regions. Third, the fintech pilots involve dynamic interaction and collaboration between regulators and enterprises so that they can jointly discover real innovation. Traditional financial pilots focus on static intervention. In conclusion, the fintech pilots and traditional financial pilots can complement each other and jointly promote financial innovation.

The fate of China's P2P industry has been decided. Fortunately, the P2P industry was a small proportion of the overall financial sector. Thus, even if the P2P industry completely disappears, it will not affect overall financial stability. However, some of the experiences and lessons from the development of the P2P industry should be reconsidered. If these lessons can help China avoid repeating mistakes in other areas of finance, the P2P experience of the past decade will prove valuable.

REFERENCES

Huang Y.P., and J.Y. Wang. 2018, "Characterizing the Media Sentiment on FinTech and Its Impact on Online Lending Market." *China Economic Quarterly* 17 (4): 1623–50.

Li, C.Y., and Shen, Y. 2018, "Information Identification and Risk Contagion: An Empirical Study Based on P2P Lending Market." [In Chinese.] *Finance Research*, no. 11: 98–117.

Shen,Y., and Wang J.Y., 2021. "Media and Immature Financial Markets—The Perspective of P2P." [In Chinese.] *Management World*, no. 2: 98–117.

Wang, J. Y., Y. P Huang, and Y. Shen. 2016."Evaluating the Regulatory Scheme for Internet Finance in China: The Case of Peer-to-Peer Lending." *China Economic Journal* 9 (3): 272–87.

6

Digital Lending in China: A Tale of Three Models

YIPING HUANG

Promotion of financial inclusion, especially providing loans to small and medium-size enterprises (SMEs), is a perennial challenge globally. The challenge is even tougher in China for a number of reasons, such as the bank-dominated financial system and repressive financial policies. In the United Kingdom, only about half of SMEs can obtain bank loans, while in China this proportion is less than one-fifth (Huang and Qiu 2021). The two primary barriers for making SME loans are (1) access to potential borrowers and (2) assessment of credit risks. SMEs are often very large in number, small in size, and scattered in location. Traditional banks reach SMEs by building a lot of brick-and-mortar branches, which is extremely costly. Banks often adopt three approaches for assessing credit risks: examining financial data, holding collateral assets, and using relationship lending. Most SMEs, however, have neither comprehensive financial data nor enough collateral assets. While relationship banking is often effective in identifying credit risks, it is also quite costly and makes it difficult to scale up the business.

For more than a decade, the Chinese government has been undertaking measures to improve financial services for the disadvantaged enterprises and households. In 2016, the State Council issued the document "Development Plan for Promoting Financial Inclusion (2016–2020)." In retrospect, China achieved a great deal in this area during those five years. Policy efforts such as setting up specialized business units within financial institutions, creating guaranteed funds for SME lending, and providing targeted liquidity support by the central bank all played important roles. But the most important and "unexpected" breakthrough occurred in the new digital financial technology, or fintech, sector. Some of the Chinese digital financial businesses, such as mobile payment, digital lending, and online investment, reached tens and even hundreds of millions of customers. In some of these business areas, China leads international innovation (Hua and Huang 2021).

Digital lending refers to the provision of loans by businesses that use digital technology such as the large technology (big-tech) platform, big data, artificial intelligence, and cloud computing. These technological tools can help with customer acquisition and risk assessment. For instance, the long-tail feature of digital platforms means near-zero marginal cost for adding additional customers once the platform is established. And analyses of big data offer a new way of evaluating credit risks. With these technological possibilities, digital lending is able to reach gigantic numbers of borrowers at extraordinary speed. For the first time in history, the dream of promoting financial inclusion is materializing. During the COVID-19 pandemic of 2020, several Chinese digital lenders continued to provide loans to SMEs without disruption, thanks to the contact-free feature of digital credit. These lenders not only supported the SMEs at a difficult time but also served as important stabilizers of the macroeconomy.

China has at least three distinctive business models of digital lending: peer-to-peer (P2P) lending, big-tech credit, and digital supply chain (DSC) financing. P2P lending refers to individuals borrowing money directly from other individuals through digital platforms, cutting out the financial institutions as the middleman (Bachmann and others 2011; Huang, Shen, and Wang 2016; Shen 2022, this volume). Big-tech credit refers to lending by big-tech companies relying on the big-tech platform, affiliated ecosystem, and big-data-supported credit risk assessment model (Cornelli and others 2020; Huang and others 2020). DSC financing refers to digital-technology-based lending solutions for enterprises that leverage their relations with existing production or sale processes (Bai and others 2020; Song 2020).

The experiences of China's digital lending businesses are quite mixed. P2P lending started in 2007, with the first platform PPDai, and experienced a period of dramatic expansion in the following eight years. After the regulators issued the regulatory policy framework in late 2015, the sector started to consolidate and was eventually reduced to zero in late 2020. Big-tech credit was initially created by the Chinese e-commerce giant Alibaba (now Ant Group) in 2010. It has become the main form of lending to SMEs and individuals, in terms of the number of loans, not the amount of loans. In recent years, big-tech companies in Argentina, India, Korea, and even the United States have adopted big-tech credit. China's big-tech credit, however, is still the largest in the world, according to estimates from a Bank for International Settlement study (Cornelli and others 2020). Compared with the first two models, DSC financing is still in the early stage of development. Although several leading big-tech companies are involved in this business, GLP Finance, a subsidiary of the logistics property giant GLP, is probably the most advanced in setting up digital technological frameworks for various lending models.

In summary, digital lending in China offers a very interesting story of three different models—P2P lending has already failed, big-tech credit is more developed, and DSC financing is emerging. Comparatively speaking, big-tech credit has been extremely successful in providing access to finance to more than 1 billion people. This is very important for financial inclusion. But big-tech loans are often quite small in size and short in duration. Even though big-tech lenders serve gigantic numbers of SMEs, they still mainly rely on business logics for consumer loans by focusing on soft and behavioral information of entrepreneurs. Meanwhile, DSC financing can only reach SMEs connected to production or sales processes; therefore, it reaches a much smaller number of customers than big-tech credit. However, by holding chattel mortgage or verifying the authenticity of transactions, DSC financing is able to provide much larger loans to SMEs, not only in the service sector but also in the manufacturing industry.

Why did some digital lending businesses in China succeed while others failed? This is the central question that this chapter intends to explore. Specifically, what was the most important driver of different outcomes: technology, management, or regulation? The key takeaway from this comparative analysis is that, at the end of the day, any viable lending business should be built on prudent credit risk management, whether using financial data or collateral assets or something else. Prudent credit risk management means there is a strong capability of reducing information asymmetry to control both the adverse selection problem and the moral hazard problem. Digital lenders should be reasonably confident that borrowers not only have the ability to repay the loans but are also willing to do so. This should be the ultimate test of the usefulness of any digital financial innovation. But this requires joint efforts by digital lenders and financial regulators.

WHY IS INDIVIDUAL AND SME LENDING DIFFICULT?

A common rule in the traditional financial industry states that the top 20 percent of customers, often the most profitable corporations and the wealthiest households, contribute about 80 percent of the market revenue. Servicing the remaining 80 percent of the customers, mostly SMEs and low-income households, is often difficult and unprofitable. This explains why promotion of financial inclusion is so challenging.

The United Nations General Assembly designated 2005 as the "International Year of Microcredit" in order to encourage more lending to SMEs. The Chinese government also made serious efforts in the following years. It approved the creation of a large number of microcredit companies. According to the People's Bank of China (PBC), China had a total of 7,118 microcredit companies at the end of 2020, with outstanding loans of CNY 888.8 billion (PBC 2021a). The authorities also undertook various measures to encourage commercial banks to increase lending to "disadvantaged borrowers." Again, at the end of 2020, the amount of outstanding loans in the area of financial inclusion was CNY 21.53 trillion, up 24.2 percent from a year ago, compared with total outstanding loans of CNY 172.75 trillion, which was up by 12.8 percent from a year ago. Of this, the amount of outstanding loans for SMEs was CNY 15.1 trillion, and that for agricultural production was CNY 5.99 trillion (PBC 2021b).

Despite some progress, SMEs' difficulties in obtaining bank loans are still widely observed problems in the Chinese economy. These difficulties may be attributable to two general challenges and two China-specific factors: the former refer to difficulties in acquiring new customers and assessing credit risks, and the latter points to ownership discrimination in lending decisions and state intervention in setting of lending rates.

At the end of 2018, China had a total of 18.07 million officially registered SMEs. A recent study using data from the mobile payment service Alipay Quick Response (QR) code payment system put the total number of registered and unregistered small businesses, which are often referred to as QR code merchants, at 97.7 million (Wang, Guo, and Li 2020). Reaching such a large number of borrowers is very difficult, especially when some of the QR code merchants do not even have fixed business locations. Traditional banks have to build many branches in order to reach their customers across the country. But that, by definition, is extremely costly. Considering that most of the SME loans are very small, serving SMEs may not be financially beneficial to banks.

Another difficulty is assessment of SMEs' credit risks. Information asymmetry is the most challenging aspect of any financial transaction. The purpose of credit risk assessment is to ensure that loans are extended to the right borrowers and will eventually be paid back. Banks often adopt three methods to evaluate credit risks. The first method is to analyze financial data, including the balance sheet, the income statement, and the cash flow table. This step is usually undertaken only with large corporations, as most SMEs do not have comprehensive and standard financial data. The second method is to hold borrowers' fixed assets as collateral in order to prevent the adverse selection and moral hazard problems. This practice is more common among SMEs, but most SMEs often do not have enough fixed assets. And the third method is to employ relationship banking—that is, banks' loan officers monitor and interact with borrowers in a comprehensive way and make lending decisions on the basis of "soft information" rather than hard financial data. As a way of assessing credit risk, this method is quite effective as, generally, the average nonperforming loan ratio of relationship lending is lower than that of normal loans. But it is not cost-effective and, therefore, makes it very difficult to scale up the business.

There are two additional barriers for lending to SMEs in China. One is ownership discrimination, as almost all SMEs are privately owned. Banks discriminate against SMEs even for commercial reasons. If a loan for a state-owned enterprise becomes bad, the government would most likely restructure the company by either injecting more capital or facilitating a merger with a stronger company. This makes it likely that the loan will eventually be paid back. However, if a loan for an SME becomes bad, it is unlikely that the loan will be recovered. Therefore, it is not surprising that banks are reluctant to lend to SMEs, as their higher volatility makes them more of a risk than large state-owned enterprises.

The other barrier is the lack of market-based risk pricing. One very important rule for financial pricing is that the reward should be compatible with the risk. Funding costs are different for major corporations and new start-ups, primarily because their levels of risk are different. SMEs are, by definition, riskier, as the average life span of Chinese SMEs is five years. In recent years, however, Chinese regulators required commercial banks to not only lend more to SMEs but also lower the lending rates. Both requirements are difficult to fulfill on a commercial basis. This is a good example of "good intention leading to a bad outcome." While large banks can cross-subsidize their SME lending businesses, it is difficult for small banks to do so.

If the difficulty of lending to SMEs is a common phenomenon, why did it make headlines in China only recently? One of the key explanations is that the Chinese economic growth model is transitioning from input driven to innovation driven. SMEs now account for more than 60 percent of GDP, 70 percent of corporate innovation, and 80 percent of urban employment. These figures imply that failure to improve conditions for SME funding will seriously endanger China's innovation, employment, and economic growth. The current financial system, which is dominated by banks and contains much state intervention, was adequate for supporting extensive growth in the past. But China has lost its low-cost advantage, and its growth needs to rely more on innovation and industrial upgrading as well as a revamped financial system. The gross inadequacy of lending to SMEs both triggered various government policies to provide more loans to SMEs and created incentives for indigenous financial innovations, including P2P lending, big-tech credit, and DSC financing.

FAILED EXPERIMENT WITH P2P LENDING

In 2006, Muhammad Yunus, founder of Grameen Bank in Bangladesh, was awarded the Nobel Peace Prize. A young man in Shanghai, Gu Shaofeng, who was then a technology manager at Microsoft, heard the news and wondered if such a microcredit model would work in China. Later that year, he and two other alumni of Shanghai Jiao Tong University created Pai Pai Dai (PPDai), the first P2P lending firm in China. PPDai was at least one of the pioneers globally in this area—together with Zopa, established in 2005 in the United Kingdom; and Prosper, established in 2006 in the United States. Ten years later, PPDai became a listed company on the New York Stock Exchange. But its story did not stop there.[1]

For several years after 2007, P2P lending remained a very small business. In 2013, when the government started to emphasize the importance of financial innovation, P2P began to be recognized as an important model of financial inclusion. As individuals can borrow from other individuals directly, cutting out the financial middleman, the P2P model was both more efficient and more inclusive than traditional financial models. Many individuals who were not covered by banks' lending businesses could now borrow from the platform, while others could invest a small amount of money and receive a higher return. Numerous P2P lending platforms sprang up across the country, with the number of operating platforms increasing from 150 in 2012 to 3,433 in 2015 (Shen 2022, this volume).

However, there was one unanswered question with this new lending business: How should credit risk management be conducted? The definition of P2P lending is that it should be a pure information intermediary, not a bank. This means that the platforms cannot provide any financial intermediation, including a guarantee. Therefore, borrowers and lenders were largely left alone to make their own decisions on such platforms. Prosper used FICO scores to mitigate the adverse selection and moral hazard problems. But the Chinese P2P lending platforms could not access PBC's credit registry system. Such a lending model is unviable in China, as lenders lack any effective means to assess credit risks. Even worse, if the borrowers do not pay back the money, there is not much the lenders can do about it. There was an extreme phenomenon that Zhang and Huang (2018) described as a "reversal bank run": some individuals intentionally borrowed from weaker platforms in the hope that if the platforms later collapsed, they would not need to repay their loans.

In order to survive and grow the business, P2P platform operators quickly added functions of financial intermediation. Hongling Capital, established in 2009 and specializing in large volumes of transactions, began to offer guarantees to lenders. Other firms followed with investment guaranteeing, fund pooling, auto bidding, and other functions. The sector grew rapidly. Total outstanding lending exceeded CNY 1 trillion in 2015. Almost all platforms were engaged in financial intermediation, but none were properly regulated. Serious problems started to emerge in 2015, when more than 1,000 platforms failed. In late 2015, one of the largest P2P lending firms, Ezubao, collapsed, which affected close to 1 million lenders/investors.

Huang, Shen, and Wang (2016) conducted an empirical analysis on which P2P lending platforms were most likely to fail. They found that platforms with the following features were often less likely to survive: lots of missing information, shorter history, smaller amounts of registered capital, fewer types of products, extreme interest rates, and provision of guarantees. This study did not offer a complete picture of why the platforms failed, but it did reveal that a lot of platforms were not properly set up and run. This is what market participants and regulators should reflect on. The financial industry is the most heavily regulated economic sector because of the potential consequences of financial risks. But apparently such regulation did not happen during the development of P2P lending.

Because of the increasing risks associated with the P2P lending industry in 2015, the China Banking Regulatory Commission published the draft regulatory policy in December of that year and later released the temporary regulatory framework in August 2016. Most important, the policy clarified that P2P lending platforms could function only as an information intermediary. Effectively, it declared the death of the P2P lending industry in China. However, a period of uncertainty followed, as regulators, fearing financial and social instability, were reluctant to abruptly shut down the sector; platform operators, meanwhile, tried all sorts of ways to transition into new businesses. At the end of 2020, the number of P2P lending platforms was zero, as many platforms had collapsed, some voluntarily shut down their shops, and others, including PPDai, switched to new businesses.

The rise and fall of P2P lending in China within a period of thirteen years was in general a failed experiment, as many people lost their savings (Shen 2022, this volume). This painful experience offered at least two important lessons. One, financial transactions in which financial risks cannot be properly managed should not exist. Lending money to somebody who otherwise would not be able to borrow from banks alone is not good enough. A viable lending business should be supported by a low default rate. If lenders do not have any means to assess credit risk, then it is not responsible lending. Without access to PBC's credit registry information, P2P lending should not have existed in China.

And lesson two is that financial transactions including P2P lending need to be properly regulated. The period between 2007 and 2016 may be described as a vacuum of regulation. It was probably difficult for regulators to act decisively at the early stage of development because the nature of the business was not yet crystal clear, the government in general was in favor of liberalization, not "control," and the regulatory division of labor was not well defined. But the result was that, for some time, no regulator wanted to touch this sector, and there was no rule. Even the "cleaning up" of the industry involved law enforcement more than regulatory authority.

BIG-TECH CREDIT'S TRANSFORMATION OF SME LENDING

Alibaba set up the online shopping platform Taobao in 2003 and then created the mobile payment service Alipay in 2004 to facilitate online transactions (Huang, Wang, and Wang 2020). In order to support development of the many online shops, Alibaba collaborated with commercial banks, hoping to provide loans for those shops selling products on Taobao. Alibaba recommended lists of promising online shops to banks, but the banks rejected almost all of them since none of the online shops satisfied the conditions for credit risk assessment. In 2009, Alibaba decided to take it upon itself to provide loans to the online shops and appointed a young staffer, Hu Xioaming, who later became the president and CEO of Ant Group in 2018, to head the project. In 2010, the project released the so-called 3-1-0 online lending model: a potential borrower completes the online application forms in 3 minutes; if approved, the loan amount is transferred to the borrower's account within 1 second; and there is zero human intervention.

This was the beginning of what is now called big-tech credit—that is, large technology companies providing loans to take advantage of their big-tech platforms and associated ecosystems and big-data-supported credit risk assessment (Frost and others 2019; Huang and Qiu 2021). While the big-tech credit model is applied by many big-tech companies around the world, including Amazon Lending in the United States, Mercado Credito in Argentina, and Paytim in India, China is the largest big-tech credit market, according to an estimation by a Bank for International Settlements study by Cornelli and others (2020) (figure 6-1). The two leading big-tech lenders, WeBank (affiliated with Tencent) and MYbank (affiliated with Ant Group), each have 2,000–3,000 employees and can make more than 10 million loans every year. Big-tech lenders can lend to a gigantic number of customers simultaneously at an extraordinary pace. Meanwhile, the average nonperforming loan ratios of both WeBank and MYbank are below 2 percent, much lower than the nonperforming loan ratios of commercial banks' SME loans (Gambacorta and others 2020).

Unlike P2P lending, big-tech credit has developed a system for managing credit risks, which contains two important pillars: the big-tech platforms and their associated ecosystems, and the big-data-supported credit risk assessment models (figure 6-2). In short, the platforms help with customer acquisition and data accumulation, while the models try to identify borrowers with both the ability and the willingness to repay loans.

FIGURE 6-1.   Big-Tech Credit in Selected Countries, 2014–2019

Millions of US dollars, logarithmic scale

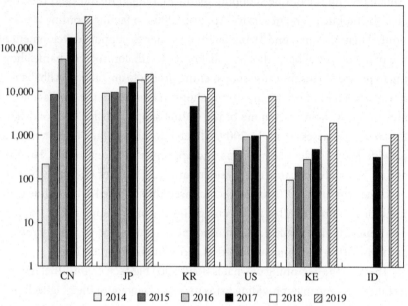

Source: Cornelli and others (2020).

Note: CN: China; JP: Japan; KR: Korea; US: United States; KE: Kenya; ID: Indonesia.

An important feature of big-tech platforms such as Tencent and Alibaba (or Ant) is the long tail, which facilitates the first function of acquiring large numbers of customers. After the platform incurs the fixed costs of construction, the marginal costs of adding additional customers are almost zero. Both Tencent's social media app WeChat and Ant's mobile payment app Alipay have more than 1 billion users. In addition, they built comprehensive ecosystems around their apps—users can organize almost every aspect of their daily lives, such as purchasing airline tickets, calling taxis, booking hotel rooms, ordering food deliveries, paying utility bills, and making doctors' appointments. The platforms and their ecosystems ensure not only that a large number of users join the "clubs" but also that they stay. Therefore, acquiring individual and SME customers is no longer a barrier.

The second function of the big-tech platforms and associated ecosystems is to record data. Users leave digital footprints on the platforms when they

FIGURE 6-2.   **Big-Tech Credit Risk Management Framework**

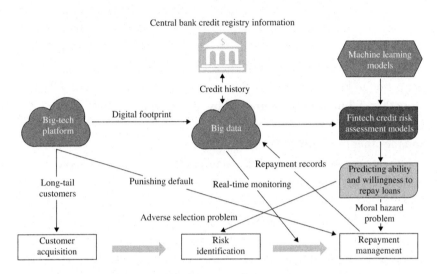

Source: Huang and Qiu (2021).

are on social media, e-commerce, or search sites. And cumulated digital foot-prints form part of the big data. Big data can be used for monitoring bor-rowers' activities and behavior. The fact that big-tech platforms have real-time data is extremely valuable for credit risk management, as it allows the big-tech lender to adjust its decisions in a timely fashion. This is almost im-possible for commercial banks, as their data often have significant time lags. More important, big data are used for credit risk assessment.

The third function of the big-tech platforms and their associated ecosys-tems is to help with management of loan repayment. Since all borrowers operate on the big-tech companies' systems, the platforms can reduce the moral hazard problem by designing schemes to encourage repayment and discourage default.

The second pillar of the big-tech credit risk management framework is the big-data credit risk assessment model. The novelty of applying nonfinan-cial data to analyze credit risk is not immediately appreciated. The pioneer-ing analysis by Berg and others (2020) shows that even simple digital foot-prints from an online furniture shop can play a role similar to a credit score. The study by Huang and others (2020), however, was the first to apply big data from a big-tech lender, MYbank, for credit risk assessment. First, they adopted a "horse race" analytical framework, under which the big-data model of credit risk assessment and the traditional bank model compete with each other. The big-data model applies big data and the machine learning method, while the traditional bank approach relies on traditional data and the scorecard method. In essence, the model that generates a more accurate prediction of loan default wins. Second, they acquired transaction data on more than 1.8 million loans granted by MYbank between March and August 2017. They divided this sample into two periods, one from March to May and the other from June to August. Data from the first subperiod were used to estimate the two models, while data from the second subperiod were applied to test the reliability of the models.

One commonly applied measure for evaluating the reliability of credit risk assessment models is the AUC (area under the receiver operating characteristics curve) (Berg and others 2020). The quality of the model is regarded as reasonable if the AUC is above 0.6 and extremely good if the AUC is above 0.8. According to Huang and others (2020), the AUC for the traditional bank model is 0.72, which is quite good (table 6-1). But the AUC for the big-data model is even better, at 0.84. These figures confirm that for the sample from MYbank, the big-data model is more reliable than the traditional bank model in predicting loan default. They also echo the observed lower nonperforming loan ratios of the big-tech credit compared with those of the commercial banks.

Outperformance of the big-data model relative to the traditional bank model may be attributable to both the data advantage and the method advantage, although the relative contribution of data and method may be sample specific. Compared with the scorecard method, the machine learning method should be more capable of capturing interactions among a large number of variables (replacing the scorecard method with the machine learning method in the traditional model raises the AUC from 0.72 to 0.80).

TABLE 6-1. **AUCs for Different Models**

	Scorecard method	Machine learning method
Traditional data	0.72	0.80
Big data	0.76	0.84

Source: Adapted from Huang and others (2020).

And compared with traditional data, big data contain two unique sets of information: real-time data and behavior data (again, replacing traditional data with big data in the traditional model raises the AUC from 0.72 to 0.76).

A more fundamental contribution of the big-data model is that it supports entry of a large number of unbanked customers but still maintains good loan quality. Of the 1.8 million transactions studied by Huang and others (2020), only about 7 percent of the customers had previously borrowed from a bank. The remaining 93 percent had never had any transactions with banks and are unlikely to obtain bank loans easily.

At the moment, there is very limited direct competition between big-tech lenders and traditional banks. Most of the big-tech credit customers are small in both business and loan sizes and are often not served by banks. So at least for now, big-tech lenders and traditional banks complement each other. But this could change over time.

RISING DSC FINANCING

Supply chain financing is not a new business. Banks can provide loans by leveraging SMEs' connections with core enterprises through production or supply processes. Supply chain financing is also an important form of financial inclusion, particularly lending to SMEs. These SMEs would not satisfy banks' requirement for credit risk assessment, as they lack both financial data and collateral assets. But they are important parts of supply chains, which enable them to borrow money from banks. For instance, a large automobile company has many suppliers of auto parts. If banks can access information about these SME suppliers' purchase, production, and sales processes and also about their cash flow through the automobile company, then they can make loans to these SMEs.

Information about product and fund flows between SME suppliers and the core enterprise serves a number of purposes: (1) it helps the banks reach the potential borrowers; (2) it supports credit risk assessment using big data to predict probabilities of loan default; (3) it can facilitate optimal use of funds, in terms of the exact amount and the exact time, in order to reduce funding cost; and (4) it is useful for management of loan repayment.

In recent years, a number of leading big-tech companies, including Ant Group and JD Digits, tried to develop DSC financing businesses by taking advantage of digital technology. So far, the most interesting case is probably

FIGURE 6-3. **Different DSC Financing Models**

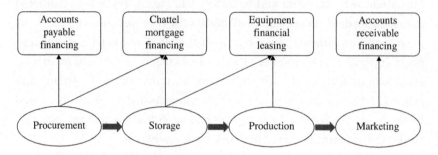

Source: Adapted from information provided by GLP Finance.

the emerging GLP Finance. GLP is a leading global investment manager and business builder in logistics, real estate, infrastructure, finance, and related technologies. It gives GLP Finance an edge over many of its peers by directly plugging into the supply chains on its own platform, already equipped with digital technology, to provide DSC financing services. With some necessary modifications, these practices may then be transplanted to other supply chains. Currently, GLP offers a range of DSC financing products, including chattel mortgage financing, accounts payable and accounts receivable financing, and equipment financial leasing (figure 6-3).

The primary pain point in supply chain financing is confirmation of authenticity of both chattels and transactions. If there is no effective way of ensuring the accuracy and reliability of information, then engaging in a lending business could be extremely risky. Did the claimed transactions really happen? Were the reports accurate? Could the chattels be reliably monitored?

One important condition for sustainable DSC financing is customers' commercial viability, which is also the common bottom line for any credit risk assessment. By taking advantage of blockchain and other digital technology, DSC financing exercises real-time monitoring of commercial flows (goods, transactions, and cash flows) for risk assessment and ensures repayment of loans by establishing a closed loop for cash flows. This business model is valuable for profitable SMEs with good accounting data, as they can use external funding and expand their businesses. Even for profitable SMEs without impressive accounting data, DSC financing can still be useful. Banks normally would not provide loans to such businesses. But it is possible for DSC financing to offer credit support, as long as the transactions themselves are profitable, authenticity of the transactions can be verified, and cash flows are managed inside closed loops.

Traditional supply chain financing faces several important barriers. For instance, double counting of chattels and transactions is a common problem in traditional supply chain financing businesses. When the steel trade financing experienced a widespread collapse in China in 2012, a number of steel companies were found to have claimed more steel for chattel mortgage than their total outputs. Others were found to have repeatedly reported the same transactions in order to obtain multiple bank loans.

DSC financing tries to reduce these problems by taking advantage of three key digital technological tools: internet of things, blockchain, and big data. First, the internet of things, like big-tech platforms in big-tech credit, provides the digital infrastructure by linking all aspects of online and offline economic activities, such as trade transactions, production processes, warehouse activities, and transportation networks. The ideal state is that all activities are monitored in real time, and all information is recorded on internet systems. If something happens, the system should know. Second, blockchain technology is applied in a P2P network of computers or servers known as nodes that both participate in and monitor the transfer of information and assets. Every transfer is recorded on each node, generating a platform of trust based on several identical copies of the ledger. The most important function of blockchain technology is to ensure authenticity of information—every entry is verified by multiple parties, and no single party can falsify the record. Once some chattels are used as mortgage, they cannot be used for other purposes. And, third, combined with external sources of data, digital footprints recorded on the system may form big data, which can be used to analyze creditworthiness and predict probabilities of loan default.

The operating mechanism of DSC financing may be explained by looking at the case of chattel mortgage (figure 6-4). An SME may use goods stored in a warehouse to borrow money. The financial institution would first verify the quality and quantity of the goods after receiving the loan application. If the loan application is approved, the financial institution would instruct the warehouse to monitor the goods and their movement full-time, until the loan is repaid. In an unlikely situation in which the borrower fails to pay back the money, the financial institution should secure the goods and try to dispose of them at a reasonable price. The logic of chattel mortgage is quite

FIGURE 6-4.   DSC Financing: The Case of Chattel Mortgage

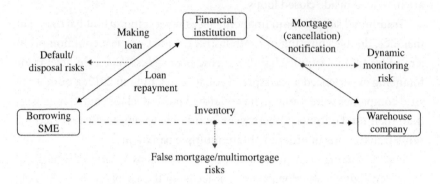

Source: Gong and Liu (2020).

similar to that of collateral lending, but it is hard to monitor the movement of the chattels, difficult to evaluate their value, and tough to dispose of them. This is why the risks of traditional chattel mortgages are quite high. With the assistance of digital technology, however, it becomes possible to reduce monitoring risk, false mortgage risk, and default risk.

EVALUATION AND COMPARISON OF THE THREE MODELS

Although the three digital lending models in China had very different development experiences, there were two common contributors to these models. On the one hand, there was a wide gap in the availability of financial services, especially those for SMEs and low-income households. All three digital lending models, whether P2P lending or big-tech credit or DSC financing, were initially created to fill that gap in the traditional financial market. At the start, they looked like revolutionary changes, as they extended to the individuals and SMEs rarely served by traditional financial institutions. Once they emerged in the market, they were enthusiastically embraced by participants. Even the authorities took a tolerant position, seeing the value of these models for financial inclusion.

On the other hand, digital technology made the impossible possible. Before big-tech platforms, big data, artificial intelligence, and cloud computing came onto the scene, it was hard to imagine that financial institutions could grant such a large number of individual and SME loans at such a rapid

FIGURE 6-5. **Comparison of Three Digital Lending Business Models**

P2P lending	Big-tech credit	DSC financing
• Origin: Informal lending	• Origin: Relationship lending	• Origin: Supply chain financing
• Main borrowers: Individuals	• Main borrowers: Individuals and SMEs	• Main borrowers: SMEs
• Technology: Platform	• Technology: Big-tech platform and big data	• Technology: Internet of things, blockchain, and big data
• Risk assessment: None	• Risk assessment: Big-tech credit risk management framework	• Risk assessment: Verification of authenticity and control of credit risks
• Current state: Disappeared	• Current state: Large	• Current state: Growing

Source: Compiled by the author.

pace and, at the same time, maintain good quality of loans. Without digital technology, these new forms of lending would not have happened.

The three digital lending models had quite different development trajectories (figure 6-5). P2P lending was originally viewed as a kind of "socialist" finance, as it provided new opportunities to both individual borrowers and individual lenders. If the two parties can successfully close deals without any financial intermediation, then there should be efficiency gains for both. After an initial stage of development between 2007 and 2012, P2P lending suddenly surged in the following three years, measured by numbers of new platforms. After the authorities announced the regulatory framework for the industry in 2016, the sector began to consolidate and disappeared completely in 2020.

The single most important lesson of the P2P lending experience is that it does not have a reliable credit risk assessment approach. P2P lending is not entirely new. In a way, informal lending or the curb market is a form of P2P lending, although it does not rely on digital technology. In many cases, informal lending works well, because informal credit risk assessment is effective. The problem with the Chinese P2P lending business was that large numbers of borrowers and lenders were moved onto a large platform. The two sides of a lending transaction never met before and probably will never meet in the future. If they are not supported by any other means of risk evaluation, then this business cannot survive.

For sure, P2P lending would not have become a mainstream lending business in China, but it did not need to die all at once, either. There are at least two possible scenarios in which some P2P lending platforms could survive. One scenario allows P2P lenders to access PBC's credit registry system. This could help the lenders identify the right borrowers and also ensure repayment of loans. In a way, this is how payday loans operate in the United States. The other scenario involves big-tech platforms, which could provide big-data-based credit scores to assist decisionmaking by individual lenders. Of course, the reality is that neither of these happened.

Of the three models, big-tech credit has been the most successful. By relying on platform and big data, big-tech lenders are able to reach borrowers at scales never seen before. Creation of the big-tech credit risk management framework is a significant financial innovation, allowing the lenders to focus on big data instead of financial data or collateral assets. While this is a completely new way to assess risk, it actually resembles, to some extent, the relationship banking of traditional banks. There, banks' loan officers focus on soft information by closely monitoring the borrowers. In a way, big data are digitized soft information.

Digital technology that helps scale up big-tech credit business could have mixed implications. On the one hand, it is now possible to realize the dream of financial inclusion. Several big-tech companies in China have more than 1 billion users. This means that financial services can reach literally anybody with a smartphone and telecom signal. On the other hand, it highlights the importance of "responsible finance." Giving a loan to whoever wants to borrow funds may not be the right thing to do. But giving a loan to whoever has real economic needs and has the ability to pay back the loans is "responsible finance." The majority of the big-tech credit borrowers are individuals, although big-tech lenders also provide loans to SMEs. These SMEs are mostly family businesses, and thus lending decisions are based more on SME owners than on the businesses. One sensitive business area is consumer loans. Consumer loans, especially those to low-income households, are an important form of financial inclusion. However, if this business continues to expand, it could cause significant risks, high household leverage ratios, and high loan defaults. At the end of the day, the only sustainable driver of consumption is income, not a bank loan.

One important challenge faced by many big-tech lenders today is the size mismatch of their balance sheets. Digital technology enables these lenders to reach very large numbers of borrowers, most of whom do not have a comparable source of funds. The PBC still does not allow remote opening of bank accounts. Therefore, the big-tech lenders do not have access to large volumes of bank deposits. This is the most important cause of the current regulatory controversies surrounding the big-tech credit business model. Big-tech lenders often look at the asset-backed securities market to raise funds; however that could easily increase their leverage ratios. They often also cooperate with other banks to grant loans, but the regulation requires that they contribute 30 percent of the loans. These regulatory concerns are valid, but they need to be addressed in a systematic fashion. Simply forcing the big-tech lenders to lower the leverage ratios and increase their own capital contribution only leads to shrinkage of their businesses.

Comparatively speaking, DSC financing is still a young business, although supply chain financing has been around for much longer. It is also relatively more resource- and time-consuming to set up the networks. In the case of Taobao or WeChat, once the platform is set up, anybody can use it. The DSC platforms need to be established for different core enterprises or ecosystems, although some of the key elements can be easily transplanted. This means that development of the DSC financing business takes more time and that it may not be able to reach similar scales of big-tech credit.

But DSC financing also has obvious advantages. First, borrowers from DSC financing are all SMEs that are directly plugged into the supply and production processes. In fact, many of them are manufacturing companies, while most of the SME borrowers from big-tech credit are from the service industry. Because the lending decision is based on actual business activities or transactions, loan sizes can also be much bigger than big-tech credit. Second, for the same reason, DSC financing's credit risk management framework is probably more reliable. In fact, in 2020, GLP Finance experienced zero nonperforming loans.

As a digital lender, DSC financing also needs to overcome some regulatory barriers. What financial licenses should DSC financing institutions use for the lending business? In what ways can DSC financing institutions cooperate with commercial banks? What is the proper division of responsibilities between DSC financing institutions and commercial banks in such joint efforts?

POLICY IMPLICATIONS

Digital lending during the past decade was probably one of the most important financial innovations in China. It provided for the realization of financial inclusion. In some areas, China is even leading international innovation in digital lending. The big-tech credit, for instance, was first introduced in China, although it absorbed important practices from other businesses, such as the online process of loan application and approval and credit scores based on nontraditional data. Today, China is the largest big-tech credit market in the world.

Of the three business models, big-tech credit is the most successful, DSC financing is still emerging, and P2P lending has already disappeared. Intentionally or unintentionally, all three models grew out of some preexisting businesses—P2P lending from the curb market (peer to peer), big-tech credit from relationship banking (soft information), and DSC financing from supply chain financing (production or supply processes). One common feature is that they all tried to apply digital technology to upgrade the business models, in order to increase the scale and reduce the risk. The ultimate determinant of success or failure is the ability to formulate an effective credit risk management framework. P2P lending failed because there was no prudent way of managing credit risks. Big-tech credit succeeded because the big-data-supported credit risk assessment model was quite reliable—at least more reliable than the traditional bank's model—for small individual or SME borrowers. DSC financing's risk management should be effective because it directly plugs into production and supply processes and ensures authenticity using digital technology. However, there are wide variations of submodels of DSC financing. It remains to be seen if the credit risk management approach is robust when applied to different businesses and different platforms.

The viability of a lending model is determined by the effectiveness of credit risk management. That has been the case for the past millennium. However, it is interesting to explore why digital technology worked for some business models but not others. It may be argued that for most P2P platforms, there was no serious application of digital technology, other than creation of the app. But then why did a business model with no effective credit risk management attract so many participants, on both the borrowing and lending sides? This raises a number of regulatory questions. First, why didn't regulators set entry requirements for P2P operators at the very beginning? It is common sense that any financial transactions need to be regulated. Second, why didn't regulators set up basic rules for the operation of P2P lending? If it was made clear that P2P firms functioning as financial intermediaries was illegal, this would have deterred many investors. Third, why didn't regulators impose the "know your client" requirement? Assuming that nobody knew whether P2P lending would work, the regulators should have been able to see the risks involved in this business, which would not be suitable for everybody. These questions are not intended to criticize the regulators. But it is worthwhile to reflect on them, especially for future policy consideration and policymaking.

Similar problems also existed in the cases of big-tech credit and DSC financing, but the consequences were less grave. The difference is that these institutional players are much more cautious and professional about credit risks, while individual investors in P2P lending lacked a sound understanding of financial risks. But this does not imply that big-tech credit and DSC financing are without problems. In late 2020, financial regulators accelerated efforts to bring all digital financial transactions under proper regulation. The first policy implication is that all financial transactions need to be regulated. The regulatory system needs to be revamped to focus on both institutions and transactions. It was not immediately clear whose responsibility it was to regulate P2P lending. That is why nobody took action. This needs to be changed.

The second policy implication is that financial regulation in the digital age also needs to innovate in order to balance between innovation and stability. If regulators see some benefits in new innovations but are not sure whether they carry serious risks, they could adopt "regulatory sandboxes" to experiment with the new financial products or business models under the close watch of regulators. If the results are satisfactory, they can issue full licenses. Otherwise, they can stop the experiment at any time. If the sandbox approach had been applied to P2P lending more than ten years, we would not have ended up in the current big mess. The good news is that the PBC has already started this policy practice, although it is called the regulatory experiment for fintech innovation.

At the same time, financial regulation also needs to apply digital technology. For digital lending businesses, old regulatory methods such as submission of balance sheet information and onsite and offsite inspections would not be timely enough to spot potential risks. Regulators need to adopt regulatory and supervisory technology (regtech and suptech) to detect and dissolve financial risks in real time.

The third policy implication is that regulators should work with digital lenders to facilitate healthy development of digital lending. Since digital lending has been the most successful business model of lending to low-income households and SMEs, the regulatory policies should be adjusted for better outcomes, without hurting financial stability. Most big-tech lenders and DSC financing providers use local microcredit licenses. But, by definition, their businesses are national. There is no stable source of funds, which seriously affects their ability to serve SMEs. Regulators may consider allowing remote opening of bank accounts to provide targeted liquidity to the digital lenders by the central bank and to open some other channels for them to raise funds from the market. And, it will be useful to explore possible means of collaboration between digital lenders and banks. The key is to control the moral hazard problem.

The final policy implication is that, for now, the regulatory priority in the digital financial industry should be regulation of unfair behavior, not antimonopoly. Big-tech platforms have a natural tendency of concentration, thanks to the long-tail feature. This is exactly why big-tech credit could be a revolution of financial inclusion. However, here, market share is often not the right criterion for determining whether there is a monopoly. Benefits of both scale and scope efficiencies may be shared with consumers or exclusively kept by the platform. The former is the ideal outcome of concentration, while the latter could be a symptom of monopoly. The key criterion should be contestability. If new entrants can still compete with the incumbent players, then a monopoly should not be a top worry for regulators. But, of course, it is always important for regulators to pay attention to unfair behavior, especially behavior that exploits borrowers taking advantage of the large platform.

NOTE

1. Shen (chapter 5, this volume) provides a comprehensive assessment of the rise and fall of the P2P industry in China.

REFERENCES

Bachmann, A., A. Becker, D. Buerckner, and M. Hilker. 2011. "Online Peer-to-Peer Lending: A Literature Review." *Journal of Internet Bank and Commerce* 16 (2): 2–18.

Bai, Y., D. Zhai, D. Wu, and X. Lin. 2020. "Blockchain-Based Optimization Strategies for Supply Chain Finance Platforms." [In Chinese.] *Financial Economics Research* 2020 (4): 119–32.

Berg, T., V. Burg, A. Gombović, and M. Puri. 2020. "On the Rise of FinTechs: Credit Scoring Using Digital Footprints." *Review of Financial Studies* 33:2845–97.

Cornelli, G., J. Frost, L. Gambacorta, R. Lau, R. Wardrop, and T. Ziegler. 2020. "Fintech and Big Tech Credit: A New Database." BIS Working Paper 887. Basel: Bank for International Settlements.

Frost, J., L. Gambacorta, Y. Huang, H. Shin, and P. Zbinden. 2019. "Bigtech and the Changing Structure of Financial Intermediation." BIS Working Paper 779. Basel: Bank for International Settlements.

Gambacorta, L., Y. Huang, Z. Li, H. Qiu, and S. Chen. 2020. "Data vs Collateral." BIS Working Paper 881. Basel: Bank for International Settlements.

Gong, Q., and Y. Liu. 2020. "Digital Supply Chain Financing." Presentation at the Institute of Digital Finance, Peking University, November 28, 2020.

Hua, X., and Y. Huang. 2021. "Understanding China's Fintech Sector: Development, Impacts and Risks." *European Journal of Finance* 27 (4–5): 321–33.

Huang, Y., and H. Qiu. 2021. "Bigtech Credit: A New Credit Risk Management Framework." [In Chinese.] *Management World* 37 (2): 12–21.

Huang, Y., Y. Shen, and J. Wang. 2016. "Analysis on the Regulatory Framework of Internet Finance: Evidence from Peer-to-Peer Lending." [In Chinese.] *Comparative Studies* 83 (2): 28–41.

Huang, Y., X. Wang, and X. Wang. 2020. "Mobile Payment in China: Practices and Its Effects." *Asian Economic Papers* 19 (3): 1–18.

Huang, Y., L. Zhang, Z. Li, H. Qiu, T. Sun, and X. Wang. 2020. "Fintech Credit Risk Assessment for SMEs: Evidence from China." IMF Working Paper WP/20/193. Washington: International Monetary Fund.

PBC (People's Bank of China). 2021a. "Statistical Report on Microcredit Companies for the Fourth Quarter of 2020." [In Chinese.] January 27, 2021, http://www.pbc.gov.cn/goutongjiaoliu/113456/113469/4172975/index.html.

PBC. 2021b. "Statistical Report on Loan Investments by Financial Institutions in 2020." [In Chinese.] January 29, http://www.pbc.gov.cn/goutongjiaoliu/113456/113469/4180902/index.html.

Song, H. 2020. "Digital Platforms Empowering Innovation of Supply Chain Finance Models." [In Chinese.] *Financial Accounting* 2020 (8): 55–63.

Wang, J., F. Guo, and Y. Li. 2020. "Estimation of Total Number of Individual Businesses in China and Evaluation of Impact of COVID-19." Mimeo, Institute of Digital Finance, Peking University.

Zhang, H., and Y. Huang. 2018. "Sentiment, Default Rate and Reversal Bank Run: Evidence from One Internet Financial Firm." [In Chinese.] *China Economic Quarterly* 17 (4): 1503–24.

7

Robo-advisors and the Digitization of Wealth Management in China

ZHUO HUANG

DEVELOPMENT OF CHINA'S ROBO-ADVISORY MARKET

Robo-advisors, also known as automated digital investment advisory programs, are algorithm-based digital tools that provide automated financial advisory services with little or no human intervention. These services have been welcomed by retail investors since 2008, when Betterment launched the world's first robo-advisor. The assets under management (AUM) of the US robo-advisory industry reached approximately US$750 billion in 2019.[1] China's first generation of robo-advisors was launched by a financial technology (fintech) company in 2014.

Compared with traditional human investment advisors, robo-advisors have several advantages, as shown in figure 7-1. First, their management fees are much lower—0.5 or 1 percent at most. They may even be free. Second, the starting investment amount is typically much lower than that required by human advisors. Third, with the help of digital and artificial intelligence (AI) technologies, robo-advisors can serve huge numbers of "long-tail" customers with diminishing marginal costs. Fourth, they provide more customized advisory services, a more transparent investment process, and a more user-friendly interface. Last, as investment decisions are made by computer algorithms, the use of robo-advisors can help avoid or alleviate human behavioral bias. Given these advantages, robo-advisors are especially

FIGURE 7-1.   **Advantages of Robo-advisors**

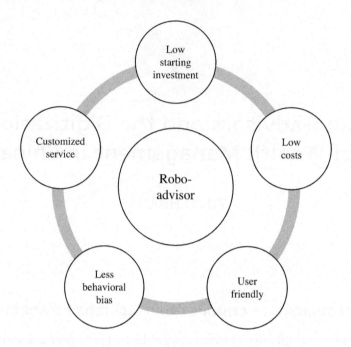

attractive to retail investors who need customized but inexpensive financial advice on managing their wealth.

Thanks to the boom in fintech and increasing demand for wealth management (WM), China's robo-advisory industry has maintained a high growth rate since 2014, when the first Chinese robo-advisor was launched. Four main types of institutions in China provide robo-advisory products: big-tech platforms, such as Ant Group; traditional investment management firms, such as mutual funds and security brokerages; commercial banks; and third-party WM companies. Approximately fifty robo-advisory products are currently available on the Chinese market.

Three Phases of Robo-Advisor Development

The development of China's robo-advisors can be divided into three phases.

Phase 1: Early Exploration by Fintech and Third-Party Companies (2014–2016). During the early phase of development, regulations on robo-advisors were not clear. In China, the robo-advisory industry is covered by three separate financial license requirements: investment advisory licensing, asset management licensing, and financial product sales or distribution licensing. Investment advisors can only provide investment recommendations; asset managers can make investment allocation decisions. According to their sales licenses, banks and third-party WM companies can sell certain financial products issued by other financial institutions, such as mutual funds, trusted plans, hedge funds, and insurance, to appropriate individual investors.

In China, unlike in the United States, investment advisory services represent only a tiny proportion of the WM industry, and the number of advisory licenses available is limited. All advisory, asset management, and distribution services and products are highly regulated, especially those designed for retail investors. The process of applying for each of the three types of licenses is complex and demanding.

In 2014, several Chinese fintech start-up companies began providing WM services through robo-advisory or AI-powered products to gain exemption from the license requirement. They attempted to replicate the regulatory arbitrage story of peer-to-peer (P2P) lending (see chapter 5) in the WM industry. Some third-party WM companies and P2P platforms also joined the robo-advisor market to reach more retail investors, hoping that the license requirement would soon be relaxed or that they could obtain a first-mover advantage in applying for a license.

Phase 2: Transaction-based Sales Model (2016–2019). As part of the movement toward tighter regulation of the fast-growing internet finance industry, the regulation of robo-advisors became more clear in 2016–2017. Learning from the P2P experience, the Chinese regulatory authorities clearly stated in several important guidelines on asset management that "the qualification as an investment advisor shall be obtained to use artificial intelligence technology for investment advisory business, and a nonfinancial institution shall not rely on robo-advisors to conduct asset management business beyond the scope of business or in disguise. Robo-advisors are subject to the same regulatory framework as traditional human advisors."[2] According to the guideline, robo-advisors operated by nonfinancial institutions, such as a technology company without a financial license, should be prohibited.

During this phase, increasing numbers of commercial banks, mutual funds, and securities brokerages in China launched robo-advisory products for various purposes. Some used robo-advisors as marketing tools to attract new clients. Some incorporated robo-advisors into their digitization strategies to improve operational efficiency and client satisfaction.

A notable robo-advisory product at this time was Machine Gene Investment, launched by China Merchants Bank (CMB) at the end of 2016. It attracted market attention as the first robo-advisory product offered by a commercial bank. CMB was well known for its successful WM business, with more than RMB 2.3 trillion in AUM in 2016.[3.] The starting investment amount set by Machine Gene Investment was only RMB 20,000, much lower than the minimum requirement of RMB 10 million for CMB's private banking WM clients. Machine Gene Investment was released to the bank's 50 million mobile users via a new version of CMB's mobile application. After obtaining information on a client's risk tolerance and investment horizon through dozens of survey questions, the AI-based computer algorithm automatically recommends a customized portfolio consisting of several mutual funds from a pool of hundreds. The proposed portfolio is well diversified, as the component funds cover equities (both active and passive index funds), bonds (both government and corporate bond funds), and commodities. When market conditions change such that the portfolio deviates from the investment target, the algorithm automatically reminds the investor to adjust the portfolio accordingly. The investor need only click a few times to confirm the initial purchase and rebalancing transactions. Within one year of its release, Machine Gene Investment had obtained RMB 10 billion in AUM.

Compared with their US counterparts, Machine Gene Investment and other advisory products in China in 2016–2019 were substantially restricted in two respects. First, while the robots provided automated portfolio recommendations, investment decisions (i.e., fund purchases) had to be made by the users themselves. Second, advisors could not benefit from clients' investment performance. They could only obtain commissions by selling funds to clients, as banks and third-party companies had fund sales licenses but not investment advisory licenses. Even mutual funds and securities brokerages during this stage were restricted in their ability to obtain performance fees.

A transaction-based business model of robo-advisory services has some drawbacks. First, it can cause conflicts of interest between advisors and their clients. Advisors make more profits from their clients if they recommend more frequent transactions or products with higher commission rates. Second, every time a robo-advisor recommends that a client rebalance their portfolio, the client has to confirm the transaction. This obviously damages the user experience.

Phase 3: Fee-based Advisory Model (2019–Present). A milestone in the development of China's investment advisory industry was the launch of the Mutual Fund Advisory Pilot Scheme by the China Securities Regulatory Commission in 2019. This brought new opportunities for the WM and robo-advisory markets by replacing the transaction-based sales model with a fee-based advisory model.

The scheme allows asset managers and fund sales companies to provide personalized investment advice. These companies can also discretionarily manage clients' investment portfolios in the mutual funds market. Robo-advisors can execute transactions automatically, without asking for investors' permission. The scheme has led to a strong shift toward a fee-based advisory model. For example, many advisors now tailor asset management services to customers' needs and charge no more than 5 percent of clients' net asset value.

Since the pilot scheme was launched, nineteen firms have been granted licenses in three rounds (see table 7-1). In the first round, in October 2019, licenses were awarded to five large mutual funds. In the second, in December 2019, licenses were given to three online fund distribution platforms, including Tengan Fund Sales and Ant Fund Sales, whose parent companies are Tencent and Ant Group, respectively. In the third round, in February 2020, licenses were awarded to three commercial banks and seven securities brokerage companies. Although licensed advisory platforms can charge advisory fees of up to 5 percent of managed assets, most charge no more than 0.5 percent.

The development of the robo-advisory market in China has been furthered by the release of HelpYouInvest, a robo-advisor jointly provided by the Chinese fintech giant Ant Group and the global asset management company Vanguard Group. This robo-advisory product is designed to serve the 1.2 billion users of the Alipay and Ant Fortune platforms, with a minimum investment threshold of only RMB 800. A service fee of 0.5 percent (annualized) is deducted from the client's account quarterly and charged at the

TABLE 7-1. Mutual Fund Advisory Pilot Scheme in China

Round of licenses awarded and date	Category	Institution
First October 2019	Mutual funds	China Asset Management
		E Fund
		Southern Asset Management
		Harvest Fund
		Zhong Ou Asset Management
Second December 2019	Third party	Tengan Fund Sales (Tencent)
		Ant Fund Sales (Ant Group)
		Yingmi Fund Sales
Third February 2020	Banks	Industrial and Commercial Bank of China
		Ping An Bank
		China Merchants Bank
	Securities	Guolian Securities
		China International Capital Corporation
		Huatai Securities
		Shenwan Hongyuan Securities
		China Securities
		China Galaxy Securities
		Guotai Junan Securities

time of transfer. HelpYouInvest acquired more than 200,000 clients and RMB 2.2 billion in assets within the first 100 days of its launch.[4] More than half of its clients are under thirty years old.

The market views this progress as part of China's efforts to further open its finance industry to the world. More global players are expected to join the competition of China's asset management and robo-advisory business.

Comparison of Robo-advisors in China and the United States

China's robo-advisors share some features with their US counterparts, such as customized advice provision, a low starting investment amount, low costs, and a user-friendly interface. However, because of differences in market development, regulatory frameworks, and investment culture between China

TABLE 7-2. **Comparison of Robo-advisors in China and the United States**

Characteristic	Robo-advisors in China	Robo-advisors in the United States
Regulatory framework	Developing, pilot scheme	Mature and clear
Main investment tool	Mutual funds	Exchange-traded funds
User objective	Maximizing return, avoiding big losses	Risk–return balance, diversification, tax planning
Investment horizon	Short to medium term	Medium to long term
Profit model	Ranges from commission to advisory fees	Advisory fees
Market players	Multiple types of financial institutions	Well-known asset and WM firms, fintech companies
Market concentration	Low	High

and the United States, robo-advisory products in these markets also differ in several respects (see table 7-2).

The regulatory framework governing robo-advisors in the United States is mature and clear. Robo-advisors must register with the US Securities and Exchange Commission and are subject to the same securities laws and regulations as human advisors, such as the Investment Advisers Act of 1940 and the Securities Exchange Act of 1934. In contrast, regulations on robo-advisors in China are still developing. Future regulatory change will depend on the performance of the Mutual Fund Advisory Pilot Scheme.

Regarding investment tools, robo-advisors in the United States rely heavily on exchange-traded funds in their asset allocation owing to the liquidity, transparency, and low transaction costs of such funds. China's robo-advisors are more likely to use passive or active mutual funds. However, this situation may soon change, as China's exchange-traded fund markets are growing very quickly.

In the United States, investors seeking robo-advisory services focus on balancing risk and return, portfolio diversification, and tax planning. In China, such investors focus more on ensuring a high rate of return and avoiding big losses. They are less patient than their US counterparts and usually hold assets for shorter periods.

The major robo-advisor providers in the United States are well-known asset management companies (e.g., Vanguard, Charles Schwab) and fintech companies (e.g., Betterment, Wealthfront). The AUM by the robo-advisor industry are currently concentrated in Vanguard and Charles Schwab, which are substantially ahead of other players. In China, the market concentration is much lower, as multiple types of financial institutions (mutual funds, securities, commercial banks, big-tech platforms, and third-party WM firms) compete for market share.

From Robo-Advisors to the Digitization of Wealth Management

Despite their rapid growth, robo-advisors in the narrow sense represent only a tiny fraction of China's overall WM market, in terms of both number of products and AUM. China's WM market is still relatively immature. However, the advancement of digital technologies will bring catch-up opportunities in all aspects of WM business for China's institutions and practitioners.

DRIVING FORCES

This section summarizes the three main forces driving the rapid development of China's robo-advisory industry and the digitization of the WM market: a huge potential WM market, the online investment behavior of young people, and the WM needs of different investors.

The Huge Potential WM Market and a Shift to Equity Assets

After forty years of rapid economic growth and wealth accumulation, China has become the second-largest asset management market in the world. With personal investable assets (excluding real estate assets) reaching around RMB 150–250 trillion in 2019,[5] the WM needs of Chinese investors have expanded considerably.

According to a report released by the People's Bank of China in 2019,[6] Chinese investors hold 59 percent of their overall wealth in the form of real estate assets. In terms of liquid wealth (excluding real estate), Chinese investors allocate about 72 percent to deposits or bank WM products (WMPs) and 20 percent to equities; the remainder is split between mutual funds and bonds. The proportion of assets allocated to equity-like assets in China is significantly smaller than that in the United States and Japan.

China's real estate market may no longer be an attractive investment instrument, for two reasons. First, the Chinese real estate industry has been subject to very strict regulations for more than five years. The central government holds that "houses are for living in and not for speculative investment." Multiple policies have been implemented to suppress house prices, such as house purchase and sale restrictions, financing constraints for real estate companies, and mortgage restrictions. Second, the homeownership rate of urban households in China is 96 percent, with 58 percent owning one house and 31 percent owning two houses.[7] Therefore, demand for housing is likely to slow down in the next decade, especially given China's high price-to-rent ratio and aging population.

China's steadily declining interest rates and regulatory changes have also made bank deposits and WMPs less attractive. A longtime problem in China's investment and WM markets is the expectation of guaranteed payment for bank WMPs. Banks create WMPs based on subprime loans in partnership with nonbank institutions such as trusts, mutual funds, and securities companies. These WMPs usually have an investment threshold (RMB 10,000–50,000) and offer a fixed rate of return and a fixed term to maturity. However, most bank WMPs are not recorded on the banks' balance sheets, as they are registered as investment or wealth management products. Investors buy bank WMPs not only because they offer higher returns than deposits but also because of the strong belief that banks will guarantee principal and interest payments. At the end of 2019, bank WMPs accounted for 30.5 percent of all AUM in China, worth RMB 79.4 trillion, while mutual funds accounted for only 18.6 percent.[8]

On April 27, 2018, the document "Guiding Opinions on Regulating the Asset Management Business of Financial Institutions" was jointly issued by the People's Bank of China, the China Banking and Insurance Regulatory Commission, the China Securities Regulatory Commission, and the State Administration of Foreign Exchange. The aim was to regulate the asset management business of financial institutions, unify regulatory standards for asset management products, and effectively prevent systematic financial risks. Importantly, "Guiding Opinions" requires bank WMPs to be distinguished from bank deposits and operated strictly as investment management products. It states that the returns of newly issued WMPs must be determined by the net value of the corresponding investment portfolios and that no payment guarantee is allowed. The document set a two- to three-year transition period to allow banks to digest existing WMPs and separate their WM business from their deposit business. By the end of 2019, sixteen commercial banks had received approval to set up WM subsidiaries. The returns of the new WMPs are more volatile than before.

For these reasons, Chinese investors are expected to continue reallocating their wealth, shifting from real estate, bank deposits, and loan-based WMPs to standard and riskier investment assets, such as equities, bonds, and mutual funds.

China's Fintech Revolution and Online Investment Trend

Since Alibaba launched the digital payment tool Alipay in 2014 to facilitate its e-commerce business, China has undergone a digital finance revolution. China now leads the world in digital payment and online lending, in terms of both technology and transaction volume.

Chinese people rely heavily on Alipay and WeChat Pay to make everyday payments. These two apps together account for more than 90 percent of the mobile payment market in China. They provide not only financial services such as digital payment, consumer lending, investment, and insurance but also one-stop services such as food ordering, transportation and travel booking, and making medical appointments.

In 2013, Alipay launched Yu'ebao, an innovative product that allows Alipay's massive user base to earn returns on their account balances and makes the funds instantly available. Yu'ebao is implemented through a money market fund managed by Ant Group's licensed asset management subsidiary Tianhong Fund. Unlike traditional money market funds, a Yu'ebao balance can be used immediately for payment and redeemed in minutes. The minimum investment threshold is only RMB 1.00, which makes Yu'ebao accessible to almost all users, especially those without money market fund experience.

The average rate of return (annualized) on investment through Yu'ebao in 2014 was 4.83 percent, more than ten times that available through bank

FIGURE 7-2.   **Yu'ebao: Number of Users and AUM, 2013–2019**

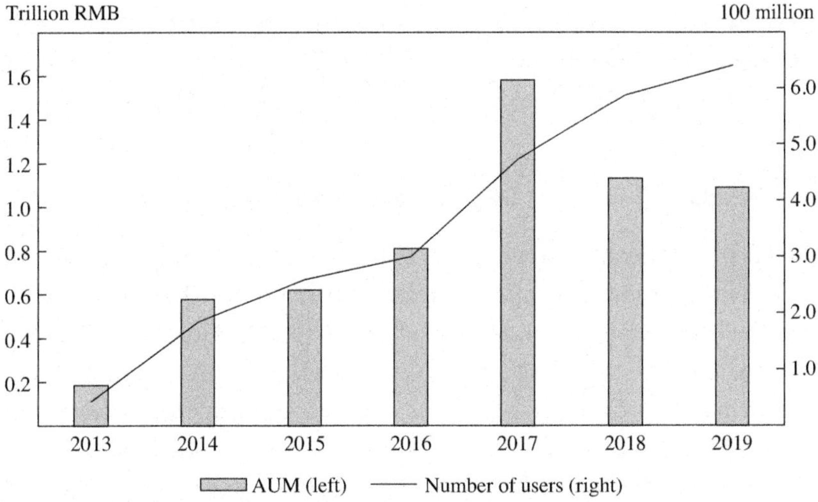

Source: Annual reports of Ant Group.

deposits. Unsurprisingly, Yu'ebao thus diverted a huge amount of money from bank deposits and forced commercial banks to raise their deposit interest rates. Within just a year of its launch, Yu'ebao had more than 100 million users and RMB 574 billion in AUM. As shown in figure 7-2, its AUM peaked at nearly RMB 1.6 trillion in 2017, and its user base exceeded 600 million in 2019.[9]

In addition to launching Yu'ebao, Alipay introduced a new function called broad investment management products, a marketplace providing easy-to-understand investment products with low investment thresholds. These products are not directly operated by Ant Group but offered by its more than 100 partners, including leading mutual fund companies, securities companies, insurance companies, banks, and other licensed financial institutions. Alipay users can choose diversified assets with different risk and return profiles from a pool of more than 6,000 investment products, including mutual funds (equity, fixed income, and balanced funds), bank deposits, fixed-term assets, and insurance.

Tencent, Jingdong, and other big-tech platforms have launched similar money market funds and investment marketplace products through their apps to compete in the new market. This has encouraged young people to start investing online. Compared with their parents, those born since the 1990s are more open to using robo-advisors and other digital WM products. Following digital payment and online lending, WM will be the next area of China's financial industry to be transformed by fintech.

WM Needs of Different Segments of Investors

China's investors can be divided into four segments according to the size of their investable assets, forming a pyramid structure. The bottom segment, with the largest population, is made up of the so-called long-tail investors; they possess investable assets worth less than US$10,000. The second segment is made up of middle-class investors, with investable assets worth between US$10,000 and US$100,000. The third segment is made up of "mass affluent" investors, with investable assets worth between US$100,000 and US$1 million. Investors in the top segment are high-net-wealth clients, with investable assets worth more than US$1 million. According to the China Banking Association, Chinese banks had more than 1 million private banking clients in 2019, with AUM of RMB 14.13 trillion.[10]

Different investors have different WM needs. For long-tail investors, who are highly risk-averse and cost-sensitive, the major concern is the security of funding. They typically allocate their assets to bank deposits or online money market funds such as Yu'ebao. In contrast, high-net-wealth investors are willing to pay large fees to enjoy the highly personalized private banking services provided by human financial advisors. It is more challenging for middle-class and mass-affluent investors to meet their WM needs. These investors are willing to accept some financial risk in exchange for a higher rate of return, such as by investing in bank WM products, mutual funds, or individual stocks. Some mass-affluent investors buy complicated financial assets such as hedge funds, private equity funds, currencies, or derivatives products. Besides asset appreciation, the WM needs of these investors are diverse; for example, they may wish to save money for their children's education, medical bills, and/or retirement. It is difficult to provide customized WM services for middle-class and mass-affluent investors in a cost-effective way.

THE ROLES OF DIGITAL AND AI TECHNOLOGIES IN WM

Standard Procedures of WM

The standard procedures of WM can be divided into five steps: client acquisition, client profiling, asset allocation, trade execution and portfolio rebalancing, and risk management (figure 7-3). The first two steps can be defined as the advisory end, with a focus on clients; the last two steps represent the asset management end, with a focus on investment products. The middle step, asset allocation (or investment strategy), is key to achieving a risk–return balance that suits the client's risk preferences and investment objectives. Commercial banks, big-tech platforms, and third-party WM firms have advantages at the advisory end, while mutual funds and securities companies are more proficient at the asset management end.

Digital and AI technologies (e.g., mobile internet, big data, artificial intelligence, and cloud computing technologies) can play important roles in all five steps. Since Markowitz introduced the mean-variance portfolio selection model in the 1950s, numerous researchers have applied quantitative models and data analysis to asset allocation, trade execution, and risk management. Computer algorithms and machine learning methods are widely used to analyze massive amounts of financial data and construct trading strategies or allocate assets. Natural language processing methods can be used with textual data, such as annual reports and social media posts, to capture market opportunities. Cloud computing supports high-frequency trading and real-time risk monitoring.

Until the recent emergence of robo-advisors, the client advisory side of WM relied heavily on human financial advisors to acquire and serve clients. Aside from fully automated robo-advisors, two main business models—robo-human advisors and wealth-tech platforms—apply digital technologies to WM advisory services.

FIGURE 7-3.   **Standard WM Procedures**

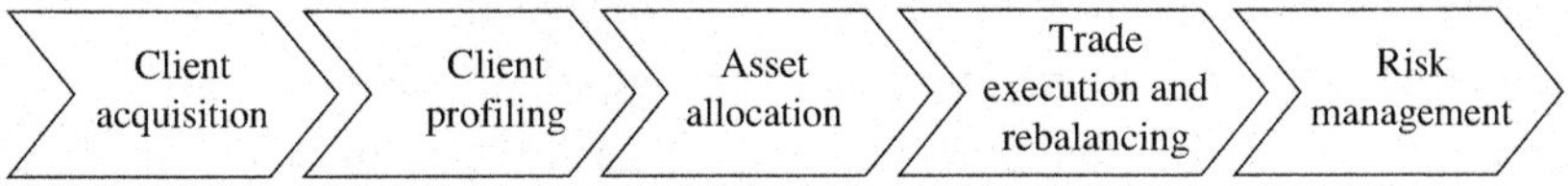

Robo-human advisors. Under this business model, now used by some traditional third-party WM institutions and securities companies in China, human advisors and robots work together to serve clients. Computer algorithms create customized portfolios, while human advisors interact with clients—for example, assessing their risk profiles, explaining investment strategies, and reminding them of portfolio adjustments. This model enhances the productivity of human advisors and reduces service costs while maintaining a "human touch" to increase client satisfaction. Computer algorithms can also be used to track and evaluate advisors' performance.

Wealth-tech platforms. Under this business model, big-tech platforms provide comprehensive WM technology solutions for traditional WM institutions, helping them access users via the platforms and meet their WM needs. A good example is the Ant Fortune app launched by Ant Group in 2017, which is an upgraded version of Yu'ebao and the WM marketplace. The AI-powered WM technology solutions provided by Ant Fortune include modules for investment product screening, assessment of investment product suitability, marketing and communication tools, and investment advisory services. Using this platform, WM institutions can increase their operational efficiency while reducing costs. By June 30, 2020, the balance of AUM enabled through Ant Fortune had reached RMB 4,099 billion.[11]

How Digital and AI Technologies Benefit WM

Digital and AI technologies have the potential to benefit WM businesses in several ways, especially on the client advisory side. This section discusses a few of these benefits.

Lowering Costs and Providing Inclusive WM Services. Technology gives long-tail investors affordable access to professional WM services. Human-based advisory services cannot be provided at scale to these investors owing to high labor costs and the limited supply of human financial advisors. In the mobile internet era, intelligent marketing technology can be used to access large volumes of users via big-tech platforms. Human–computer interaction and machine learning technologies can be used for identity authentication and client profiling. Through these digital technologies, robo-advisors and digital WM services can easily serve mass investors, as the marginal cost of adding one more client is close to zero.

Improving Customized Asset Allocation and Risk–Return Trade-offs. The key goal of WM is to recommend the most suitable investment products to the right clients. To achieve this, financial advisors first need to know clients' risk profiles and investment horizons and objectives; this principle is referred to as "know your client." Aside from the usual method of obtaining information from questionnaires, algorithms can combine relevant information from external data sources to improve client profiling and ensure matching between clients and WM products. Lufax, a leading wealth-tech company in China, has implemented such an upgraded "know your client" system, which blocks about 30 percent of unsuitable investments.

In the asset allocation step, robo-advisors and digital WM services typically use the mean-variance model or more advanced financial models to construct portfolios. Compared with human advisors, computer algorithms can cover more investable assets to achieve greater diversification and avoid human behavioral biases. Furthermore, algorithms can continuously monitor portfolio performance and make real-time adjustments when market conditions change.

Developing User-friendly WM Products to Improve Customer Satisfaction. Digital WM institutions have learned from internet companies to focus on the user experience and create user-friendly products. Investors can enjoy one-stop WM services through the integration of multiple functions in mobile apps. AI technology can also be used to create personalized content communities and provide interactive investor education.

Remote interaction technologies can remove the restrictions of space and distance from WM services. Such technologies became especially valuable in early 2020, when lockdown restrictions during the COVID-19 pandemic made face-to-face interactions impossible. One example of a company that benefited from these technologies during the crisis is CreditEase Wealth, the WM subsidiary of China's leading fintech company, CreditEase. Most of its employees and clients were isolated at home; in response, CreditEase Wealth accelerated its digitization strategy. Remote technologies were used to assist its financial advisors, and the company implemented remote WM services such as account opening, online qualified investor certification, and investor education. In February 2020, the AUM and the number of new clients of CreditEase Wealth showed month-on-month growth of 8 and 23 percent, respectively, despite the adverse situation.

HOW ROBO-ADVISORS CHANGE INVESTOR BEHAVIORS

Reducing the Behavioral Bias of Individual Investors

Behavioral finance research suggests that individual investors often exhibit behavioral biases in their financial investment and WM decisions. Rather than being rational beings who attempt to optimize outcomes, investors often make decisions based on emotions and cognitive biases, which are subject to cognitive limitations of information processing. This section lists some of the most common behavioral biases of individual investors and discusses how they influence investment performance.

Overconfidence and excessive trading. "Overconfidence" refers to an investor's propensity to overestimate one's knowledge, ability, and accuracy of judgment. It explains why investors tend to engage in excessive trading and favor active investment strategies. Investors in developing countries are particularly prone to overconfidence and excessive trading. In 2017, the average turnover rates of China's stocks and equity mutual funds were 428 and 297 percent, respectively—much higher than the corresponding US figures of 116 and 26 percent.[12]

Insufficient diversification. Diversification that covers a wide range of asset classes can deliver lower portfolio risks while maintaining the same expected returns. In practice, individual investors usually hold underdiversified portfolios. For example, a typical Chinese investor holds only a few familiar stocks, which they buy and sell repeatedly.

Herding effect. The herding effect is a phenomenon in which investors ignore their own information and instead follow the decisions of other investors. It explains why investors often collectively buy overpriced stocks in bull markets and sell them off in bear markets, which causes asset bubbles or market crashes. Empirical studies suggest that in China's stock market, both individual investors and mutual fund managers exhibit herding behaviors.

Focusing on returns and neglecting risk. The mean-variance portfolio selection model suggests that investors should aim to balance risk and returns when constructing portfolios. In practice, investors tend to focus on returns and neglect risk, which results in the overweighting of high-risk assets.

These behavioral biases result in deviations from portfolio optimization and harm investment performance. By delegating investment decisions to algorithms and reducing human participation, robo-advisors can potentially reduce investors' irrational behaviors and improve investment performance. Using data from India, D'Acunto, Prabhala, and Rossi found that robo-advisors can help underdiversified investors increase the number of stocks in their portfolios.[13] Such improved diversification decreases their portfolio volatility and improves their market-adjusted performance. Robo-advisor adoption also substantially reduces investors' behavioral biases, including the disposition effect, trend chasing, and the rank effect. Rossi and Utkus found that a major US robo-advisory product eliminates investors' home bias by increasing international equity and fixed income diversification.[14]

A Robo-advisory Product Case Study

Using a real case from China, Shaowei Shen and I show that robo-advisory products can substantially reduce investors' turnover rates.[15] This effect is more pronounced for male (vs. female), less experienced, and younger investors, as well as those living outside Beijing, Shanghai, and Guangdong.

We use data on a robo-advisory product jointly issued by a large commercial bank and a well-known mutual fund in late 2018. The minimum investment threshold is RMB 10,000. The data cover 7,427 randomly chosen clients of the robo-advisor. Of the sampled investors, 64.84 percent are female; and 52.19 percent live in the metropolitan areas of Beijing, Shanghai, and Guangdong. The variables include personal information such as gender, age, education, and city. We also have the trading records of these investors from 2010 to 2019, including their traded investment assets within commercial banks and mutual funds. Thus, we can compare the average turnover rates of these investors before and after they began using the robo-advisory product.

Figure 7-4 compares the turnover rates of male and female investors before and after they began using the robo-advisor product. The turnover rate of male investors dropped by 28.90 percent, which is much greater than the 15.96 percent reduction for female investors. Research shows that male investors tend to be more overconfident and that they trade more frequently than female investors. Our findings suggest that the use of robo-advisors may further increase this behavioral bias among male investors.

Figure 7-5 presents changes in the turnover rates of investors in different age groups. Robo-advisors had the strongest negative effect on turnover for the group of investors under thirty years old (63.8%), followed monotonically

FIGURE 7-4.   **Changes in Investors' Turnover Rates by Gender**

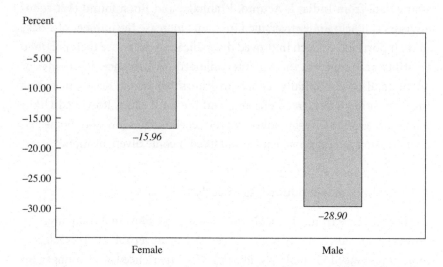

Data source: Data from a major commercial bank in China.

FIGURE 7-5.   **Changes in Investors' Turnover Rates by Age**

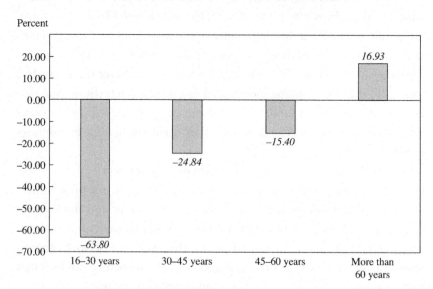

Data source: Data from a major commercial bank in China.

FIGURE 7-6.   **Changes in Investors' Turnover Rates by Investment Experience**

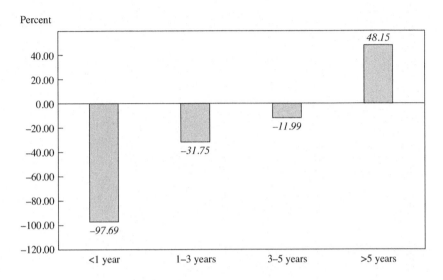

Data source: Data from a major commercial bank in China.

by those aged thirty to forty-five and forty-five to sixty. Interestingly, robo-advisors increased the turnover rate of investors over sixty years old by 16.93 percent. Older people may benefit more from the increased trading convenience offered by robo-advisors.

Figure 7-6 shows that the negative impact of robo-advisor use on turn-over rate was inversely related to investors' trading experience, as measured by the duration of trading with the bank or mutual fund. For investors with less than one year's investment experience, the robo-advisory product low-ered their turnover rate by 97.69 percent. For investors with more than five years of experience, the robo-advisor actually increased their turnover rate. This suggests that experienced investors use robo-advisors to find market opportunities and therefore make more transactions.

Figure 7-7 illustrates the changes in turnover rates of investors living in different areas. We found that the negative impact of the robo-advisory prod-uct on turnover rates was negligible for investors living in Beijing, Shang-hai, and Guangdong but substantial for investors living in other areas. The divergence might be explained by the financial knowledge of investors from different regions.

FIGURE 7-7.   Changes in Investors' Turnover Rates by Location

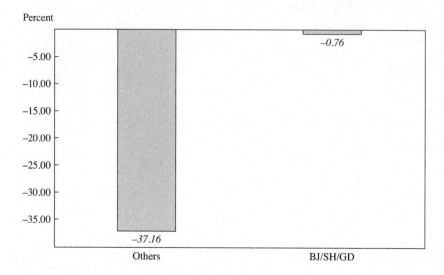

Data source: Data from a major commercial bank in China.

TRENDS IN CHINA'S DIGITAL WEALTH MANAGEMENT MARKET

Strategies of Competition and Cooperation Adopted by Different Market Players

Given their respective strengths and weaknesses, traditional wealth managers, big-tech platforms, and independent fintech firms in China seek a healthy balance between competition and cooperation in the digital WM market.

Traditional Wealth Managers: Cooperating to Speed Up Transformation. Traditional wealth managers (mutual funds, securities, commercial banks) are further opening up and cooperating with fintech companies and internet giants to accelerate the implementation of smart applications. Commercial banks have a large customer base and can accurately capture customer characteristics and understand customer needs based on accumulated historical data. Through professional investment research and rich portfolio management strategies, fund companies and securities companies can provide high-quality fiduciary WM services for investors. However, institutional constraints hamper innovation and transformation, preventing major traditional institutions from sustaining competitive advantages in the WM market. Therefore, such institutions are forming alliances with fintech and internet giants to upgrade all aspects of WM to offer more efficient and personalized WM services to a broader customer base using cloud computing, big-data analytics, and blockchain technologies.

Fintech Companies: Providing Smart Solutions and Partnering with Traditional Wealth Managers. Fintech companies use advanced technologies such as big data, AI, and machine learning to provide financial institutions with smart WM-tech solutions, which range from risk control to smart interaction services. However, because they lack a large user base and relevant financial licenses, many fintech companies strategically cooperate with traditional wealth managers to provide customers with personalized WM planning. In this way, they offer smart solutions that cover the entire value chain.

Big-tech Platforms: Establishing a New Financial Ecosystem. Big-tech platforms such as Ant Group, Tencent Financial Technology, and Lufax have the technological expertise, large user base, and financial licenses needed to lead the industry forward. In addition to cooperating with traditional wealth managers as product or service providers, they aim to become open platforms working with users to establish the foundation for a new financial ecosystem and provide technical expertise to the players within it.

Ongoing Refinement of the Regulatory Framework for the Digital WM Industry

Since 2016, China's financial administrative authorities have issued a series of important regulations for the fintech sector and asset management businesses. The most important is "Guiding Opinions" (issued in 2018), which sets out a comprehensive regulatory framework for asset management businesses. At the time of writing, detailed regulations for specific types of digital WM businesses are due to be issued. This ongoing refinement of the regulatory framework for China's digital WM industry will ensure its healthy development through the implementation of further licensing requirements, look-through regulations, and a regulatory sandbox mechanism.

License Regulation. The license requirements set out in "Guiding Opinions" are designed to foster the healthy development of digital WM. Without these requirements, digital technologies would do little to enhance the end-to-end smart capability of asset management. They could even cause market chaos, amplify financial risks, harm investors, and hinder the healthy development of the WM industry. "Guiding Opinions" sets out stringent license requirements concerning the sale of asset management products via the internet. It eradicated unlicensed financial platforms and helped create a sound environment for the healthy development of digital WM.

Look-Through Regulation. The use of digital technologies has facilitated the development of a look-through regulation for WM. The digital transformation of WM helps wealth managers expand their customer bases, optimize their business processes, and improve their service efficiency. "Guiding Opinions" introduced a look-through regulation for asset management products, allowing regulators to examine the products' funding sources, structure, and underlying assets. This has facilitated the real-time supervision of businesses and helped wealth managers accurately identify financial risk and protect investors' interests.

Regulatory Sandbox to Balance Risk and Innovation. The regulatory sandbox mechanism creates a healthy balance between risk and innovation. A regulatory sandbox is a framework that allows fintech companies to test innovative projects under regulators' supervision. This both stimulates innovation and improves efficiency with controllable risks. Introducing the regulatory sandbox mechanism to innovative WM projects aids in identifying potential risks and reducing regulatory costs before a marketing push. To date, the regulatory sandbox mechanism has been piloted in nine Chinese cities/areas: Beijing, Shanghai, Chongqing, Shenzhen, Xiongan New Area, Hangzhou, Suzhou, Chengdu, and Guangzhou. The full implementation of this mechanism would stimulate innovation and increase vitality in China's WM market.

CHALLENGES AHEAD

Despite its rapid growth and bright prospects, China's digital WM market faces several major challenges, which should be addressed through the joint efforts of the industry, academics, and regulators.

Privacy Protection and Data Security

Compared with traditional WM services, robo-advisors and other digital WM products typically collect much more information from investors, such as data on their risk preferences, investment horizons, and objectives. Customized digital WM services may even require the collection, storage, and analysis of more private information, such as age, education background, family assets, and health conditions. When WM products are jointly offered, such private information may be shared between the cooperating institutions. Therefore, it is necessary to establish comprehensive rules for data security and privacy protection in China's WM industry.

Technical Risks

For investors, the operation of robo-advisors and other digital WM services resembles a black box, as major investment decisions are made by computer algorithms and other digital technologies. This results in unpredictable and unexplainable risks. When such risks arise, it is difficult to determine who should be held accountable under the existing technical framework. AI, cloud computing, big data, and blockchain technologies have enabled WM institutions to serve a large base of investors. However, it is crucial to ensure stable performance and improve system compliance under these conditions. In addition, if markets are dominated by a large number of robo-advisors that follow predefined strategies and react in the same ways to trading signals, a financial shock to the market might be amplified into a market crash or systematic risk.

Inadequate Investor Education

The importance of investor education has been widely recognized by both academics and practitioners. To ensure the success of WM, investors must have sufficient financial knowledge, especially when using robo-advisory products. Familiarity with concepts such as return-risk trade-off, diversification, and long-term investment help investors understand how WM products work and deal rationally with market fluctuations. However, investor education in China has long been inadequate. Most Chinese investors have insufficient financial knowledge owing to a historical emphasis on implicit guarantees and a culture of speculation in the stock market. Younger generations of investors, who have not directly experienced stock market crashes, tend to focus on return and neglect risk. Behavioral biases such as excessive trading, herding, and the disposition effect largely offset the benefits of WM services.

Digital asset management offers several opportunities to improve China's investor education. First, user-friendly digital interfaces facilitate interactions with investors. Second, algorithms can efficiently analyze investors' trading history and remind them to avoid behavioral bias. Third, investor education modules can be incorporated into digital WM product design to allow investors to gain financial knowledge through real investment practice.

Shortage of Technical Talent

WM is a data- and talent-driven business. A shortage of technical talent may create a bottleneck in the digital transformation of China's WM market. China's WM institutions currently employ a very small proportion of the world's technical talents, compared with US giants such as Vanguard and Charles Schwab. Goldman Sachs, a leading investment bank with assets under supervision of US$2.1 trillion, even regards itself as a tech company, considering its proportion of technical employees and R&D expenditure.

The WM industry must compete with many other industries for high-end talent with AI and big-data skills. To capitalize on digitization opportunities in the fintech era, it will be critical for China to nurture individuals with technical talent who can apply cutting-edge digital technologies to WM. Chinese universities should offer more interdisciplinary programs and tech nical and quantitative courses in WM and related subjects.

NOTES
The author gratefully acknowledges the research assistance of Pingping Wang, Yue Zhao, and Shaowei Shen.

1. Lufax, "Lufax and iResearch Release White Paper on Levels of Intelligence in Wealth Management," July 10, 2019, https://www.prnewswire.com/news-releases/lufax -and-iresearch-release-white-paper-on-levels-of-intelligence-in-wealth-management -300882301.html.

2. "Guiding Opinions on Regulating the Asset Management Business of Financial Institutions," People's Bank of China, April 27, 2018, http://www.pbc.gov.cn/goutongjiaoliu/113456/113469/3529606/index.html.

3. China Merchants Bank, *China Merchants Bank 2016 Annual Report (China A-Shares)*, March 24, 2017, https://pdf.dfcfw.com/pdf/H2_AN201703240435007007_1.pdf?1547214260000.pdf.

4. Huimin Li, "Assets under Management (AUM) of HelpYouInvest Reached RMB 2.2 Billion," *China Securities Journal*, July 20, 2020, http://stock.10jqka.com.cn/20200720/c622043182.shtml.

5. Estimated by the author based on reports by BCG, Lufax, Creditease, and the People's Bank of China.

6. Research Group on Assets and Liabilities of Chinese Urban Households, "2019 Survey on Assets and Liabilities of Chinese Urban Households." Research Group on Assets and Liabilities of Chinese Urban Households, https://baijiahao.baidu.com/s?id=1664830535681198027&wfr=spider&for=pc.

7. Ibid.

8. Financial Stability Analysis Group of the People's Bank of China, *China Financial Stability Report, 2020*. Beijing: China Financial Publishing House, http://www.gov.cn/xinwen/2020-11/07/5558567/files/d7ba5445e5204c83b37e3f5e07140638.pdf.

9. Tianhong Asset Management Company, *Tianhong Yu'ebao Money Market Fund 2020 Annual Report*, December 31, 2019, http://eid.csrc.gov.cn/fund/disclose/instance_show_pdf_id.do?instanceid=179593.

10. "China Private Banks Report (2020) and White Paper on Risk Management of Wealth Management Industry," China Banking Association and Tsinghua University PBC School of Finance, https://www.sohu.com/a/448457604_121015326.

11. Ant Group, *Initial Public Offering Report*, August 24, 2020, http://www.sse.com.cn/disclosure/listedinfo/bulletin/star/c/688688_20201027_2.pdf.

12. Sohu, "Yugen Xun: The Current Transformation Path of China's Capital Market from the Perspective of the United States in 1980," May 30, 2018, https://www.sohu.com/a/233400664_313170.

13. F. D'Acunto, N. Prabhala, and A. G. Rossi, "The Promises and Pitfalls of Robo-advising." *Review of Financial Studies* 32, no. 5 (2019): 1983–2020.

14. A. G. Rossi and S. P. Utkus, "Who Benefits from Robo-Advising? Evidence from Machine Learning." SSRN Working Paper, https://ssrn.com/abstract=3552671 or http://dx.doi.org/10.2139/ssrn.3552671.

15. This case is drawn from a joint research project with Shaowei Shen titled "The Impact of Robo-advisors on Trading Behaviors of Chinese Investors" (forthcoming).

8

The Digitization of Commercial Banks

XUANLI XIE

In its analysis of the digitization of commercial banks, this chapter addresses the following questions: What is the current status of the Chinese commercial banking industry, and how has it been impacted by the development of digital technology? How have commercial banks been transformed by and adapted to the digital challenge? What are the key obstacles in the digitization process? What are the future directions and related policy implications of digitization?

The modern Chinese commercial banking industry started from the economic reform of China. As a result of continual reform efforts, the major state-owned banks have been restructured and publicly listed, and the barriers to entry for private and foreign banks have been reduced. While some Chinese commercial banks now occupy the top ranks globally in terms of size, their competitiveness is lagging. Chinese commercial banks are used to doing business in a monopolized market with a regulated interest rate. Their business model relies heavily on the interest margin and large corporate clients. Although the reform has brought increased competition, the overall rules of the game have not changed.

The recent development of digital technology and the mobile internet enabled the creation of financial technology, allowing big-tech platforms and numerous new technology entrants to enter the banking business, mainly through payments and lending. Because of the convenience and competitive pricing provided by financial technology, the business of commercial banking has been threatened and the competitive landscape of commercial banks has changed dramatically.

Facing this critical challenge, commercial banks have responded in several ways, one of which was to divest assets that no longer generate value. For example, the number of bank branch closures increased tenfold from 2015 to 2019. Cutting the head count was also significant for reducing cost. At the same time, many banks started building online channels such as internet banking and mobile banking.

While channel innovation was one of the early strategic responses, more and more banks gradually realized that the challenge was not only about the channel but also about the digitizing of the entire business. To achieve this goal, new capabilities must be built, including investing in R&D, hiring staff with technology backgrounds, and establishing alliances with technology firms. To support the reconfiguration of organizational capability, banks' internal organizational structures have also been altered.

In short, facing the disruption of financial technology, commercial banks are adapting and transforming. We quantify their digital transformation by developing an index, which shows significant overall progress in digitization.[1]

The chapter is structured as follows:

1. Introduction to the commercial banking industry in China

2. Emergence of financial technology and its impact on commercial banks

3. Digitization of commercial banks

4. Digitization strategies of commercial banks

5. Obstacles and challenges in the digitization of commercial banks

6. The future of commercial banking and implications for policies

INTRODUCTION TO THE COMMERCIAL BANKING INDUSTRY IN CHINA

The modern commercial banking industry of the People's Republic of China started with the separation of commercial banking from the Central Bank of China, the People's Bank of China, in 1979, along with the country's economic reform. The first restored bank was the Agricultural Bank of China, and the next was the Bank of China. By 1987, three other major state-owned banks, China Construction Bank, Industrial and Commercial Bank of China (ICBC), and Bank of Communications, were established or restored. These five large state-owned banks form the foundation of China's commercial banking industry.

The past three decades witnessed the continual reform and transformation of China's banking industry. After a series of restructures, the five major state-owned banks were publicly listed. Twelve nationwide joint-stock banks were established. Urban credit cooperatives were restructured into city commercial banks, which can better serve regional financial needs. And since 2014, nineteen licenses have been issued for private banks, allowing private firms to enter the industry. These banks are part of the policy design to use the internet and financial technology to meet the needs of the underserved microfinance market. They are allowed to operate nationwide but only through the internet. In 2019, the restriction on foreign ownership of Chinese banks was removed to reduce the entry barrier for foreign banks. By the end of 2020, there were 6 major state-owned banks (the most recent addition was the Postal Savings Bank of China), 12 nationwide joint-stock banks, 134 city commercial banks, 19 private banks, 1,485 rural commercial banks, and 41 foreign banks, with total assets of RMB 23.9 trillion.[2] Commercial banking has been one of the most important components of China's financial system.

Although the reform has brought increased market competition and fast development of Chinese banks, the old rules of the game still dominate. This leads to several issues. First, while Chinese banks have grown in size and scale, they are not yet strong in financial service capabilities. The banks rely heavily on revenues from the interest margin. For example, the interest margin makes up more than 70 percent of the revenue of the major state-owned banks. This ratio is much higher than that of banks in Western countries, such as JPMorgan Chase, which has less than 50 percent income from interest.

Second, in China, the banking sector still faces the challenge of inclusion. According to a report by the World Bank, in China, there are only 19 bank accounts per 1,000 adult population, compared with the world average of 52 and the US average of 91.[3] This difference indicates that the banking sector in China is undersupplied. Because banks are accustomed to serving large corporate clients, the small and medium-size enterprises have been underserved.

Moreover, as the industry remains tightly regulated, banks can take advantage of their position. Thus, they have limited motivation to build core competences or develop a customer-oriented culture. As the reform progresses and interest rates gradually become marketized, the average industry return has been declining with a rising nonperforming loan (NPL) ratio. Figure 8-1 shows that from the first quarter of 2011 to the third quarter of

FIGURE 8-1.   **Declining Bank Returns with Rising NPL Ratio, 2011–2019**

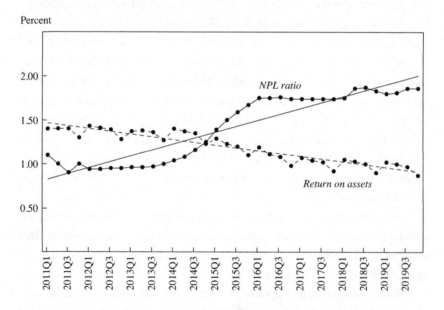

Percent

Source: "Quarterly Banking Regulatory Statistical Indicators (2019)," China Banking and Insurance Regulatory Commission, February 17, 2020, http://www.cbirc.gov.cn/cn/view /pages/ItemDetail.html?docId=890466&itemId=954&generaltype=0.

2019, the average bank return on assets decreased from about 1.5 percent to less than 0.9 percent.[4] At the same time, the NPL ratio almost doubled, from 1 percent to nearly 2 percent.

The Chinese commercial banking industry seems to be in great need of further reform and transformation. Would the emerging financial technology be the savior?

EMERGENCE OF FINANCIAL TECHNOLOGY AND ITS IMPACT ON COMMERCIAL BANKS

Over the past decade, China has experienced tremendous growth in financial technology, mainly because of the dominance of internet giants and the underserved domestic financial market.

Digital payments led the first wave of disruption. Alibaba, one of the internet giants, introduced Alipay in 2003 as a key component to fulfill its e-commerce business model. Tencent followed suit with its own payment product in 2005. The real competition was during the early 2010s when the prevalence of smartphones made mobile payments a reality. The two big-tech platforms saw mobile payments as a key portal and provided huge subsidies to gain users. By the end of 2019, the two companies occupied more than 90 percent of the third-party payments market. In 2019, a total of 630 million people, or more than 85 percent of Chinese internet users, used online payments. However, only about 10 percent of these transactions were made through banks.[5] The payment function of banks has been significantly challenged.

Similar scenes can be found in savings and lending. In 2013, Ant Finance introduced its epoch product, Yu'ebao, which is a money management fund product. Because of its higher interest rates and greater flexibility for withdrawals, it poses a direct challenge to bank savings. By June 2020, it had 670 million users and managed more than RMB 1 trillion in assets,[6] becoming the largest public fund in China. It is estimated that by 2020, the scale of online wealth management reached RMB 15.5 billion, about 10 percent of total savings in commercial banks.[7]

Credit can also be obtained online. The financial branch of Alibaba, Ant Finance, started providing *hua bei* and *jie bei*, which are consumer credit and microcredit, respectively, through its Alipay app. Tencent's development of *weili dai* (microcredit) through its most popular app, WeChat, was immensely successful. These online products can issue credit within seconds of application. The credit evaluation is based on big data gathered online, which is a disruptive model compared with banks' traditional risk control approach.

Because of the competitive pricing and convenience it provides, the new financial technology soon gained ground, especially among young and less wealthy individuals, who had not received adequate service from banks in the past. The new generation of customers who grew up in the internet age wanted to do everything online. Traditional brick-and-mortar bank branches were visited less frequently. In 2018, for the first time, the banking industry witnessed a negative increase in bank branches, with 1,005 net closures. This number increased to 1,465 in 2019 (figure 8-2).[8] Along with branch closures, bank staff has been reduced. The major state-owned banks reduced employment by almost 83,000 over the past four years.

From this evidence, it is obvious that the competitive landscape of commercial banks has been dramatically changed. On the demand side, members of Generation Z (those born between 1995 and 2009, during the internet age) are digital natives and tech-innate. Traditional commercial banks are not fully prepared to serve these potential customers. On the competi-

FIGURE 8-2. **Bank Branch Establishment and Closure, 2015–2019.**

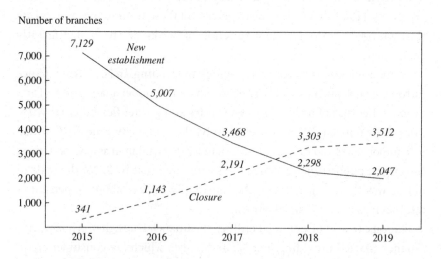

Source: "Financial License Information," China Banking and Insurance Regulatory Commission, http://xkz.cbirc.gov.cn/jr/.

tion side, financial technology is blurring the boundaries of the banking industry and threatening the positional advantages of commercial banks. How should commercial banks respond to such a challenge?

DIGITIZATION OF COMMERCIAL BANKS

The competitive pressure from financial technology forced commercial banks to change and adapt. Some saw the intrusion of financial technology as a threat, and others sensed an opportunity. To capture such variations in bank responses, we quantify bank digitization by developing an index of digital transformation. The index consists of three dimensions (subindexes). The first dimension is managerial cognition of financial technology, which is captured using content analysis of bank annual reports. A series of keywords, including *internet, digitization, financial technology, intelligence, big data, e-bank, cloud computing, blockchain, inclusive finance,* and *open banking,* are used to count the frequency of these keywords in bank annual reports. The higher the frequency of these keywords, the greater the awareness of financial technology among bank management.

Second, the index captures organizational change. This dimension includes the establishment of a department to oversee digitization, the proportion of top management and members of the board of directors with technology backgrounds, and the formation of external alliances and collaborations with technology firms.

The third dimension of the index measures bank digital innovation. This dimension covers digital channels, digital products, and fintech patents. The digital channel includes online banking, mobile banking apps, and WeChat banking. Digital products include lending products and savings products that are provided online and do not need offline human intervention. Fintech patents form the foundation of the new products.

Finally, these three subindexes are normalized to form a composite index. Table 8-1 lays out the structure of the index.

We collected data on Chinese commercial banks for 2010–2018.[9] The sample includes the full population of the major state-owned banks, joint-stock banks, city commercial banks, and private banks. Fifty-one rural commercial banks and twenty-four foreign banks are also included in the sample. After deleting missing data, we had a sample of 228 banks, which are representative of the commercial banking industry in China, as they account

TABLE 8-1. **Bank Digital Transformation Index**

First-level indicator	Weight	Second-level indicator	Measurement	Weight
			Percent	
Cognition digitization index	6.60	Frequency of keywords on digital finance	The number of keywords in every 10,000 words in the text of the annual report	100
Organization digitization index	47.40	Organizational structure	Department of Digital Finance	14.94
		Management background	Proportion of directors with IT backgrounds on the board of directors	26.56
			Proportion of executives with IT backgrounds in the top management team	24.89
		External collaborations	Digital finance–related investment, alliances, and mergers and acquisitions	33.61
Product digitization index	46.00	Digital channel	Development of mobile banking and WeChat banking	10.90
		Digital product	Development of internet financing products, internet credit, and e-commerce products	23.23
		Digital patents	Number of digital finance–related patents in recent three years	38.94
			Proportion of invention patents in digital finance–related patents	26.93

for more than 97 percent of the total assets of the industry. Based on these data, the final index is calculated and shown in figure 8-3.

Figure 8-3 shows that there has been a significant increase in the digitization of commercial banks. The index rose from 7.6 in 2010 to 39.4 in 2018, a more than fivefold increase. The figure also reveals that while the increase in digitization was consistent over the decade, the rate of increase varied.

FIGURE 8-3.   **Bank Digital Transformation Index, 2010–2018**

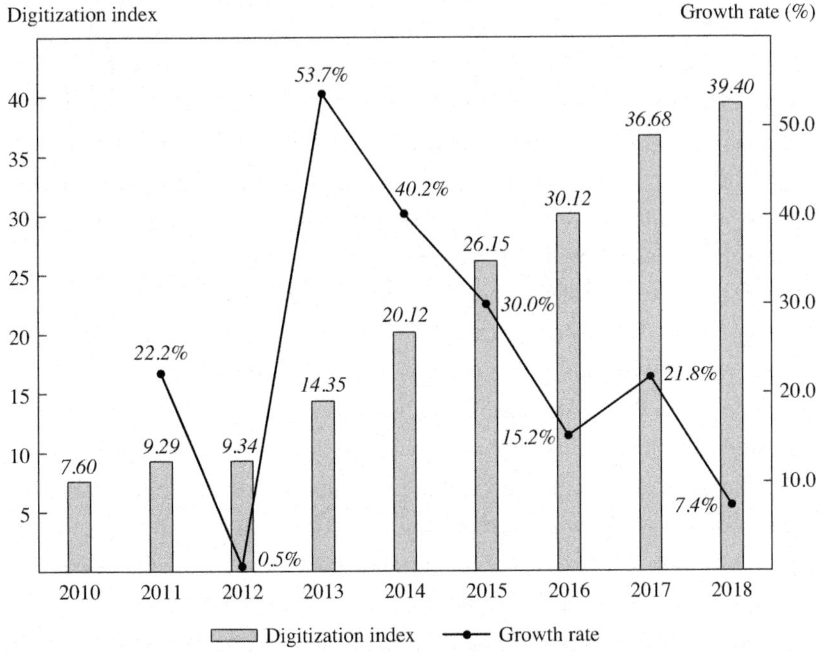

Source: Compiled by the author.

Time Differences in Digitization

In the early years, few banks engaged in digitization. The first peak in the growth rate of digitization, at 53.7 percent, appeared in 2013. This was the year when Alibaba introduced Yu'ebao, which was an instant hit in the market. During this time, the development of smartphones and mobile internet provided the foundation for online and mobile banking. The success of Yu'ebao stirred the waves in the commercial banking industry. Some banks with foresight followed the changes quickly. For example, ICBC (also known as Cosmos Bank), the largest bank in China, initiated its e-ICBC strategy in 2014. The core of this strategy was to develop three online platforms: Rong E Gou, Rong E Lian, and Rong E Hang. Rong e Gou (Easy Shopping) is an e-commerce platform. Many people may question the strategy of diversifying into the e-commerce business. But the goal of ICBC was not to replicate the success of Alibaba but to collect data on individual and business consumption, which banks lack. Rong E Lian (Easy Connect) is a social network platform for users to communicate and engage in social networking—some call it the WeChat of ICBC. Rong E Hang (Easy Banking) is the direct banking branch of ICBC, the first direct bank among the state-owned banks. These three platforms together combine information flow, money flow, and merchandise flow, providing well-rounded data that are critical for further analysis to capture user behavior and develop innovative financial products.

In 2014, "internet banking" was even mentioned in the state government report. The popularity of internet banking achieved a new peak as thousands of firms entered the peer-to-peer (P2P) lending market, which had a yearly growth rate of over 200 percent. However, problems were fermenting. In 2016, one of the P2P platforms, E Zu Bao, was overdue and convicted for financial fraud. Soon other P2P platforms were found to have similar problems. The government quickly tightened its supervision of the industry, and a series of new regulations were announced. Coincident with these events, the growth rate of the digitization of banks cooled down, from the peak of 53.7 percent in 2013 to 40.2 percent in 2014 and 15.2 percent in 2016.

However, technology development continues to progress. Artificial intelligence (AI), blockchain, cloud computing, and big data have matured and provide new opportunities for innovations in the financial industry. In 2017, the Central Bank of China established a committee on financial technology to focus on the importance of technology adoption in the financial sector. This strong, positive signal reversed the declining trend of growth in digitization and formed a second peak of growth at 21.8 percent.

This dynamic change in digitization can also be found in the keywords mentioned in banks' annual reports. Using the word cloud generator in Python, the most frequently mentioned keywords in bank annual reports are shown in figure 8-4. The figure shows that the emphasis on bank digitization strategies changed over time. In the early period before 2013, e-banking was the dominant concept. At that time, most of the bank digitization entailed using information systems for banking services. After 2013, *internet* became the most popular keyword, suggesting that the target changed to providing banking services over the internet. From 2016 to 2018, new keywords, such as *artificial intelligence, big data*, and *digitalization* become more dominant, suggesting that bank digitization has grown from focusing on the internet to focusing on financial technology.

FIGURE 8-4.   **Word Cloud of Bank Annual Reports, 2010–2018**

2010–2012

2013–2015

2016–2018

Overall, it seems that the digitization of banks is closely intertwined with the development of financial technology and driven by the maturity and legitimacy of the technology. Recently, the legitimacy pressures that motivate banks to make the digital transformation have been especially relevant. In 2020 the government started to officially encourage digitization, and the Central Bank of China emphasized that financial institutions should speed up the process of digitization. In 2021, the "14th Five-Year Plan for National Economic and Social Development" listed digitalization as one of the long-term goals for China. Under such a backdrop, every bank must consider digitalization as one of its most important strategies.

Regional Differences in Digitalization

Just as China's economic development is not evenly distributed, the digital transformation of banks also exhibits regional imbalance (figure 8-5). The eastern region has taken the lead in bank digitization, and the western and

FIGURE 8-5.   **Regional Variation in Banking Digitization, 2010–2018**

Percent of banks

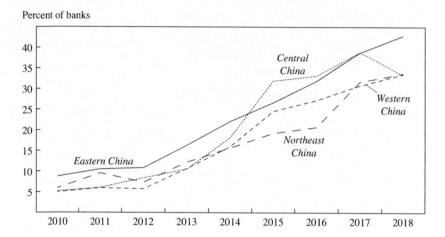

Source: Compiled by the author.

northern regions have fallen behind. The gap has even widened slightly in recent years. The central region shows significant growth and caught up with the eastern region during 2015–2017.

The regional variation in banking digitization mirrors regional economic development as well as the development of digital finance. According to Peking University's Digital Financial Inclusion Index, the development of digital finance is also most advanced in the eastern region and has gradually spread to inner China. This suggests that the degree of bank digitization could be related to the level of fintech development in the region. Two mechanisms might help explain this relationship. The first is the demand view. A higher level of fintech development indicates that more users have experience with financial technology. Banks are drawn by such demands to change to digital finance. The second mechanism is based on the competition view. The more advanced development of financial technology also suggests that there is greater availability of financial technology products offered by technology firms. This competition poses a direct threat to traditional banks. Thus, this substitution effect may also push banks to make changes. These two views could explain why banks' digitization varies across regions.

Differences in Digitization by Type of Bank

Despite the overall strong trend in digital transformation, there has been significant variance across banks in terms of the degree, strategy, and process of digitization. Figure 8-6 shows the variation of the digitization index across different types of banks. The data suggest that state-owned banks led the digital transformation in all time periods, while small, regional banks, such as city and rural commercial banks, are lagging. Joint-stock banks lie somewhere in the middle. The advantage of scale in digital transformation is obvious.

The above discussion of the differences in bank digitization by time, region, and bank type paints an overall picture of the digitization of commercial banks. The next section discusses in more detail the specific digitization strategies behind this picture.

DIGITIZATION STRATEGIES OF COMMERCIAL BANKS

This section provides details on bank digitization. It introduces bank adaptation and transformation strategies from the cognition, organization, and

FIGURE 8-6.   **Bank Digital Transformation Index, by Bank Category, 2010–2018**

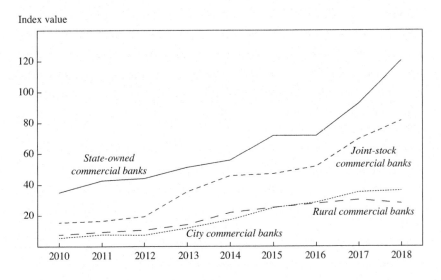

Source: Compiled by the author.

product aspects. Specific cases of bank digital innovations in wealth management and lending are provided, along with the impact of digitization on bank performance.

Managerial Cognition and Digital Banking

Managers exert important influences on firms. Because of the bounded rationality in decision making, managers rely heavily on their cognitive map to filter and process information. Managerial cognition thus plays a central role in organizational change.

New technologies, especially disruptive technologies, may have distinct differences compared with the existing technologies of incumbent firms. These technologies may not be mature at the beginning, and they may cater to different groups of customers or be based on new business models that diverge from incumbents' current customer and supplier networks. As the incumbents in the financial industry, banks may not correctly identify the value of new technology; thus, they may not respond to the change in the environment in a timely fashion. Cognitive inertia has been found to be one of the most important reasons incumbent firms fail in facing disruptive technologies.

While managerial cognition is an important determinant of firm strategy, the key challenge is to correctly identify and measure managerial cognition. With the development of big data and machine learning technology, content analysis of textual documents produced by managers has been used as a new methodology to capture managerial cognition. Research has used the frequency of new technology mentioned in text to measure managerial attention to the new technology, which is an important part of managerial cognition and a cause for organizational change. Following this method, the results are presented in figure 8-7.

Figure 8-7 suggests that state-owned banks showed the earliest awareness of digital finance. Compared with state-owned banks, joint-stock banks were slow to react in the beginning (almost no attention in 2012 and earlier), but they caught up quickly and kept pace with state-owned banks after 2016. The managerial attention paid to digital finance among city commercial banks and rural commercial banks was significantly lower than that of state-owned and joint-stock banks. This late and limited managerial attention could hinder their digital transformation.

FIGURE 8-7.   **Managerial Cognition of Digital Finance, 2010–2018**

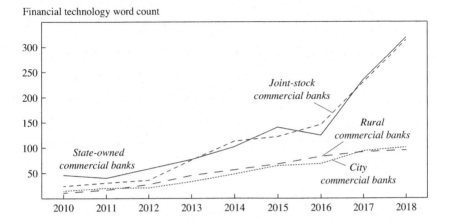

Financial technology word count

Source: Compiled by the author.

Organizational Changes for Digitization

Organizational adaptations are important to support the digitization strategy. Just as they led on managerial cognition, larger banks seem to be the leaders on organizational changes as well (figure 8-8). However, their advantage is less obvious in later stages. By contrast, joint-stock banks became the most active in making organizational changes. State-owned banks can be characterized as a "big ship that is difficult to turn around." And this might explain their difficulty in making organizational changes.

Organizational change has three aspects. First, a new department or committee might be helpful in coordinating the digitization strategy. On the one hand, the new department can facilitate interdepartmental collaboration; on the other hand, it can create symbolic meaning in the organization. The innovative capabilities of traditional commercial banks are often constrained by the historical burden of an old organizational structure and departmental interests. Therefore, changes in the organizational structure will help traditional commercial banks implement the digital transformation more smoothly and effectively.

The data suggest that more and more banks are establishing a new organizational department to oversee the digital transformation. The percentage of banks that have such a department rose from 20 percent in 2010 to 76 percent by the end of 2018. Specifically, from 2010 to 2012, most of the

FIGURE 8-8.   **Organizational Changes for Digitization, 2010–2018**

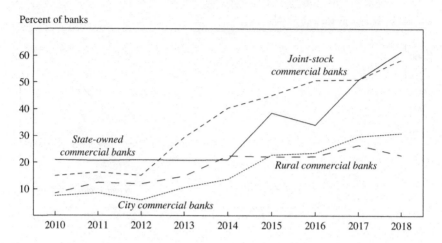

Percent of banks

Source: Compiled by the author.

digitization function was carried out by various departments (such as the information technology department, the retail business department, and so forth), and having a department focus on digital finance was rare in the industry. From 2010 to 2012, only 20 percent of the banks in the sample set up a dedicated digital finance–related department, and these were mainly state-owned banks and joint-stock banks. After 2013, the number gradually increased. In 2015, more than 50 percent of the banks in the sample had set up a digital finance–related department, which has become a "mainstream" practice since then.

Second, to formulate and implement a digital strategy, banks need to have adequate managerial capabilities. With the advent of the information age and the popularization of digital technology, the importance of information technology in bank operations has increased. Managers with a technology background can better understand financial technology and integrate technology into financial services. The regression analysis shows that banks that have managers with these skills achieve better financial results in digitization.[10] This confirms the critical role of managerial capability in digitization.

The data show that managers with a technology background have become more and more common on bank top management teams and boards. By the end of 2018, about 45 percent of banks had hired at least one manager with a technology background for the top management team or as a member of the board of directors. The proportion of senior executives with an information technology background remained at 17–21 percent from 2010 to 2016, with small fluctuations. In 2017 and 2018, there was a big jump, rising to more than 30 percent. The proportion of directors with an information technology background was 12–13 percent over the years 2010–2014; the proportion started increasing in 2015 and reached 23.4 percent in 2018. The recent increase was mainly driven by the contributions of city commercial banks, rural commercial banks, and private banks. Still, more than half of the banks in the sample do not have any managers or board members with a technology background. This lack of managerial talent in banks may become a barrier for them to engage in digitization.

Third, in addition to internal adaptations, external alliances or investments may be a source of learning and capacity building. Through cooperation with technology firms, commercial banks can combine their financial expertise with the technology and data advantages of technology firms.

By 2018, one quarter of the banks had established such external collaboration with technology firms. From 2010 to 2013, only a few banks made digital finance–related alliances and investments. An upward trend began in 2014, which is consistent with the rise of financial technology firms such as Ant Financial. From 2015 to 2018, external cooperation gradually became more popular, mainly on the part of state-owned banks, city commercial banks, and private banks. In terms of the number of cooperative relationships, most banks carry out only one or two each year. Only a few banks have carried out multiple alliances or investments in a single year. For example, China Merchants Bank carried out six collaborations in 2015 and 2016. Hua Xia Bank carried out more than five from 2016 to 2018. Industrial Bank and China CITIC Bank each conducted more than ten in 2017. Thus, it seems that the joint-stock banks are more active in external collaborations and more open in their interactions with technology companies. Most commercial banks need to be more open-minded in order to create value from building ecosystems in the new digital era.

Digital Innovation in Products

The overall digital transformation in products exhibits an upward trend from 2010 to 2018 (figure 8-9). State-owned banks and joint-stock banks have a higher level of product digitization than smaller banks. The state-owned

FIGURE 8-9. **Product Digital Innovation, 2010–2018**

Number of innovations

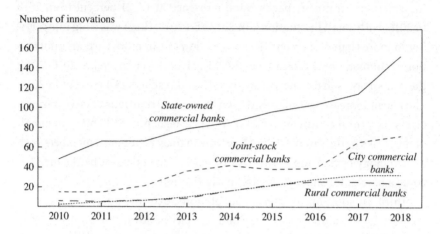

Source: Compiled by the author.

banks are particularly advanced in this area, mainly due to their heavy investment in technology and patents.

The first strategy in product digitization is to develop online channels, such as mobile apps or WeChat mini apps. As consumers have moved online, banks have had to adapt in order to maintain access to their customers. In 2010, only about 28.3 percent of banks had developed mobile banking channels. But by 2018, 97.7 percent of the banks either had a banking app or offered WeChat banking (figure 8-10). For the China Construction Bank, ICBC, and Agricultural Bank of China, the number of users of banking apps exceeded 300 million in 2018.

In the years 2010–2012, most banks did not have mobile banking channels, and only some major banks had developed mobile banking apps. After 2013, the development of apps and WeChat banking entered the "fast lane." By 2016, more than 70 percent of banks had both mobile banking apps and WeChat banking, and this proportion rose to 81.3 percent in 2018. Some banks directly adopted WeChat banking without developing banking apps. Considering the heavier investment and low user stickiness of bank apps, this "lightweight" channel may become a trend in the future.

Another area of change is investing in R&D to build technology capabilities. In 2019, the major state-owned banks, on average, invested tens of billions (yuan), about 2 percent of their revenue, in technologies. China Mer-

FIGURE 8-10. **Bank Online Channel Penetration, 2010–2018**

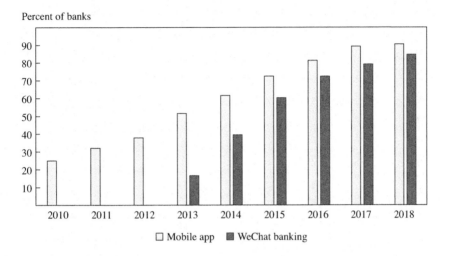

Source: Compiled by the author.

chants Bank, which is a top joint-stock bank, led the industry by investing 3.72 percent of its revenue in financial technology. Along with the increase in R&D, there has been an increase in patent applications, especially in recent years (figure 8-11).

In addition to the mobile channel and technology innovation, banks have introduced financial products online, including online savings/wealth management, online credit/loans, and e-commerce. Figure 8-12 shows the penetration of these digital products in the financial industry. About one-third of the banks have introduced such digital products, growing from almost zero in 2010. The overall industry penetration rate of digital products is still low.

Digital Innovation in Wealth Management. Although commercial banks have previously launched wealth management products offline, these products usually had an investment threshold (RMB 50,000) and a fixed term with little flexibility for withdrawal. This product design is not attractive to younger consumers with limited funds and a preference for online access. While this group of customers may not be the most affluent group at this time, they are precisely the group with the greatest future potential. Thus, their wealth management needs constitute a new growth path for commercial

FIGURE 8-11. **Bank Fintech Patent Applications, 2010–2020**

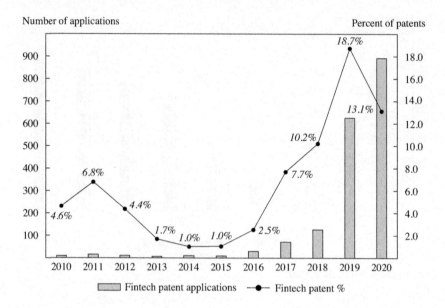

Source: Compiled by the author.

FIGURE 8-12. **Digital Products Penetration Rate, 2010–2018**

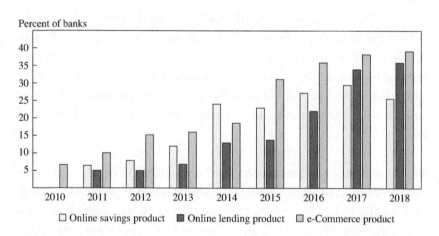

Source: Compiled by the author.

banks. Digital wealth management products offer a new solution. Because of the use of AI instead of human service, the management cost could be lowered to reduce the entry threshold. Moreover, investors can purchase their favorite wealth management products online, for immediate saving, and make withdrawals using any bank card. This innovation was so welcomed by customers that commercial banks have followed suit and introduced their own versions of digital wealth management products.

From 2010 to 2013, the proportion of banks that developed online wealth management products was low, at only about 10 percent, and they were dominated by joint-stock banks and city merchant banks. After 2014, owing to the impact of Yu'ebao, banks began to take note of the importance of such products, and the penetration of online wealth management products doubled to 20 percent.

Take Machine Gene Investment, for example. This is a product that integrates China Merchants Bank's more than ten years of wealth management practice and fund research expertise. It uses machine learning algorithms that automatically calculate and scan the entire market to carry out fund screening, asset allocation, and risk analysis. In China, robo-advisors began to appear in 2014 and proliferated during 2016–2017. China Merchants Bank launched Machine Gene Investment, the first robo-advisor in the commercial banking sector, in December 2016. After that, Industrial Bank and ICBC introduced their own robo-advisor investment products.

Machine Gene was developed by the wealth management department of China Merchants Bank and is based on the bank's firsthand observation of the Chinese wealth management market. On the one hand, investors are immature and have not learned to invest long-term or in a portfolio. On the other hand, the investment consultancy service still relies heavily on humans, which is not only costly but also inefficient. Motivated by the passion to change the status quo and taking advantage of the new financial technology, Machine Gene emerged as a bottom-up innovation that later received support from the bank headquarters.

It is not just a single product or a simple portfolio of fund products but a complete set of financial services, including "know your customer," portfolio construction, portfolio tracking reports, risk warning reminders, dynamic risk adjustment, and so forth, all integrated in the banking app and provided online. Customers can perform most functions with one click. AI services greatly improve the efficiency and lower the entry barriers for customers.

Machine Gene also provides relatively complete, personalized after-sales service. For example, monthly operation reports allow investors to monitor the performance of their portfolios. When the market fluctuates sharply or major events occur that cause the customer's portfolio to deviate from the optimal state, Machine Gene will provide the customer with dynamic portfolio suggestions. Customers can use "one-click optimization" to make adjustments.

Building on the brand effect and huge customer base of China Merchants Bank, Machine Gene Investment was instantly popular upon its introduction. As of the end of May 2018, the number of users exceeded 150,000, and the fund has exceeded RMB 11 billion. It has established the leading position in the robo-advisory market, especially in the banking sector.

Digital Innovation in Credit and Loans. Efficient loan service based on financial technology is a path that banks must take in the digital era. But it also presents challenges as the traditional risk control model relies on collateral or human relationships. Ping An OneConnect (a subsidiary of Ping An Group, which also owns Ping An Bank) is on the frontier of innovation in this area.

In 2017, OneConnect released a smart loan solution called Gamma. Gamma revamped the traditional loan models in terms of customer acquisition, review, approval, and system development. Its smart dual recording technology, which uses facial recognition, voiceprint recognition, fingerprint recognition, and online document verification, greatly simplifies the complex and inefficient customer identity authentication process under the existing loan model. These technologies free up staff in a large number of processes, such as face-to-face review, verification, and contract signing, making the entire loan process paperless.

Gamma has also integrated the technology into an offline terminal that can be placed in bank branches, retail stores, or large factories. Because the machine is a noncash device and there are no printed consumables, the cost of security and management is relatively low. A customer who needs a loan can go to the machine and do a face-to-face signature. If the signature is accepted, the loan funds are made available to the customer immediately, with no manual intervention throughout the whole process. The machine can check physical certificates onsite to avoid fraud, such as the use of someone else's electronic materials; at the same time, it can record the signing process to meet regulatory requirements. This has obvious advantages in cities below the second tier, where the threshold for a loan application is relatively high and obtaining a loan could take weeks or even months.

Currently, Chinese government policies require financial institutions to practice inclusive finance. However, the development of online financial services is plagued by a particularly high rate of fraud. OneConnet's analysis revealed that 50 percent of online NPLs are fraudulent, and the other 50 percent are credit risks. Credit risk will change according to the income of the borrower, the economic cycle, and other factors, and some smart risk control methods can be used to minimize the possibility of default. However, the implementation of anti-fraud measures must be a constant task in order to contend with the escalating methods of fraud. Thus, it is of great importance to develop antifraud technologies for banks seeking to develop an online credit product.

Gamma is designed to solve this issue for banks. One of its core technologies is a micro–facial expression assistance system, which was independently developed by OneConnect. The head of the development team of the micro-facial expression assistance system is a PhD graduate from MIT, and many graduate students from prestigious overseas universities are team members. A professor of psychology from Fudan University and criminal investigation experts from the Ministry of Public Security were invited to jointly establish a model that recognizes small changes in facial expressions through a remote video camera, and intelligently makes judgments on potential fraud. For example, if a borrower lies during the face-to-face review, it is not an instant facial expression, but a process. The individual may be surprised at first, then blush, followed by embarrassment and a smirk, and the whole process may take half a second to a second. The machine then reads the relevant information through the facial feature library and provides feedback. Before the system was officially put into use, the OneConnect team retrieved more than 100,000 face-to-face review videos, which were accumulated by the Ping An Group in the past, and continually trained the model across several different dimensions. This large amount of data allowed for more precise machine learning, thereby training a better model. According to expert evaluations, Gamma currently performs better than 80 percent of human face-to-face interviewers, and with further data accumulation, it will continue to be optimized. Considering the volume of the verification process in the loan business and the limited supply of senior interview experts, Gamma could help solve this issue by substituting for or facilitating relatively junior interviewers and provide risk prompts.

Overall, the application of financial technology can simplify the loan application process and greatly improving business efficiency. For example, the application time for small loans has been drastically shortened from a few hours or even days to three to five minutes. The improvement in efficiency directly saves staff and material resources, and it provides a better customer experience. At the same time, the introduction of financial technology has improved the consistency of loan decisionmaking and the ability to identify fraud risks. Not only does it directly help financial institutions reduce loan operating costs, but it also significantly enhances their capabilities for market expansion and for providing inclusive finance because of improved risk control capabilities.

Impact of Digitization on Bank Performance

Would digitization benefit firm performance? We find that bank digitization has a positive and significant effect on bank performance, measured by returns on assets and returns on equity.[11] In addition, this positive effect is more pronounced in banks with a larger number of managers who have a technology background and in banks headquartered in cities with a higher level of development of digital finance. Further investigation on other aspects of bank operations suggests that digitization reduces bank risk, helps banks transform their business, and increases their market share. These results support the critical role of digital transformation in capability upgrading and sustainable operation for Chinese banks.

OBSTACLES AND CHALLENGES IN THE DIGITIZATION OF COMMERCIAL BANKS

Despite the fast spread and growth of digitization, there are still major obstacles that need to be overcome by commercial banks.

First, digitization is not only about shifting from offline to online channels; it should be about the transformation of the entire organization. The data show that most banks have been focusing on digital transformation by developing banking apps. Yet this strategy has not proved to be very effective, as banking apps are often used in low frequency. Most individuals use banking apps only once a month to pay bills, so user stickiness to the apps is relatively low. For instance, while some banking apps claim to have a large installed base, they may not have a large number of active users. In China, only two banking apps, those of China Merchants Bank and ICBC, have more than 100 million monthly active users. This number is only one-tenth of the monthly active users of WeChat or Alipay. Moreover, digitization is not only about putting offline products online, as most banks are now doing this. Real digitization means building digital capabilities to create digitized products and even reshape the value chain and redefine the business model. For example, technology firms use big data, blockchain, and the internet of things to conduct risk control, which have revamped the old collateral-based credit model. Such kinds of digital innovation would require sustained investment in technology and innovation as a core capability.

Second, the small banks have fallen behind and face the greatest challenges in digitization. The data show that regional banks are lagging in all aspects of digitization. They do not have the scale economy and deep pockets for technology investment. It is also difficult for smaller regional banks to attract technology talents, as these individuals are concentrated in large cities. Even worse, the regional banks are also losing their local markets, which used to be a critical source of their competitive advantage, to the technology firms and larger banks. The small regional banks need to find their way in this new digital age.

Finally, digitization requires reform of the internal organization of banks. Among the three aspects of digitization, organization transformation is relatively behind the cognition and product aspects, yet greater organization adaptation is what is most needed for the digital transformation of banks (figure 8-13).

For example, digitization often relies on technology personnel. However, banks cannot compete with technology firms on salaries or career development paths. Traditional banks usually have a hierarchical system with many levels, which inevitably leads to some inefficiencies. Because the wage distribution is based on job levels, and not on contributions, there are few incentives for young employees. In addition, most traditional bank departments have too many staff members, but there are few positions at the level

FIGURE 8-13. **Bank Digital Transformation Subindexes, 2010–2018**

Index value

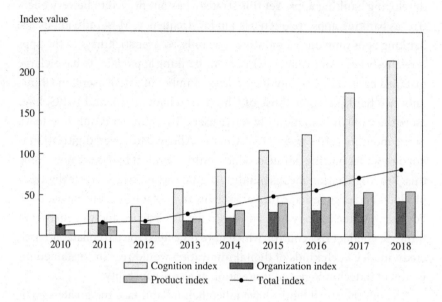

Source: Compiled by the author.

of department leaders, and young employees have little room for growth. This further reduces the enthusiasm of young employees.

Whether in terms of wages, working environment, or job atmosphere, the conditions of banks are not as good as those of internet companies. So, technology talents are more inclined to work at internet companies. In addition to disadvantages in recruitment, banks have not yet formed a complete and long-term mechanism for training. As a result, even if technology workers are recruited, there is no best way to use their talent, which results in serious brain drain.

These problems have caused a shortage of workers with technology talent in banks, which in turn has restricted the technological transformation of banks.

Moreover, in the digital age, technological innovation is changing with each passing day, and the speed of product upgrades is getting faster and faster. The division of responsibilities in traditional banks is usually based on a matrix structure. The long decisionmaking chain and complicated processes no longer fit the new demand in product innovation, and appropriate changes are urgently needed. To keep up with the pace of innovation, banks need to learn from technology firms and practice agile product development methods. Banks can adapt to changes in the new era by flattening the hierarchical structure, using cross-functional teams, and creating a culture of innovation.

For example, the technology department of Minsheng Bank initiated the "Light Organization" reform in 2016, in which the old department structure was replaced by decentralized task-oriented teams. All employees can compete for the team leader position, breaking the old hierarchy. A research center and an innovation incubator were established to encourage learning and experiments. The goal is to construct a flexible and efficient organizational structure, form a human resource pool, and improve the efficiency of resource allocation.

The department was split into many small units, each with only seven or eight people. Every young person in a unit can take charge of a project, focusing on the project goals and breaking the original administrative barriers to build a decentralized organizational structure. In project reporting, employees can skip reporting levels according to project needs.

Pay and bonuses are based entirely on work performance rather than seniority, to make sure those employees who work harder to earn more. With the reform, the bonus can reach as much as 55 percent of an employee's yearly salary. In other words, a person who has a very high administrative level but no performance contribution will not receive a bonus; they will receive only the salary portion, reflecting their historical contribution.

Minsheng Bank has also begun to implement a flexible work system, project points system, and open competition mechanism. Employees can arrange work in a manner that best suits the conditions of the work and no longer need to follow traditional methods, which are not conducive to innovation.

Within three months of the restructure, performance increased by 10 percent. To further unleash the productivity potential, Minsheng spun off its technology department to create an independent financial technology company in 2018. This practice can help a division break away from the rigid bureaucratic structure of the parent company, as the new subsidiary can start everything new and have more leeway in head count and compensation policies.

By the end of 2020, twelve banks had established affiliated financial technology companies; five of these were state-owned banks, six were joint-stock banks, and one was a city commercial bank. Yet, while establishing a

new subsidiary might help in some instances, it does not solve the root problem in the parent bank. The organizational change is still a barrier that
must be overcome.

THE FUTURE OF COMMERCIAL BANKING
AND ITS POLICY IMPLICATIONS

Future Directions

In the past decade, banks have changed and transformed from physical
buildings to internet portals to mobile apps. In the future, banks will continue to evolve. It is predicted that the future of banking will be open banks,
which means that banks will become boundaryless and banking as a service
could be integrated into every living scenario. Because it is supported by the
technology of application programming interface (API), it is also called API
banking. For example, when online streaming service customers want to
open a VIP account to skip advertisements, a virtual wallet with banking services would be generated. This would allow the customer to make a deposit to
pay for the VIP expense with interest or apply for consumer credit.

This new form of banking has several advantages. First, banking will be
more convenient for users because it can be accessed anywhere at any time.
Thus, the goal of financial inclusion could be within greater reach because
the banking service is greatly expanded beyond the limits of physical banks.
Open banking also expands access to customers beyond banking apps. This
will not only solve the low-frequency and stickiness issues of banking apps
but also provide a new route for the development of newly formed private
banks that do not have an established customer base or offline branches. For
example, the private bank XW Bank has used the open banking model to
achieve fast growth. XW Bank has registered capital of RMB 3 billion; and
its shareholders include New Hope Group, Xiaomi, and Hongqi Chain. Compared with the shareholders of WeBank (by WeChat) and MYbank (by Alibaba), XW Bank's shareholders do not have a large internet platform. However, this apparent "disadvantage" has brought more room for the business
development of XW Bank. Specifically, XW Bank opens up to other promi-
nent internet platforms, such as Didi, JD, ByteDance, and Meituan, to meet
the financial needs of customers in multiple life scenarios, such as automo-
biles, tourism, consumption, and travel. For example, online credit products

such as Didi's "Di Shui Dai," China Mobile's "He Bao Dai," and JD's "JD Gold Bar" are all provided by XW Bank. By embedding itself in these online platforms, XW Bank is able to acquire customers and realize the integration of financial and life scenarios.

Second, the openness and collaboration between different parties could create an innovation ecosystem and become a source of innovations. An innovation ecosystem is multiple companies that combine their products to create a unified, customer-oriented innovative solution through collaborative arrangements. An innovation ecosystem enables the creation of value that no one company can create alone. In the context of the financial industry, banks and technology companies are highly complementary in their resources and capabilities. On the one hand, traditional banks have deep financial knowledge and a large customer base with data on their financial transactions. However, they may have limited technological capability. On the other hand, technology companies have comprehensive behavioral data, active users, and the most cutting-edge technologies, yet limited financial service experience. The collaboration between traditional banks and technology companies will cross-fertilize and achieve a win-win situation, creating greater value for customers.

Open banking may be a strategy particularly well suited to smaller banks. They can develop their digital banking through external alliances with other banks or technology companies. For example, Ping An OneConnect developed a new business model to transfer Ping An Bank's technology capability, financial products, and operational expertise to other small and medium-size banks. OneConnect has helped forty-two small and medium-size banks develop direct banking and mobile banking. Helping small and medium-size banks establish direct banking is only the first step, as the relationship also includes subsequent product design, operation, and maintenance. OneConnect brings not only competitive financial products but also the marketing and product capabilities from Ping An Bank to these small banks. By the end of 2019, their clients covered 99 percent of city commercial banks in China.

Policy Implications

The digitization of commercial banks, which has been pushed by the threat of financial technology firms and pulled by the surge of customer demand, has received strong support from the government. In May 2017, the People's Bank of China established the FinTech Committee to strengthen the research planning and overall coordination of financial technology.

In August 2019, the People's Bank of China officially issued the "FinTech Development Plan (2019–2021)," which pointed out the importance of financial technology as a route to promote financial transformation and upgrading, provide financial services to the real economy, and develop inclusive finance. The plan clearly puts forward the goals and priorities of financial technology development, including, by 2021, "establishing and improving the 'four beams and eight pillars' of China's financial technology development, enhancing the technology application capabilities of the financial industry, and achieving deep integration and coordinated development of finance and technology."[12]

In 2020, the first meeting of the FinTech Committee of the People's Bank of China emphasized that financial institutions need to accelerate digital transformation and continue to enhance their technology application capabilities. In October 2020, Guo Shuqing, secretary of the Party Committee of the People's Bank of China and chairman of the China Banking and Insurance Regulatory Commission, emphasized that "all financial institutions must step up digital transformation."[13] In November 2020, State Council Circular #43 encouraged commercial banks to use big data and other technologies to establish risk pricing and control models. It is clear that the application of financial technology and digitization of commercial banks have been strongly promoted.

The digitization of commercial banks can be viewed as a part of the overall reform of the banking industry. As the interest rate marketization has not been realized and entry barriers to the banking industry remain in place, digitization could help enhance the competitiveness of commercial banks, providing the foundation and a new possibility for achieving the reform goals in the future.

However, digitization also poses great challenges to regulators. First, the digitization of small banks may need greater guidance. There are thousands of rural credit unions and village banks. This group of banks not only lags in digitization but also has not been fully reformed. Policymakers should carefully consider the goals and development strategies of these banks and carry out further reform in this area. For example, some of these regional banks, in the process of digitization, collaborated with internet companies to offer credit and saving products over the internet. In February 2021, the China Banking and Insurance Regulatory Commission issued the "Notice on Further Regulating the Internet Loan Business of Commercial Banks," requiring that commercial banks independently carry out risk control of internet loans. Commercial banks are forbidden to outsource this task to internet firms, and regional banks are not allowed to conduct business outside the region where they are registered. If small regional banks cannot expand through the internet and rely on technology partners for digital capabilities, then they must reformulate their strategies for digitization.

Second, as the industry becomes more digitized, and thus more open, the boundaries of banks become blurred. Regulators need to expand their monitoring capability and pay attention to increasingly complex banking transactions. This requires regulatory agencies to build stronger digital capabilities for improved understanding of digital finance and to oversee the continuous innovation in the industry.

Finally, data are the building blocks and key input factors in digital finance, yet there is still great ambiguity and risk associated with the use and transaction of data. On the one hand, weak or unprotected bank technology systems may become targets of attack through API. On the other hand, data ownership remains a complex issue in open banking transactions. This requires policymakers to complete the infrastructure for digital finance, including new legislation on data ownership and transactions and a shared credit reporting system. With these infrastructures as the solid foundation, the banking industry could achieve steady and far-reaching development in digitization.

NOTES

1. X. Xie, and S. Wang, 2021. "The Digitalization of Chinese Commercial Banks: Measuring its Degree and Impact." National School of Development, unpublished working paper.

2. "List of Legal Persons of Banking Financial Institutions (as of December 31, 2020)," China Banking and Insurance Regulatory Commission, March 16, 2021, http://www.cbirc.gov.cn/cn/view/pages/govermentDetail.html?docId=970966&itemId=863&generaltype=1.

3. World Bank Financial Development Database, https://www.worldbank.org/en/publication/gfdr/data/global-financial-development-database.

4. "Quarterly Banking Regulatory Statistical Indicators (2019)," China Banking and Insurance Regulatory Commission, February 17, 2020, http://www.cbirc

.gov.cn/cn/view/pages/ItemDetail.html?docId=890466&itemId=954&general
type=0.

5. "The General Situation of the Payment System in 2019," People's Bank of
China, March 17, 2020, http://www.pbc.gov.cn/zhifujiesuansi/128525/128545/128643
/3990497/index.html.

6. Tianhong Fund Management, *Interim Report of Tianhong Yu'ebao Money
Market Fund in 2020*, https://static.howbuy.com/gkxx/ggfile//2020/2020-8/2020-08
-31/2027929.pdf.

7. China Academy of Information and Communications Technology (CAICT),
The White Book on Digital Inclusive Finance, 2019, https://max.book118.com/html
/2019/1109/6214023150002122.shtm.

8. "Financial License Information," China Banking and Insurance Regulatory
Commission, http://xkz.cbirc.gov.cn/jr/.

9. X. Xie and S. Wang, "The Digitalization of Chinese Commercial Banks:
Measuring Its Degree and Impact." National School of Development, 2021, unpublished working paper.

10. W. Bian, X. Xie, and S. Wang, 2021. "How Valuable Is FinTech Adoption for
Traditional Banks?" Sungkyunkwan University and National School of Development, 2021, unpublished working paper.

11. W. Bian, X. Xie, and S. Wang, "How Valuable Is FinTech Adoption for Traditional Banks?" Sungkyunkwan University & National School of Development,
2021, unpublished working paper.

12. "FinTech Development Plan (2019–2021)," http://www.pbc.gov.cn/zheng
wugongkai/4081330/4081344/4081395/4081686/4085169/2019090617242730910.
pdf.

13. "The Central Bank Issued a Three-Year Plan for Financial Technology to
Achieve Deep Integration of Finance and Technology by 2021," *China Daily*, August 23, 2019, https://baijiahao.baidu.com/s?id=1642638050501965051&wfr=spid
er&for=pc.

9

The Digital Divide and the Trickle-Down Effect

XUN ZHANG

The information and communications technology sectors have experienced unprecedented development over the past decades that has led to the digital divide. The digital divide refers to the different amounts of information available to those with and without access to the internet. This divide is quite serious in China and in the rest of the developing world, and it is expected to aggravate the universal challenge of worsening income distribution and potentially exacerbate poverty. One option to alleviate the detrimental impact is to allocate public resources to help the disadvantaged. This chapter provides another possible option: the emergence of the digital economy, especially the fast growth of financial technology (fintech). Fintech offers cheaper, more transparent, and more inclusive financial services than the traditional financial sector and has changed the way people engage in economic activity. Such engagement contributes to economic growth, generating jobs and benefiting all citizens, not just those with internet access. This is the trickle-down effect provided by fintech development. The chapter also discusses prerequisites and limitations of the trickle-down effect. On the one hand, there must be a certain scale of internet coverage for the trickle-down effect to be fruitful. On the other hand, the development of the internet may not have spillover effects on wage income. Moreover, some population subgroups without access to the internet, such as the elderly and individuals with lower levels of human capital, are more likely than other groups to be negatively affected by the development of fintech. The chapter ends with some policy implications.

DEVELOPMENT OF INFORMATION AND COMMUNICATIONS TECHNOLOGY

As is well known, the information and communications technology sectors have seen unprecedented development over the past decades. The inventions of the telegraph, telephone, radio, and computer have enabled communication over great distances. More important, the advent of the internet marked a new era. It serves as an infrastructure and a means of information provision and allows individuals to interact with each other regardless of their geographic locations. The marginal cost of information broadcasting has become quite low. The internet also enables people to share multimedia messages such as pictures and videos, which are generally more straightforward to understand and more informative than texts.

The explosive growth in internet usage started in 1995; before then, the internet was mainly used in the technology and military fields. In 1995, the commercialization of the internet quickly enlarged the number of users. According to a report from the US Department of Commerce, from 1995 to 1998, the number of internet users increased by 50 million.[1] By contrast, it took seventy-five, thirty-eight, sixteen, and thirteen years, respectively, for the telephone, radio, personal computer, and television to reach the same number of users. In light of this, the governments of the United States, the European Commission, and Japan put forward the national strategy of accelerating the popularization of the internet, which was regarded as the key factor for strengthening national competitiveness in the twenty-first century.[2] Therefore, with the support of governments and driven by the power of technology, the market, and globalization, the internet has expanded at an unprecedented speed on a global scale. Figure 9-1 clearly shows that the number of internet users is growing at an exponential rate. The latest statistics show that in 2017, the number of internet users climbed to 3.68 billion, nearly 49 percent of the world's population.

The development of the internet brings in information. With the help of the internet and thus information, there is a clear trend of accelerating urbanization over time. Figure 9-2 shows the number of years various countries took

FIGURE 9-1.   **Number of Internet Users Worldwide, 1993–2017**

Users (millions)

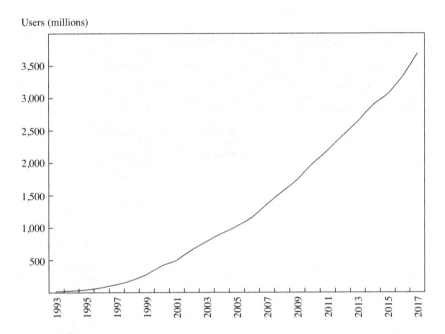

Source: World Development Indicators database, https://databank.worldbank.org/source /world-development-indicators (accessed August 1, 2020).

to go from about 10 percent to about 50 percent urbanization. That number is more than 400 for the earliest starters, such as Portugal, Poland, Switzerland, Sweden, France, and Great Britain. It reduces to just over 100 when counting countries that began the urbanization process in the mid-nineteenth century (e.g., Romania, Norway, Greece, and Germany). For the late starters in Asia (e.g., China, Indonesia, and Thailand) and Africa (e.g., Cameroon, Côte d'Ivoire, and Liberia), it took only about 60 years. This phenomenon is not unique to fast-growing economies like China and Indonesia; it is also applicable to the least developed countries, such as Togo and Angola. The acceleration trend can also be measured by how fast a major city grows. For example, it took London 130 years to grow its population from 1 million to 8 million, but only 45 years for Bangkok and 25 years for Seoul.[3]

The development of the internet has led to the emergence of the digital economy, especially in China. According to statistics from the Cyberspace Administration of China, the value of e-commerce transactions in China

FIGURE 9-2.   **Years to Move from 10 to 50 Percent Urbanization,
Selected Years, 1500–2050**

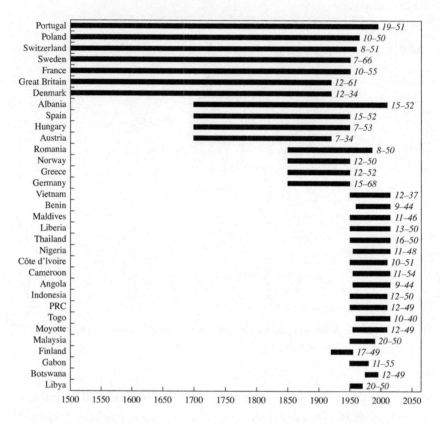

Source: G. Wan and Y. Zhang, "Accelerating Urbanization Explained: The Role of
Information," ADBI Working Paper 674 (Tokyo: Asian Development Bank Institute, 2017).
Note: The urbanization rate is defined as the ratio of urban population to total population.
PRC: People's Republic of China.

reached RMB 20.8 trillion in 2015, achieving an annual average growth rate of
more than 35 percent between 2011 and 2015.[4] This amount further climbed
to RMB 34.81 trillion in 2019. Among the e-commerce transactions, the value
of online retail sales was about RMB 4 trillion in 2015 and RMB 10.63 trillion
in 2019, ranking first in the world. This tremendous growth has attracted attention in the context of the slowing down of global economic growth.

The emergence of the digital economy has allowed digital finance (or fintech) to thrive in China. Over the past ten years, traditional financial insti-

tutions have improved access channels for households and significantly reduced their budget constraints. With the rapid expansion of fintech, China has seen an even more dramatic transformation in the accessibility and affordability of financial services, particularly for formerly financially excluded sectors of the population. Fintech has offered low-cost services to hundreds of millions of underserved people and thus may be beneficial to the development of financial inclusion.

Two examples illustrate the role of fintech in people's lives and economic development. First, fintech development offers a more convenient way for people to make online payments and stimulates e-commerce transactions, especially online retail sales (detailed analysis is provided in the next section). Nowadays, most families in China shop on online platforms such as JD and Taobao. Second, fintech development helps support innovative residents (especially those who were formerly members of lagging groups) and facilitates their ability to borrow and become entrepreneurs. Before the development of fintech, entrepreneurs who wanted to borrow from traditional financial institutions usually had to have a credit check to determine whether they had good credit. However, because most residents in developing economies do not have credit records, traditional finance methods often cannot solve the start-up funding problem. Fintech can help with this. In modern China, residents can use mobile phones to pay for most transactions, including shopping in local commercial markets or online, dining in restaurants, and paying utility bills, even if they do not have a credit card. More important, most mobile phone transactions can help residents gain a fintech-defined credit record and thus facilitate residents' borrowing through fintech channels. Therefore, fintech can increase the probability that residents will become entrepreneurs.

To sum up, development of the internet drives the emergence and expansion of the digital economy and digital finance (fintech), which have become a new engine of economic growth, especially in China.

THE DIGITAL DIVIDE AND ITS EFFECTS

The Digital Divide: Some Facts

Along with the rapid development of the information and communications technology sectors and the internet, the problem of the digital divide has emerged. This problem is present in developed and developing countries, and it is more severe between developed and developing countries.

The Digital Divide across World Regions. Figure 9-3 shows the geographical distribution of global internet penetration. The figure presents internet coverage rates among regions from 1996 to 2017, during which the information and communications technology sectors underwent unprecedented development. The geographical distribution of global internet penetration is extremely unbalanced. The leading regions in internet development are North America and Europe/Central Asia. As of 2017, the internet coverage rates in these two regions were 87.8 and 74.6 percent, respectively. These rates were much higher than those in other regions. The economic gap between Europe/Central Asia and North America is relatively small; thus, the gap in internet penetration between these two regions started to narrow around 2010.

FIGURE 9-3.   **The Digital Divide across the Continents, 1996–2017**

Individuals using the internet
(percent of population)

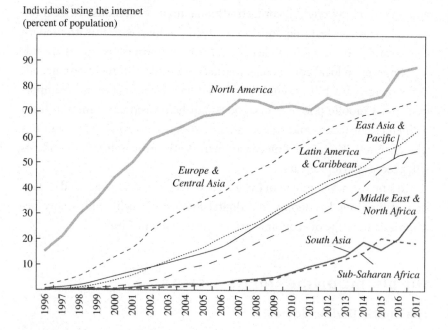

Source: World Development Indicators database, https://databank.worldbank.org/source/world-development-indicators (accessed August 1, 2020).

The second echelon of internet penetration includes Latin America and the Caribbean, East Asia and Pacific, and the Middle East and North Africa. Although these regions are still far behind the leading regions (around 55 percent in internet coverage rate), some countries and subregions, such as Mainland China, Hong Kong, India, Japan, Korea, Singapore, and Taiwan, have the potential for network popularization and development. Thus, the three regions in the second echelon are catching up with the leading regions, and the subregions are likely to drive network development in their regions. As we have observed in recent years, the digital economy and digital finance in China have been progressing rapidly. The coverage rates in South Asia and sub-Saharan Africa are among the lowest, although that of South Asia has begun to increase. As of 2017, the internet coverage rate of sub-Saharan Africa was only 18.7 percent, about one-fifth the level of North America. Moreover, if we look at the trends, we find that the coverage gap between high-level and low-level popularization areas has widened, and the imbalance in the popularization and development of the internet and fintech among different geographical regions is further aggravated, indicating that the digital divide between regions is a serious problem to be solved.

The Digital Divide across Countries with Different Income Levels. To explore the digital divide problem across countries at different income levels, I use the World Bank's World Development Indicators database and calculate the cross-country inequality in GDP per capita (in constant 2010 US prices) and the internet coverage rate. Table 9-1 shows the three main results. First, inequality in per capita income among countries in the world has decreased slightly. The Gini coefficient of GDP per capita was 0.675 in 2000 and decreased to 0.641 in 2015. Second, compared with that of GDP

TABLE 9-1. **Inequality of Income per Capita and Internet Penetration**

Indicator	Gini coefficient			
	2000	2005	2010	2015
GDP per capita (constant 2010 US prices)	0.675	0.661	0.654	0.641
Internet coverage rate	0.698	0.577	0.452	0.338

Source: World Development Indicators database, https://databank.worldbank.org/source /world-development-indicators, and author's calculations (accessed August 1, 2020).

per capita, inequality in internet coverage rates among countries decreased more. The Gini coefficient of internet penetration in 2000 was 0.698, higher than that of GDP per capita, but it dropped to 0.338 in 2015, suggesting that internet penetration in less developed countries is improving. Third, although the inequality of internet popularization among countries has decreased, it was still as high as 0.338 in 2015, indicating that the problem of the digital divide still exists.

I directly compare the digital divide among country groups at different income levels. This could be seen as a comparison of the digital divide between the North and the South, which refers to the difference in the level of internet penetration between high-income countries and low-income countries. The results in table 9-2 show that GDP per capita has increased dramatically in high- and low-income countries. In 2000, the GDP per capita of high- and low-income countries was US$25,102.9 and US$323.9, respectively, and it quickly climbed to US$39,730.9 and US$860.6 in 2015. Moreover, the income ratio of high over low decreased from 77.5 to 46.2, suggesting that income inequality has been narrowing in recent years. At the same

TABLE 9-2. **Income and the Digital Divide across Country Income Groups**

Group	2000	2005	2010	2015
GDP per capita (constant 2010 US prices)				
High income	25,102.88	33,172.20	38,650.14	39,730.92
Upper-middle income	1,878.12	2,953.44	6,089.42	7,695.50
Lower-middle income	565.86	859.90	1,542.65	1,886.73
Low income	323.89	423.57	734.20	860.57
High-low ratio	77.50	78.32	52.64	46.17
Internet coverage rate				
High income	29.911	57.813	71.540	79.374
Upper-middle income	2.373	10.756	31.880	50.160
Lower-middle income	0.518	3.661	10.447	22.617
Low income	0.081	0.970	4.984	12.239
High-low ratio	29.83	56.84	66.56	67.14

Source: World Development Indicators database, https://databank.worldbank.org/source/world-development-indicators (accessed August 1, 2020).

time, although the internet coverage rates of these two country income groups increased from 29.91 and 0.08 percent to 79.37 and 12.24 percent, respectively, the gap has grown from 29.83 to 67.14 percent. The growing gap indicates that the digital divide between high- and low-income countries is increasing, although income inequality is decreasing.

Next, I investigate the problem of the digital divide within high-income countries—that is, countries in the North. Although the differences in the level of economic development among developed countries are relatively small, there is still a digital divide between them (see figure 9-4). Take the popularization of the internet in the twenty original countries of the Organization for Economic Cooperation and Development (OECD) as an example. The latest statistics (in 2017) show that the internet coverage rate of Luxembourg is as high as 97.36 percent, while that of Italy is only 63.08 percent, a difference of 34.28 percentage points. The difference suggests that the gap

FIGURE 9-4.   **Income and the Digital Divide among the Original OECD Countries, 2017**

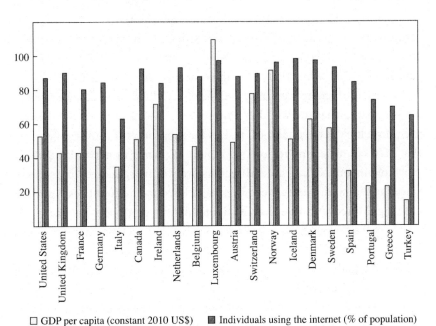

☐ GDP per capita (constant 2010 US$)　■ Individuals using the internet (% of population)

Source: World Development Indicators database, https://databank.worldbank.org/source /world-development-indicators (accessed August 1, 2020).

TABLE 9-3. **Inequality among Low-Income Countries**

Indicator	Gini coefficient			
	2000	2005	2010	2015
GDP per capita (constant 2010 US prices)	0.233	0.233	0.243	0.208
Internet coverage rate	0.579	0.567	0.554	0.418

Source: World Development Indicators database, https://databank.worldbank.org/source
/world-development-indicators, and author's calculations (accessed August 1, 2020).

in the level of economic development (already high income) cannot fully explain the digital divide among countries and that other factors are influencing the formation of the digital divide, which needs further exploration.

Finally, we explore the digital divide problem within low-income countries—that is, countries in the South. As was done in table 9-1, we calculate the cross-country inequality in GDP per capita (constant 2010 US prices) and the internet coverage rate. In 2000, the Gini coefficient of per capita GDP of low-income countries was 0.233, while that of the internet coverage rate was 0.579, much higher than the gap in economic development (see table 9-3). Thus, income inequality and the digital divide have been increasing over time, although the latter is still much higher than the former. In 2015, income inequality, as measured by the Gini coefficient of GDP per capita, was 0.208, while that of the internet coverage rate was 0.418.

To sum up, income inequality and the digital divide have decreased overall, suggesting that the world is now connected to a greater extent. However, if we look at the analytical results for subgroups of countries, we find that a few countries and regions are rapidly digitizing or networking, while most low-income countries and regions are still marginalized or isolated, since the digital divide between high- and low-income countries is still increasing. Moreover, I find that the digital divide within low-income countries is still a serious problem. On the one hand, it is larger than the global level of the digital divide; on the other hand, it is larger than within-group income inequality. In other words, increasing access to the internet within high-income, upper-middle-income, and lower-middle-income countries may have resulted in the recent development in internet popularization. Low-income countries still have a long way to go before they are connected to the world.

Determinants of the Digital Divide

The digital divide is certainly not an exogenous given. Moreover, the digital divide may cause additional negative impacts on economic and social development. It is thus essential to know why the digital divide exists, so that policies can be implemented to reduce or mitigate its negative impacts.

The digital divide is determined by inequality in several economic and social factors. Discussing the determinants of the digital divide is equivalent to discussing those of internet development. In general, the factors that affect internet development can be classified into three categories. *Economic development* is the most fundamental factor that drives internet development. It not only forms the endowment for an economy to construct communications infrastructure but also stimulates individuals' demand to connect to each other. *Human capital* is a prerequisite for internet development. Individuals with higher education have a higher demand for connecting to the internet for information. *Openness* is important because an open economy is more willing to accept information and technology from others; thus, it will demand a higher level of internet development.

Effects of the Digital Divide

There is no doubt that the existence of the digital divide has negative impacts, both economic and noneconomic, on individuals who do not have access to the internet. One need look no further than the recent pandemic for an example of how lacking access to the internet can inconvenience one's life. To prevent the spread of the COVID-19 virus, every province in China has requested that upon entering a public place, each person show a QR (Quick Response) code from his or her internet-connected mobile phone indicating his or her health status and travel record. Although to a great extent this measure has been effective in containing the outbreak, it has also disrupted the lives of the elderly, many of whom are not familiar with using mobile phones, let alone showing their QR codes. This may result in their being barred from buses or denied entry to supermarkets, causing them much inconvenience.

The digital divide also generates negative economic impacts. Research has demonstrated that the digital divide aggravates the universal challenge of worsening income distribution when a significant proportion of the population is deprived of access to various services and opportunities. For example, in the past, job seekers had similar avenues to obtain information on employment opportunities. Now, however, those without access to the internet may lose earning opportunities to their counterparts, possibly worsening the poverty problem. Similarly, the digital divide has created or enhanced inequalities in training, education, and borrowing.

The presence of the digital divide and its negative impacts has been observed in many countries. The United States, which is at the highest level of internet application and popularization, was the first country to note the imbalance of internet development. The National Telecommunication and Information Administration of the United States has reported on the problem of the digital divide within the country more than four times since July 1995. Further, it treats the problem as the top economic and human rights issue in the country. The United States has raised this issue to such an important level because it aims to enable all Americans to integrate into the network economy and network society. By vigorously promoting the internet, the United States is working to improve its national competitiveness in the twenty-first century. With the gradual deepening of the understanding of the digital divide, more governments, international organizations, and political leaders of various countries have begun to realize the huge growth potential of the internet. Thus, the existence of the digital divide is likely to become a new source of unbalanced development among and within countries.

Table 9-4 briefly illustrates the problem of the digital divide in China. Column (1) compares the proportion of employment of the working-age population within groups with and without access to the internet. Employment here covers not only those who are employed by firms but also those

TABLE 9-4. **Impacts of the Digital Divide on Employment, Income, and Consumption in China**

Status	Employment rate (%)	Income (RMB)	Consumption (RMB)
Have internet access	89.4	23,903	68,863
Do not have internet access	87.5	14,266	28,138

Source: China Family Panel Studies and author's calculations.

who are self-employed in any sector. I use household survey data from the China Family Panel Studies, a nationally representative survey of communities, families, and individuals that was conducted biennially from 2010 to 2018. The survey covers 162 counties in 25 provinces. It provides information on individual and household economic activities, educational outcomes, family relationships, health conditions, and so on. The results show that the employment rate of those with access to the internet is 89.4 percent, which is higher than that of those without access to the internet, at 87.5 percent. The difference implies that access to the internet indeed provides additional information, such as on job opportunities, and thus raises the proportion of employment. Further, more opportunities for employment lead to greater income and thus consumption. Columns (2) and (3) show that individuals without access to the internet have lower incomes and consumption and may therefore be more likely to live in poverty.

I have found that individuals without access to the internet are less likely to be employed and more likely to have lower incomes than those with access to the internet. Column (3) in table 9-4 further shows that lacking access to the internet could result in a lower level of consumption. The negative impact of the digital divide on consumption could be attributed to two reasons. First, as shown in the first two columns of the table, individuals who lack access to the internet have fewer employment opportunities and lower income; thus, their consumption would be lower, since consumption relies on income. Second, fintech, especially the payment technology brought about by the commercialization of the internet, could further enhance consumption, especially in China. Individuals no longer need to bring cash or a credit card to shop, dine, or conduct other consumer behaviors. People can use their mobiles to pay for anything with the help of a payment app. This could further stimulate consumption, as time spent on shopping is reduced. This channel is not related to income, indicating that access to the internet could increase the proportion of consumption over income. In other words, the digital divide reduces the level of consumption.

Excessive savings in China and other net exporting economies is often cited as the cause of the US subprime crisis and the European sovereign debt crisis. For instance, Ben S. Bernanke argues that an important factor in the global savings-glut story is the sharp reserve accumulation by developing countries.[5] Alan Greenspan alleges that the high Chinese savings rate was the culprit in the recent US subprime mortgage crisis because it caused low interest rates in world financial markets, which pushed Americans toward excessive consumption and housing financing.[6] Therefore, the finding above that the level of consumption could be increased if more people had access to the internet suggests that reducing the digital divide may also contribute to global rebalances and thus more sustainable economic development.

THE TRICKLE-DOWN EFFECT OF FINTECH DEVELOPMENT

Given that the digital divide generates negative impacts on people's lives and economic development, it is necessary to mitigate its effects. But how do we bridge this gap or alleviate its detrimental impacts? In general, there are two possible options. The first is to directly increase internet coverage or popularization. In other words, allocate public resources to help those who do not have access to the internet, such as building additional communications infrastructure. This option aims to not only increase access to the internet but also improve people's ability to cope with useful information online, which usually requires high-quality access.

China has already made efforts to help the disadvantaged so that most people will have access to high-quality internet. Since China launched its public computer interconnected network in September 1994, it has achieved a major breakthrough in network infrastructure construction. However, slow speed and low coverage restricted the further development of the Chinese economy. This problem was solved in August 2013, when the State Council of China proposed the Broadband China plan, which aimed to speed up China's internet and enlarge its coverage. As of 2016, three groups of cities were participating in the Broadband China pilot. The first batch, announced in 2014, had a total of thirty-nine cities (city clusters), including Beijing, Shanghai, and Guangzhou. The second and third batches of cities were announced in 2015 and 2016, respectively, and eventually, most cities in China will enter the plan. The main technical route of Broadband China is to coordinate the construction of access networks, metropolitan area networks, and backbone networks; comprehensively use wired and wireless technology; combine the technology with requirements of the next generation of scaled commercialization of internet-based on Internet Protocol Version 6 (IPv6); and promote the development of a broadband network in a phased system. Since 2016, the speed of China's broadband and mobile networks has improved dramatically.

Obviously, China tries to allocate public resources to build high-quality internet infrastructure that allows most people—even those located far from cities—to have access to the internet and enhances the connectivity of the disadvantaged. However, this requires a huge fiscal expenditure, including costs of construction and maintenance. Therefore, the first option is not always feasible, especially for governments with limited fiscal resources.

The second option is to continue to let the market drive resource allocation and economic activities. But this option is feasible only if certain aspects of development produce what is called a trickle-down effect,[7] to ensure that the disadvantaged also gain. The trickle-down effect in the case of the digital divide would be for the economic gains of internet development, such as increased employment, income, and consumption, to benefit those who do not have access to the internet. This is analogous to the controversial trickle-down effect in the context of poverty reduction—poverty can be reduced through growth, not just redistribution.

In some cases, we observe a significant trickle-down effect provided by internet development, especially when internet development drives the emergence and expansion of the digital economy and fast growth of digital finance (fintech, new tech that seeks to improve and automate the delivery and use of financial services), when individuals can realize economic gains from using the internet. Here, the trickle-down effect happens when the digital economy and development of digital finance not only benefit those with access to the internet but also have spillover effects on those without access to the internet. In this case, the economic gain from the digital economy and the development of digital finance driven by internet popularization trickles down to the disadvantaged and thus generates the so-called trickle-down effect.

The agriculture industry in China offers an example of the trickle-down effect. Agricultural cooperatives in China are a possible platform through which internet development could generate the trickle-down effect. The cooperatives are constructed on the basis of the will of individuals and managed through joint ownership and democracy. They are built with an aim to increase the incomes of the farmers, helping them eliminate hunger and improve their nutritional status. Agricultural cooperatives have played an important role in promoting sustainable agricultural development in China. China has more than 1.2 million agricultural cooperatives, with an average of more than two in each village.[8]

Agricultural cooperatives can influence farm performance through production and marketing. A first major pathway of their positive effect is that agricultural cooperatives improve farmers' access to better technologies and inputs and assist farmers in using inputs in an efficient manner to increase the technical efficiency of agricultural production. The second pathway is that agricultural cooperatives provide farmers with information such as marketing channels and market prices, which enables them to sell their produce at higher prices.

Both pathways require that agricultural cooperatives have an information advantage over farmers themselves; otherwise, farmers would not have an incentive to join the cooperatives. One way that agricultural cooperatives could have an information advantage is through connection to the internet, while farmers are not connected. When agricultural cooperatives are connected to the internet, they can perform like rural e-commerce platforms. Through the internet, agricultural cooperatives could help farmers sell their products online, and thus potentially raise farmers' income. In this process, agricultural cooperatives themselves must have access to the internet, but rural residents do not need to have access. Farmers who have access to the internet can use it to promote their products. Additionally, families without internet access (most of them are expected to be farmers) can take advantage of the e-commerce platform of agricultural cooperatives to increase their sales and revenue. In this case, the gains from internet development, especially the so-called rural e-commerce platforms, trickle down to farmers who do not have access to the internet, as long as the agricultural cooperatives to which they belong do have access.

To rigorously demonstrate the causal impact of fintech development on agricultural operating income, I combine the index of digital financial inclusion proposed in chapter 2 with data from the China Family Panel Studies. I find that, in general, fintech development has significantly raised agricultural income for those without access to the internet, and that this effect is larger than that of those with access to the internet, suggesting that internet development could generate a trickle-down effect on agricultural operating income. As stated, the setup of agricultural cooperatives is the platform through which the digital economy and fintech could generate such an effect. The reason why fintech development had a smaller effect on agricultural operating income for those with access to the internet may be that agricultural operating income is overall low in those areas with high internet coverage.

The fact that development of the digital economy and fintech could generate a trickle-down effect on agricultural operating income implies that fintech development could raise agricultural productivity, pushing "redundant" rural residents to urban areas and thus stimulating structural transformation from the agriculture sector to the nonagricultural sector. Analysis of the data shows that fintech development had a positive impact on nonagricultural employment for families who do not have access to the internet, thus generating a positive trickle-down effect.

Finally, given that development of the digital economy and fintech has a trickle-down effect on income and employment, we expect that the consumption of those without access to the internet could also increase with the help of the internet. Rigorous data analysis confirms that the consumption of those without access to the internet increases with the help of fintech.

To sum up, development of the digital economy and fintech could help mitigate the negative impact of the digital divide. Fintech offers cheaper, more transparent, and more inclusive economic and financial services than the traditional sectors and has changed the way in which people engage in economic activity. Such engagement contributes to economic growth, generating jobs and benefiting all citizens, not just those with internet access. The benefits include increased levels of employment, income, and consumption. This is the trickle-down effect provided by internet development.

PREREQUISITES OR LIMITATIONS OF THE TRICKLE-DOWN EFFECT

I have found that development of the digital economy and fintech could generate a trickle-down effect. The next question is whether the trickle-down effect is always fruitful. After all, it is possible that under certain conditions the trickle-down effect may not work. This section briefly discusses prerequisites and possible limitations of the trickle-down effect.

Two conditions must be in place for a trickle-down effect to be fruitful. First, there has to be a certain scale of internet coverage. This is intuitive, as we have discussed that development of the digital economy and fintech relies on internet popularization. If the internet coverage rate is low, the digital economy and fintech, let alone the trickle-down effect, cannot develop.

Looking again at the case of China, its digital economy and fintech have been developing in recent years. From the country-wide perspective, since the Broadband China policy was implemented, there have been significant increases in internet coverage of the Chinese people. This increased coverage not only helps individuals with internet access enjoy economic gains and convenience in their lives from the digital economy, but also has spillover effects on those without internet access. The latter also benefit from development of the digital economy and fintech.

Even in the less developed rural area, China has implemented a targeted poverty alleviation policy and mitigated the negative impact of the digital divide by promoting e-commerce activities. Specifically, according to the announcement by China's president Xi Jinping, by the end of 2020, more than 130,000 administrative villages will be equipped with optical fiber networks, the coverage rate of optical fiber in poor villages and that of broadband in deeply poor villages will reach 98 percent, and e-commerce will have achieved full coverage among the 832 deeply poor counties. It is noteworthy that such a high coverage rate in county and village levels does not indicate that families in these areas will have access to the internet,[9] but at least they can take advantage of the e-commerce platform (through agricultural cooperatives as mentioned earlier) to increase their sales and revenue. Thus, as long as there is a certain scale of internet coverage, fintech development could generate a trickle-down effect.

Some population subgroups may not be able to enjoy the trickle-down effect provided by development of the digital economy and fintech. Thus, the second condition is that individuals should have the ability to earn, without which the benefits of internet development may not take effect. This may be illustrated by focusing on the effect on wage income, which is the type of income that most correlates to "earning ability." Data analysis shows that internet development fails to generate a trickle-down effect on wage income. Moreover, wage income is negatively correlated with fintech development for those without access to the internet. This means that compared with those with internet access, those without internet access have decreased bargaining power in labor markets, possibly due to information disadvantage. Further heterogeneity analysis shows that the digital divide mainly affects individuals with lower human capital, reducing their wage incomes, while individuals with higher human capital may still benefit from the trickle-down effect on wage income provided by development of the digital economy and fintech. Moreover, the elderly are negatively affected by the internet, especially with the development of fintech.

IMPLICATIONS FOR POLICIES

In its analysis of the problem of the digital divide and its solution, this chapter uncovered several key findings. First, although the digital divide continues to decrease around the world, it is still severe within and among low-income countries. Second, the digital divide could reduce employment, income, and consumption (rate), which may in turn cause further global imbalance. Third, the solution to the digital divide involves either huge expenditures on communications infrastructure to connect people, or reliance on the trickle-down effect provided by development of the digital economy and fintech. Fourth, the trickle-down effect with the emergence and fast growth of the digital economy and fintech is powerful in mitigating the negative impact of the digital divide and helps increase agricultural income, employment, and consumption for those without access to the internet. Fifth, there are prerequisites and limitations of the trickle-down effect: on the one hand, there must be a certain scale of internet coverage for the trickle-down effect to be fruitful; on the other hand, the development of the internet may not have spillover effects on wage income. Sixth, some population subgroups without access to the internet are more likely to be negatively affected by the development of fintech—for example, the elderly and individuals with lower levels of human capital.

Based on the discussion above, the policy implications of this chapter are straightforward. First, the government should step up efforts to build digital infrastructure across the country to reach more people and promote the adoption of digital technology such as smartphones. Second, since the development of the digital economy and fintech could generate a trickle-down effect and alleviate the negative impact of the digital divide, I recommend promoting improvement of the digital economy and fintech to a greater extent. Third, to stimulate the trickle-down effect, special attention should be paid to the mechanism underlying the effect. For instance, the setup and smooth functioning of agricultural cooperatives are essential for generating the trickle-down effect from the digital economy to agricultural operating income. Fourth, given that the trickle-down effect has some limitations, a special focus (such as social policy) should be placed on those who do not have access to the internet and therefore would not directly benefit from its development. Finally, in addition to the digital divide, it is important to consider the privacy protection issue, especially for those who have access to the internet but lack internet security awareness.

NOTES

1. U.S. Department of Commerce, *The Emerging Digital Economy, 1998* (Washington: Author, 1998), https://www.commerce.gov/sites/default/files/migrated/reports/emergingdig_0.pdf.

2. On February 26, 1998, US president Bill Clinton delivered a speech titled "New Cyber Policy," which emphasized the important role of the internet. In December 1999, the European Commission proposed a political initiative to create "Cyber Europe." In 2000, Japan's president Mori Yoshiro further forwarded the concept of "Japanese-Style IT Society."

3. Of course, figure 9-2 may be misleading because urbanization depends on various drivers. Table 9-1 reports preliminary regression results, showing that the coefficients for the decadal dummy variables are all positive, significant, and increasing over time. These confirm that urbanization has indeed been accelerating, even after controlling for the conventional determinants.

4. Cyberspace Administration of China, *E-Commerce in China*. Beijing: Ministry of Commerce of the People's Republic of China, 2019, http://images.mofcom.gov.cn/wzs2/202007/20200703162035768.pdf.

5. Ben S. Bernanke, "The Global Saving Glut and the US Current Account Deficit." Remarks at the Sandridge Lecture, Virginia Association of Economists, Richmond, VA, March 10, 2005, https://www.federalreserve.gov/boarddocs/speeches/2005/200503102/default.htm.

6. Alan Greenspan, "The Fed Didn't Cause the Housing Bubble," *Wall Street Journal*, March 11, 2009, A15.

7. The trickle-down effect refers to the phenomenon of gains from economic development flowing from the upper classes to the lower classes in a society.

8. Rural Development Institute and Chinese Academy of Social Sciences, *Green Book of Rural Area: Analysis and Forecast on China's Rural Economy (2019–2020)* (Beijing: Social Sciences Academy Press, 2020).

9. According to *47th China Statistical Report on Internet Development* (Beijing: Cyberspace Administration of China, 2021), the internet coverage rate of rural families is only 55.9 percent.

10

China's Central Bank Digital Currency: Facts and Future Directions

YUAN XU

Since the emergence of bitcoin in 2009, people have realized that the current monetary system is under reform. The idea initially originated in the tech-oriented cryptocurrency community and has gradually spread to the general public. Even the policy discussion community now publicly admits that the current monetary system is not sustainable. For example, in a speech at the Jackson Hole Symposium in August 2019, the former Bank of England governor Mark Carney acknowledged there will be a change in the unsustainable monetary system.

By now it is also clear to both the academic and policy community that private cryptocurrencies, such as bitcoin, Litecoin, and Ripple, cannot be the main currencies of the future monetary system, for at least three reasons. First, blockchain-based cryptocurrencies cannot handle large amounts of simultaneous transactions. Second, cryptocurrency will influence the effectiveness of monetary policy in an unknown way. Third, and most important, the privilege to issue money has to be in the hands of governments (Yermack 2015; Böhme and others 2015). Therefore, although cryptocurrencies have achieved great success, they do not represent the future of the monetary system.

Confronting this change and challenge, worldwide central banks begin to initiate projects on central bank digital currencies (CBDCs). According to a survey of sixty-six central banks released in January 2020 by the Bank for International Settlements, a full 80 percent of surveyed central banks engage in research, experimentation, or development of CBDCs. Among them, Norway, Sweden, Finland, Canada, the European Central Bank, England, Singapore, and China are at relatively more advanced stages. The Federal Reserve of the United States lagged a bit early on, but it officially began to conduct research on CBDC in early 2020 and has also resumed the project on Fedcoin.

This chapter looks at the developments of China's CBDC. The discussion can be split into two parts. The first part looks at what we already know about China's CDBC. The discussion is based on publicly available information; I simply compiled publicly released facts. The second part discusses possible future evolutions of CBDC. In this part, I allow more space for inferences and speculations. I wish to acknowledge upfront that these inferences and speculations could be quite inaccurate. Future evolutions may take alternative paths that are quite different. However, given the importance of CBDC and the lack of actual data, I argue that these inferences and speculations are still necessary and could be crucial.

Before delving into the details, it is helpful to preview the key features of China's CBDC:

1. It is referred to as Digital Currency/Electronic Payment (DC/EP) in the research progress. Its final name is e-CNY, meaning electronic Chinese yuan. e-CNY will have the same value as traditional CNY with the same face value.

2. Technically, e-CNY is simply encrypted character strings. Given the current stage of computing power and encryption technology, e-CNY's encryption can be considered safe in the sense that it cannot be decrypted in a reasonable amount of time.

3. Monetarily, e-CNY is supposed to be M0 (currency in circulation) and gradually replace traditional paper cash and coins. This is why its official name is e-CNY.

4. e-CNY will be distributed via a two-layer system consisting of the central bank and financial institutions, mainly commercial banks and possibly big-tech companies.

5. e-CNY will help improve domestic financial monitoring—of corruption and tax evasion. It may also help policy implementation such as subsidy distribution.

6. e-CNY's role in RMB internationalization will be limited in the near future.

The rest of this chapter is organized as follows. The first section briefly reviews the history of e-CNY research and development. The second section introduces the key features of DC/EP, compiled from publicly available information. The third section compares DC/EP with other digital currencies such as bitcoin. The fourth section discusses some potential influences of DC/EP, and the final section summarizes the chapter.

CHINA'S CBDC: A BRIEF RETROSPECT

The People's Bank of China (PBC) began to look into digital currency as early as 2014. Zhou Xiaochuan, then the governor of the PBC, was an enthusiastic proponent of CBDC. As an institutional support, the PBC set up the Institute for Digital Currency in 2017.

Research and development of CBDC was sped up in 2019. In July of that year, the State Council officially authorized the research and development of CBDC and designated PBC to take the lead on this project. PBC conducted the work with the help of market institutions, including commercial banks and fintech (short for financial technology) companies such as Tencent and Alibaba. The three major telecommunication companies—China Telecom, China Mobile, and China Unicom—were also involved in the research and development.

In the next few months, discussions about China's CBDC began to heat up and attract more attention. PBC officers began to disclose more information about its research and development. The DC/EP name was officially used in public forums and writings. For example, Mu Changchun, director of the Payment System Department of PBC, announced in a public forum at Yichun, Helongjiang, that China's DC/EP was in an advanced stage and that the product (e-CNY) was "almost ready." Fan Yifei, the vice governor of PBC, also wrote publicly to introduce and promote DC/EP (Fan [2018, 2020a, 2020b]). By official statistics, PBC's Institute for Digital Currency had obtained seventy-four patents by August 21, 2019. Private companies such as Alibaba also obtained patents related to digital currencies.

In the next step, China tested e-CNY by issuing the currency to a relatively large number of users in a contained environment. This was achieved by sending e-CNY to randomly selected residents in cities sponsoring the experiments.

The experiment in Shenzhen, China, took place on October 8, 2019. Ten million worth of e-CNY was sent to 50,000 randomly selected Shenzhen residents, each of whom received 200 yuan. The money could be spent freely at 3,389 offline shops in Shenzhen, and any remaining money would be collected by noon on October 18. The big-four state-owned commercial banks—Industrial and Commercial Bank of China, Agricultural Bank of China, Bank of China, and China Construction Bank—participated in the experiment. To differentiate themselves from each other, the four banks designed their digital wallets in different colors.

A similar experiment was conducted in Suzhou, China, on December 15, 2020. Twenty million in e-CNY was sent to 100,000 randomly selected residents, doubling the size of the experiment in Shenzhen. Unspent e-CNY was collected on December 28. This time, in addition to more than 5,000 offline shops, the money could also be spent on JD.com, a large online digital shop. It also supported offline payments via Bluetooth and Near Field Communication. Two other state-owned commercial banks, Bank of Communications and Postal Savings Bank of China, joined the experiment; thus, the big-six state-owned commercial banks all participated in this experiment. The important role that commercial banks will play in China's e-CNY system will be discussed later.

In these two experiments, 150,000 residents tried a total of 30 million worth of DC/EP in both offline and online shops. Such experiments will help accumulate a large amount of data for further examination. Swedish CBDC (e-Kroner) has also been tested in an isolated environment since March 2020, but the experiments in China appear to be the largest to date.

In retrospect, the year 2020 may well mark the first year of CBDC issuance. Given the potential importance of CBDC, this is a landmark year for human monetary history. In 2020, the world's attention was focused on the COVID-19 pandemic. In a few years, the pandemic will be long over and probably forgotten. However, CBDC will be issued in many countries and will greatly affect the whole financial system. It may well be the case that 2020 is not the year of COVID but the year of CBDC.

WHAT DOES e-CNY LOOK LIKE?

Many important facts about e-CNY have been compiled in official lectures and writings of PBC officers. This section draws heavily on published papers of PBC officers, including (Fan [2018, 2020a, 2020b]), Yao (2018, 2019), and Mu (2019). As we will see, e-CNY is structurally similar to RScoin, proposed by the Bank of England in 2015 (Danezis and Meiklejohn 2015; Broadbent 2016). It is digital cash operated by the existent double-layer banking system.

First, the nature of e-CNY is digital cash. Technically, it is encrypted character strings. Because of the progress made in asymmetric encryption, it is very difficult to decode the encrypts. With careful designs and before further developments are made in computing technology, such encryption can be considered safe in the sense that it cannot be decrypted in a reasonable amount of time.

Monetarily, e-CNY can be considered a digital version of traditional paper cash. Therefore, its final name of e-CNY is a better fit than DC/EP, which was used in earlier stages and is now used to refer to the whole research scheme. By design, e-CNY will replace traditional paper cash. Such replacement will be gradual since a large proportion of people do not use smartphones. This is especially true for older people and people in underdeveloped areas, such as in rural areas or in western China. According to data from the China Internet Network Information Center, there were about 0.9 billion smartphone users by the end of 2019.[1] In other words, about 0.5 billion people in China still do not use smartphones. Fan Yifei, PBC vice governor, confirmed that e-CNY and CNY (traditional Chinese yuan) would coexist for a very long time.[2]

Second, e-CNY is token-based rather than account-based. As mentioned earlier, e-CNY is encrypted character strings. Therefore, it has to be stored in a smartphone app, which naturally can be linked to an account. However, the token can be separated from the account in the sense that independent character strings can be examined and accepted (or denied) by another smartphone. This is especially useful when both phones are offline (i.e., not connected to the internet). This feature is also referred to as semi-account-based—that is, it is related to an account but can also be independent of the account.

Third, e-CNY will be distributed and supported by a double-layer operating system, including the central bank as the root and commercial banks as the trunk and branches. The central bank issues the money to commercial banks. Then the commercial banks deal with households, firms, and other entities. When commercial banks get e-CNY from the central bank, they need to deposit 100 percent cash as reserves. In other words, e-CNY will not affect M0 supply directly. Indirectly, M0 may further reduce M0 because faster money circulation and less "cash" are necessary.

According to top PBC officers' public speeches, it is possible that noncommercial banks, such as big fintech companies and telecommunication companies, also participate in distributing e-CNY to the general public. If so, they also need to deposit 100 percent reserves. However, without a banking license, they can only provide payment services. They cannot absorb deposits from the residents or issue loans to firms and households.

This discussion tells us one possible important change after e-CNY is introduced. Traditionally, commercial banks have provided three lines of service: deposits, payment, and loans. After the fast development of third-party payment in recent years, it is clear that payment services can be split out from commercial banks. Actually, deposit services can also be split out from commercial banks. Residents can buy investment services directly from specialized providers such as mutual funds. Loans can be split out as well. Whoever has information about firm credibility can help facilitate loan issuance. In fact, big-tech companies such as Alibaba already play an important role in loan issuance. With the introduction of e-CNY, fund flows will be more precisely recorded and could be made accessible to a wide range of data analysts. Loan issuance can be conducted based more on data analysis and less on local soft information such as personal connections. This may be a bit of a stretch, but I speculate that the future banking business will be quite different from the past.

In addition to the double-layer system, an alternative single-layer system, in which the central bank issues e-CNY directly to residents, has been discussed but was quickly abandoned. Obviously, given the large population of China, the alternative plan is technically very complicated and challenging. It is very difficult to design a system that can satisfy the vast amount of simultaneous resale transactions. For example, on November 11, the date of an annual shopping carnival recently popularized by Alibaba (called Singles Day), the peak transaction volume reaches 544,000 per second. The OceanBase system of Alibaba can support up to 61 million transactions per second. This is just an example of how large resale transaction volume can be. With further economic growth, urbanization, and digitization, future transaction volume can be much bigger. Therefore, it is very difficult to construct a single system to support all the transactions.

In addition to the technical difficulty, a single-layer system has two other shortcomings. First, it distracts the central bank from the central mission of monetary policymaking. In the modern era, central banks have split themselves from daily commercial banking services and specialize in monetary policymaking and financial monitoring. A single-layer system will be a setback on such specialization. Second, a single-layer system also directly exposes the central bank to any unknown risks e-CNY may bring. As a brand-new and potentially potent instrument, e-CNY may have unforeseeable bugs and problems that could pose significant risks if they spread into the whole monetary system. A double-layer system helps eliminate or at least reduces the risks. In an emergency, a firewall can be set up.

Fourth, e-CNY will not be blockchain based at issuance but is technology neutral in distribution. With the help of bitcoin and other cryptocurrencies, the merit of blockchain technology is widely recognized. In the core, blockchain is a distributed ledger technology (DLT) that is decentralized, traceable, and un-rewritable. Such a technology can build trust among unfamiliar parties. Such trust is obtained at the cost of redundant computations and storage, which makes it unsuitable for resale transactions. Therefore, e-CNY cannot be based on blockchain at issuance. It is simply not technically feasible. It is also not necessary. Central banks, commercial banks, and other big-tech companies are not strangers but creditworthy players in the modern economy. Their credit can be used to replace part of the redundant computing and storage.

However, when distributing e-CNY into the monetary system, commercial banks and big-tech companies can choose to use any technology, including blockchain. This is similar to existing stablecoins such as Tether (USDT) and USD Coin (USDC). It is also similar to Libra, a new stablecoin proposed by Facebook.

The virtue of such a design is twofold. First, the central bank can specialize in money issuance and central data management. Second, the double-layer system can introduce competition among commercial institutions and promote technological progress. Whichever institution has a better technology can grasp a larger share in this future important market.

HOW DOES e-CNY COMPARE WITH OTHER DIGITAL INSTRUMENTS?

When people talk about digital payments in China, they are usually referring to Alipay, WeChat Pay, stablecoins, or cryptocurrencies. e-CNY is a new species in the family. A comparison of e-CNY and other digital instruments reveals three important differences.

First, e-CNY is issued by the central bank. Therefore, it is the official currency supported by governmental laws. By law, all residents must accept e-CNY as a legal form of payment when they have the equipment. On October 23, 2020, the PBC published the revision plan of Act of People's Bank of China. In this revision, digital currency will be officially included in legal forms of payment, together with traditional paper cash and coins. After the revision, people cannot refuse to accept e-CNY if they have the facilities.

In comparison, other forms of digital currency, including Alipay and WeChat Pay, are not official currencies. Therefore, people can choose not to accept them. Strictly speaking, Alipay and WeChat Pay are not currencies but third-party payment facilities.

Tech-based cryptocurrencies such as bitcoin are not issued by the central bank or other government agencies. They are produced by an algorithm operated by an internet community. Since the government cannot control its supply, a cryptocurrency will necessarily compete with the government for the privilege of money issuance. This is why many governments do not welcome tech-based cryptocurrencies. As long as modern social life is still organized around state governments, the space of tech-based cryptocurrencies will be limited. Here I use the term *tech-based cryptocurrencies* to refer to cryptocurrencies not issued by central banks. Familiar examples include bitcoin, Litecoin, and Ethereum.

Second, e-CNY supports offline transactions. In contrast, all other digital currencies and third-party payment instruments require both transaction parties to be online. Offline transactions are supported by Bluetooth and Near Field Communication technologies. Nowadays most smartphones have these functions. In the future, offline transactions may account for only a small percentage of all transactions. However, this function is still necessary because e-CNY is an official currency; therefore, it must consider rare scenarios in which people do not have an internet signal or the signal is of low quality. It should also be noted that offline transactions will probably be limited to small-value transactions for reasons of convenience as well as to prevent risk. Finally, although these transactions are offline, the information can still be uploaded and recorded when the internet becomes available.

Third, e-CNY supports semi-anonymity. Transaction parties do not need to know the identity of the counterparty. The transaction is secured by the underlying system, which verifies the transaction and prevents the problem of double spending. This process is similar to paper cash verification using verification equipment. In contrast, tech-based cryptocurrencies often support total anonymity. In fact, one reason bitcoin and other encrypted currencies have become popular is that they offer total anonymity, although it is possible to detect the real identities of the transaction parties.

Semi-anonymity is quite different from total anonymity: in the former, anonymity is only between transaction parties; the parties are not anonymous to the central bank. Technically, the central bank can trace all transactions and store all the data in its clearing system. Even offline transactions are recorded in the database. By using this database, all transactions of all parties can be monitored and realized. It is not yet clear how the data will be used. Ideally, rules about data accessibility can be set up to protect transaction privacy as well as maximize the value from the data resource. Otherwise, it will be either a tremendous risk or a tremendous waste.

It is also helpful to compare e-CNY with other countries' CBDCs. As mentioned earlier, many central banks have engaged in research, experimentation, or development of CBDCs, including the Federal Reserve of the United States, the Bank of England, the European Central Bank, the Bank of Japan, and the Bank of Canada. The main difference between e-CNY and these CBDCs is that e-CNY is not based on DLT or blockchain. PBC explained that DLT cannot satisfy the vast amount of simultaneous retail transactions in China. DLT may be more appropriate in a smaller economy or in particular scenarios.

Among these CBDCs in discussion, the closest to e-CNY is the RScoin, proposed by the Bank of England in 2015 (Danezis and Meiklejohn 2015; Broadbent 2016). RScoin as proposed is also a digital cash operated by the existent double-layer banking system. Interestingly, most CBDCs will adopt a double-layer banking system.

WHAT ARE POSSIBLE INFLUENCES OF e-CNY?

By now we have a relatively clear idea of what e-CNY will look like. Next, this section discusses the possible consequences of the introduction of e-CNY. Here is where people's opinions widely diverge. Some people think that since most payments are already online, the influence of e-CNY will be minor. Some people believe that since Alipay and WeChat Pay are so convenient and user friendly, e-CNY will not be a popular choice. In fact, some people doubt the necessity of e-CNY. At the other extreme, some people think e-CNY will bring about radical changes and even help RMB internationalization. My opinion is somewhere in between. I argue that although e-CNY will not have a visible effect in some areas, its potential effect in other areas could be quite significant and potentially unmeasurable. As to RMB internationalization, I would say its short-term effect is probably quite limited.

First, the effect of e-CNY on resale payments can be somewhat limited. This is because digital payments such as Alipay and WeChat Pay are already prevalent. It is not clear why people would switch to an e-CNY wallet unless it is at least equally user friendly. Otherwise, people will continue to use Alipay and WeChat Pay.

One common misunderstanding is to treat e-CNY as a competitor of third-party payment facilities. In fact, they are more like vertical cooperators than horizontal competitors. The relationship between e-CNY and third-party payment facilities is more like that of US dollar and stablecoins such as USDT. Third-party payment facilities can peg to e-CNY in the same way they peg to paper cash.

Second, e-CNY may have significant effects on financial monitoring and economic policy implementation. This is because all transactions can be traced and recorded in PBC's database. Such a database can be useful in many areas, including anticorruption, anti–money laundering, and anti–tax evasion.

As an example of fighting against corruption, public servants could be required to use e-CNY for all their daily transactions. This requirement could help popularize e-CNY and improve user friendliness. As another example, e-CNY can be used in subsidy distribution. It often happens that subsidies to particular groups, such as low-income and older people, are redirected to other uses or delayed for long periods. With e-CNY, such subsidies can be issued directly to the targeted groups. The after-payment flow of the money can also be monitored and analyzed, possibly leading to the discovery of corruption and fake accounts. Additionally, future monetary and fiscal policies could be better monitored and improved.

Third, the effect of e-CNY on RMB internationalization will be quite minor, at least in the near future. RMB internationalization depends on RMB's acceptability in the international community, especially among neighboring countries and trade partners. e-CNY can help facilitate RMB when it is willingly accepted. Until that time, its role in RMB internationalization will be limited.

History tells us that people are slow to accept a new international currency. For example, the United States has been the world's largest economy since around 1870, but the US dollar did not replace the British pound as the leading international currency until 1945—a gap of seventy-five years. Right now, China's GDP is only about two-thirds that of the United States. Even after China becomes the largest economy, it still has a long way to go before RMB can become a top international currency. Right now, it is unclear what the future international monetary system will look like. I speculate that the US dollar will continue to dominate the international monetary system and serve as the anchor of the international economy for a very long time. The best that RMB can expect is to become a second-tier primary currency, similar to the euro, pound, and Japanese yen. In the short run, gradual acceptance in neighboring economies and trading partners is a reasonable expectation. This can help China's international trade, especially export companies.

SUMMARY

This chapter introduced China's development of CBDC. Since China's CBDC has not been officially launched, a relatively clear picture of what it will look like was compiled from publicly available information. A comparison was made with other digital instruments, and its potential influences were discussed.

The official name of China's CBDC is e-CNY. It is digital cash designed to replace traditional paper cash and coins (M0). It is currently at the stage of contained experiments in selected areas. It will be distributed into the monetary system via a double-layer system with the central bank as the root and commercial banks and big-tech companies as the trunk and branches. It is not blockchain based at issuance but is technology neutral in distribution. Commercial banks and technology companies will play a major role in developing and operating the infrastructure and managing money accounts.

People have been debating the relationship between e-CNY and existing digital payment facilities. They are not competitors but vertical cooperators in monetary services. After the introduction of e-CNY, existing payment facilities can peg to e-CNY as they peg to traditional money. People can choose not to switch to e-CNY. e-CNY can also compete for a market share in electronic payment.

Until the RMB is more widely accepted in the international community, the effect of e-CNY on RMB internationalization will likely be limited in the near future. e-CNY can help RMB internationalization after it is better accepted internationally, but not vice versa.

NOTES

The author thanks colleagues at the Institute of Digital Finance, Peking University—especially Jing Chen, Yiping Huang, and Huixuan Li—for helpful comments and discussions. The author is solely responsible for any errors or inaccuracies.

1. China Internet Network Information Center, *The 45th China Statistical Report on Internet Develoment*, April 29, 2020, http://www.cnnic.net.cn/hlwfzyj/hlwxzbg/hlwtjbg/202004/P020210205505603631479.pdf.
2. People's Bank of China, "The R&D Progress of China's Digital RMB White Paper," July 16, 2021. [In Chinese.] http://www.gov.cn/xinwen/2021-07/16/5625569/files/e944faf39ea34d46a256c2095fefeaab.pdf.

REFERENCES

Böhme, Rainer, Nicolas Christin, Benjamin Edelman, and Taylor Moore. 2015. "Bitcoin: Economics, Technology, and Governance." *Journal of Economic Perspectives* 29 (2): 213–38.
Broadbent, Ben. 2016. "Central Banks and Digital Currencies." Speech at the London School of Economics, March 2.
Danezis, George and Sarah Meiklejohn. 2015. "Centrally Banked Cryptocurrencies." arXiv preprint arXiv:1505.06895.

Fan, Yifei. 2018. "Several Considerations about Central Bank Digital Currencies." In *Digital Currency: A Reader for Leading Cadres*, edited by Ren Zhongwen. [In Chinese.] Beijing: People's Daily Press.

———. 2020a. "About the Policy Implications of e-CNY's Role as M0," *Financial Times*, January 26, 2020.

———. 2020b. "Several Opinions on Digitalization of the Payment Service Industry." Speeches on the Ninth China Payment and Clearing Forum, Beijing, September 24.

Mu, Changchun. 2019. "Fintech Frontier: Libra and Outlook for Digital Currencies." Dedao App, https://www.dedao.cn/course/mlEA1baQN7WKeRBsZyV8L9OgkryvYw.

Yao, Qian. 2018. "Experimental Study on Prototype System of Central Bank Digital Currency." *Journal of Software* 29 (9): 2716–32.

———. 2019. "Central Bank Digital Currency: Optimization of the Currency System and Its Issuance Design." *China Economic Journal* 12 (1): 1–15.

Yermack, David. 2015. "Is Bitcoin a Real Currency? An Economic Appraisal." In *Handbook of Digital Currency*, edited by David Lee Kuo Chuen, 31–43. Waltham, MA: Academic Press.

11

The Implications of Digital Technology for Financial Regulation

QIANQ GONG and YAN SHEN

China has achieved remarkable development in digital finance in recent years. Digital technology has been deeply integrated with financial services and widely applied in many fields, including payment, financing, wealth management, insurance, and settlement. Financial services have become widely available, and the depth and efficiency of the financial system have improved. For instance, WeBank, Mybank, and other online banks operate entirely online and conduct business remotely through mobile terminals, effectively broadening the availability of financial services. Mybank's 3-1-0 loan model means that it takes an applicant less than 3 minutes to fill out an online application and less than 1 second to receive the money once approved, and there is no manual intervention in the whole process. The development of digital finance mainly benefits people who do not have access to traditional financial services. Digital finance plays an increasingly important role in alleviating the financial exclusion of small and medium-size enterprises and low-income residents.

Despite tremendous achievements in the development of digital finance in China, its regulation is still dominated by traditional interim and ex post supervision, making it difficult to guard against new and more complex risks. The development of digital finance thus faces a significant challenge. Huge controversies related to digital finance have involved the collapse of peer-to-peer (P2P) lending companies, initial coin offerings (ICOs) turning out to be Ponzi schemes, leading digital finance companies monopolizing customer data and traffic, principal–agent problems in co-lending, misuse of private customer data, and the cross-border operations of large technology companies causing risk spillovers, to name but a few problems of concern to the general public.

CHALLENGES IN THE DEVELOPMENT OF DIGITAL FINANCE

Significant risks arising in the recent development of digital finance in China include, but are not limited to, the following.

Abrupt Collapse of the P2P Lending Industry

P2P online lending companies were initially positioned as financial information intermediaries, but in reality the vast majority of these companies carried out credit and wealth management business. According to statistics collected by the China Banking Regulatory Commission (CBRC) for 2020, more than 10,000 P2P lending platforms were launched in the past fourteen years, with more than 5,000 operating simultaneously and the annual volume peaking at RMB 3 trillion.[1] However, the bad debt rate was exceptionally high in P2P lending. In 2015, for example, the amount of money involved in the Ezubao case reached 74.568 billion yuan, affecting the welfare of 909,500 people.

Provisions and High Leverage

In loan facilitation, third parties, such as e-commerce platforms and technology companies, rely on big data to act as information intermediaries. The third parties introduce customers with borrowing demands to commercial banks and promise that they themselves can be the guarantor of debts, although they cannot take risks. Once the credit risk appears, it is immediately transmitted to the cooperative banks and leads to systematic financial risk. The highly unequal shares of co-lending allow some unsecured third-party institutions to slacken their risk management. Increased bank leverage also introduces risks to the digital finance industry.

Surge in Financial Fraud under the Guise of Cryptocurrency

A variety of cryptocurrencies have appeared since bitcoin brought wealth to the first cryptocurrency speculators. With terms such as *blockchain* and *artificial intelligence* adding to the excitement, investors have been attracted by the high returns promised by the platform, failing to recognize the Ponzi essence of bitcoin's "borrow new to pay old" scheme and pouring money into the sinkhole of cryptocurrencies. The number of financial fraud cases in the cryptocurrency category is growing exponentially, with the associated loss in China being as high as 13,522 yuan per capita, ranking such fraud first among all types of financial fraud. SpaceChain, PlusToken, and HeroChain are typical scams involving online pyramid schemes under the guise of cryptocurrency.

Loopholes in Customer Privacy Protection

Owing to the lack of clarity in laws and regulations regarding data scales, data boundaries, and data property rights related to digital finance, banking software applications overcollect customer information in an unauthorized manner. Some technology companies use the excuse that "users are willing to trade privacy for convenience" in order to overcollect and abuse corporate and personal data and even use the data for loan collection. Some data are illegally sold on the black market, and some payment software applications and online shopping platforms have privacy loopholes. These loopholes give criminals the opportunity to carry out telecom and internet fraud, causing default among college students and, in extreme cases, their death by suicide, and senior citizens to lose all or part of their savings. In other words, the lack of customer privacy protection has severe social consequences.

China's financial regulatory system is constantly being reformed with the development of digital finance. Since 2015, China's financial regulators have been reforming and improving the regulatory framework to adapt to modern financial markets. Financial institutions are regulated primarily by the CBRC, securities and financial markets by the China Securities Regulatory Commission, and insurance by the China Insurance Regulatory Commission. China's central bank—namely, the People's Bank of China (PBC)— also has important regulatory responsibilities, in addition to its work in formulating and implementing monetary policies. In 2018, the National People's Congress reformed the new regulatory structure by merging the CBRC and the China Insurance Regulatory Commission into the China Banking and Insurance Regulatory Commission to cope with comprehensive financial services created through digital finance innovation. Initially, these regulators seemed to take a wait-and-see attitude toward emerging financial technology innovations; however, they became more cautious about potential risks after the abrupt collapse of the P2P lending industry in China. In November 2018, the Financial Stability and Development Committee was established under the State Council to strengthen the responsibilities of the PBC in macroprudential management and systemic risk prevention. However, the boundaries and responsibilities of financial regulators are ambiguous because digital finance has both technological and financial attributes. Thus, some problems may not be addressed in a timely manner, resulting in significant losses for customers.

ONLINE LENDING SUPERVISION: FROM P2P LENDING TO LOAN FACILITATION

In November 2020, the number of P2P lending platforms operating in China fell to zero, marking the end of China's P2P lending industry after thirteen years of dramatic growth. China's P2P lending industry, which once flourished throughout the nation with nearly 5,000 operating platforms at its peak, had substantial financial risks hidden behind its expansion, such as Ponzi schemes and self-financing. A large number of platforms declared insolvency, and investors suffered heavy losses.

After the first year of China's P2P regulation beginning in 2016, the industry went through a period of in-depth rectification. Many platforms self-regulated their businesses or even left the marketplace, and a few compliant platforms actively sought transformation. For example, PPDai, China's first P2P lending platform, announced that it had completely shut down its P2P lending business and tried to transform into a loan facilitation business. How was China's P2P lending industry regulated? What lessons has the experience had for the development of China's digital finance? What issues and regulatory requirements will online lending face after the transformation of loan assistance? This section answers these questions from the perspective of financial supervision.

Development and Regulation of P2P Lending in China

Zopa, the world's first P2P lending platform, was established in the United Kingdom in 2005. Prosper and LendingClub, the two largest P2P lending platforms in the United States, were then founded in 2006 and 2007. China first established a P2P lending platform, PPDai, in 2008. PPDai preserved the original features of P2P lending—that is, the platform did not directly participate in lending but provided a matching platform for borrowers and lenders, making a profit by charging fees in matching transactions. At that time, P2P lending essentially played the role of an information intermediary.

As the market demand continued to increase, the P2P lending industry in China began to expand at an incredible rate and deviate from its original form. From 2012 to 2015, P2P lending platforms maintained rapid growth. The number of P2P lending platforms peaked at nearly 5,000 nationwide in 2015. However, this rapid growth came with risks. To gain investors' trust and attract more funds to expand their businesses, P2P lending platforms promised to cover all losses in the event of default. This provision was first proposed by Hongling Capital, the platform with the highest trading volume, and it was quickly adopted by other P2P lending platforms and gradually became common practice in the P2P lending industry. However, this rigid redemption commitment had an adverse effect. P2P lending platforms operated funds from investors in a capital pool and conducted rollovers by borrowing short-term assets to make long-term loans, which presented multiple potential risks, including platform self-financing, fund diversion, and the creation of Ponzi schemes. In 2015, Ezubao, a one-year P2P lending platform, was convicted of illegal fundraising for collecting 74.568 billion yuan from more than 909,000 investors. Furthermore, Ezubao's failure fueled panic, the panic quickly became contagious across regions of the P2P lending industry, and supervision was imminent.

Regulation Clampdown. With the insolvency of many P2P lending platforms from 2016 to 2017, a comprehensive regulatory framework for the P2P lending industry was formulated and endorsed. The CBRC and other government departments put in place four regulatory standards and laws for overall qualification, registration, third-party custodianship, and information disclosure. At the end of 2017, regulation authorities had largely completed the 1 + 3 (one standard and three guidelines) regulatory framework, providing an institutional basis for the prudential regulation of China's P2P lending industry.

In August 2016, the CBRC and three ministries jointly drafted "Interim Measures for the Administration of Business Activities of Online Lending Information Intermediations," which officially announced that the P2P lending industry had entered a stage of comprehensive supervision. This law stipulates thirteen business red lines that online lending information intermediaries cannot cross—for example, intermediaries are not allowed to finance themselves directly or in guise, absorb public deposits, pool lenders' funds to establish a fund pool, or lend directly or in guise.

Supervisory actions are ongoing. In November 2016, to further strengthen interim and ex post supervision, the CBRC and the three ministries issued guidelines on the registration and administration of P2P lending platforms, stipulating the application procedures and filing requirements for the registration of new P2P platforms. In February 2017, to prevent the risk of P2P lending platforms misappropriating funds, the CBRC sanctioned guidelines on the custodian policy of P2P lending platforms, which stipulate that funds on P2P platforms should be handed over to commercial banks for separate depository management. In August 2017, to set a standard for the disclosure of information by P2P lending platforms, the CBRC released guidance on the disclosure of information for P2P lending business activities, strengthening the supervision of the disclosure of information by P2P lending platforms to the public and investors and thus better protecting the legitimate interests of investors.

With the implementation of regulatory rules, the P2P lending industry has begun to rectify the accumulated risks. During a trust crisis, many platforms broke out large-scale withdrawals and runs during the rectification period. Most of the platforms were at the end of the road owing to their inability to pay. Since 2016, the number of P2P operating platforms has fallen off a cliff, and no more than 300 remained in 2019. The final historical shutdown of the P2P lending industry was in mid-November 2020, and there are now no P2P platforms in China.

Should Ineffective Regulation Be Held Responsible for the Failure of P2P Lending in China? In revisiting the rise and fall of China's P2P lending platforms, the failure of P2P lending should be attributed to the unsustainable business model of the platforms rather than regulatory policy to some extent. The business model of China's P2P lending industry suffers from at least two flaws.

From the perspective of investors, P2P investors in China seriously deviated from investor suitability requirements. There were few requirements for participation in China's P2P lending platforms, and most of the market investors were therefore individuals. However, lowering the investment threshold is not always a good thing. With the temptation of guarantees promised by many platforms, there was an influx of retail investors with insufficient risk identification and risk-bearing capacity, which was not conducive to a stable lending relationship. From this perspective, China may need to learn from the regulatory approach adopted in the United States. The US Securities Regulatory Commission has strict requirements for the qualification review and registration of P2P investors. The vast majority of investors are therefore institutional investors with far-reaching risk identification and risk-bearing capacity. For individual investors, this can prevent the herd effect of the retail market to a certain extent.

From the perspective of borrowers, imperfect credit information made the risk management capabilities of China's P2P platforms seriously inadequate. Most of China's P2P lending platforms disclosed minimal information about borrowers. Without big data to support risk management, the risk management capability of P2P lending platforms is far inferior to that of traditional financial institutions, such as banks. However, P2P lending platforms bear much higher credit risk. In this case, subprime borrowers can easily take advantage of the loopholes in risk management and pour into the market, but it is difficult for lenders to distinguish prime borrowers from subprime borrowers. Information asymmetry is further magnified, and the platforms inevitably fail to fulfill the promise of rigid payment in the end. Meanwhile, there is the malicious behavior of reverse bank runs on P2P lending platforms. Some borrowers expect the default cost to decline in the future, and so they will take out more loans when there are negative shocks on P2P lending platforms. These borrowers also hope that no one will collect their debts and that they can enjoy a proverbial free lunch when the platforms go bankrupt, which accelerates the collapse of the platforms.

China is not the only example of a nation where P2P lending has declined. In the United States, even the largest P2P lending platform, LendingClub, was accused of conducting illegal lending to manipulate profits. In response,

LendingClub announced the shutdown of its retail P2P lending offerings. A few P2P lending platforms that survived in China turned to loan facilitation, starting their next journey in online lending.

Development and Supervision of the Loan Facilitation Business

Since the entire P2P lending industry began to decline, many digital finance companies with a P2P lending background have poured into the loan facilitation market. Here, loan facilitation refers explicitly to cooperation between commercial banks and third-party institutions (e.g., e-commerce platforms and digital finance companies). The platforms serve as customer traffic portals; rely on big data; and use cloud computing, machine learning, and other means to apply first risk management to the credit applications of customers. Through risk management screening, commercial banks conduct second risk management and decide whether to lend. Some leading platforms with loan funds and licenses provide loans with financial institutions in proportion, which is referred to as co-lending. With the development of internet finance, the demand for funds has increased dramatically. The platforms have rapidly expanded their scales of operation to obtain greater profit margins, and this expansion has introduced many problems.

Risk of Provision. One reason for the rise of loan facilitation is that banks and other financial institutions need to expand their businesses. While third-party institutions have advantages in marketing, information technology, overdue clearing, and other aspects, banks and loan facilitators cooperate directly with each other. Before 2018, in the absence of rigorous regulations, there were many institutions without licenses or secured qualifications in the lending industry. According to P2P Eye Platform, as of November 2017, there were at least 2,000 operating internet financial platforms. However, there are only 249 online microfinance licenses in the industry, which means that more than 87 percent of operating platforms lack online microfinance licenses. Companies without licenses conduct loan business in the name of loan facilitation. What is worse is that many banks prefer making easy and fast money, so loan facilitators usually offer a provision agreement to obtain bank funds easily. This means that the platform pays a deposit to the bank first, and the bank provides ten to twenty times the amount of the loan as leverage for lending.

In reality, most credit facilitators do not have the ability to salvage bad loans. Confronted with bad debts, lending agencies do not have a complete provision system. In pursuing the expansion of the customer pool to obtain traffic, they lower risk management and customer quality standards so that the high reborrowing rate and borrowing from multiple sources make the nonperforming cash loan rate as high as 20–50 percent. Moreover, they use high annual interest rates and overdue penalties to cover the same high ratio of bad debts and platform operating costs. They even resort to violence in collecting debts, which results in serious criminal cases. At the same time, there are situations where customers and lending institutions collude maliciously, using false projects to obtain loan funds from the funder. Even worse, many banks outsource risk management to loan facilitators, which means that the bank does not conduct substantive risk management but becomes a capital channel. Once the credit risk erupts, these risks flow back to banks and generate heavy losses.

In response to the risks posed by provision, the Office of the Leading Group for the Special Campaign against Internet Financial Risks issued a notice on the regulation and rectification of the cash loan business at the end of 2017. The notice highlights that when a banking financial institution cooperates with credit facilitators, it is illegal for the institution to outsource aspects of its core business, such as credit investigation and risk management. Loan facilitation activity should return to the information intermediary, and banking financial institutions should not accept credit enhancement services provided by loan facilitators without guarantee qualifications. To meet these regulatory requirements, loan facilitators seek cooperation with financing guarantee companies or insurance companies, which reduces their profits. However, third-party guarantees cannot always fend off credit risks and salvage bad debts. Loan facilitators thus switch to a profit-sharing model: commercial banks undertake the responsibility of risk management and due diligence, and loan facilitators provide services such as customer recommendation and risk management assistance. The two parties share profits according to a pre-agreed profit-sharing contract. Such a profit-sharing model forces banks to build their own online lending risk management systems, which is beneficial to the long-term development of the financial industry.

Concern about High Leverage. Although the provision problem has been resolved, the problem of high leverage remains imminent. Credit facilitators can often leverage a large proportion of funds from commercial banks with a very small proportion of funds. Taking the example of the originator of co-lending, Weilidai made loans of 3.7 trillion yuan in 2019, but its financial statement shows that the balance of various loans is only 1,629.66 billion yuan, accounting for about 4.4 percent of the amount issued. If the risk management capability of the credit facilitator is insufficient, once the co-lending risks arise, they are ultimately borne by the bank. Additionally, the credit risk caused by excessive leverage is a hidden concern.

Reducing leverage has become a top priority. In November 2020, the China Banking and Insurance Regulatory Commission and PBC issued interim measures for the management of online microfinance businesses. These interim measures significantly reduce the leverage ratio of co-lending and the exposure of commercial banks to credit risk. The measures stipulate that the balance of the funds collected by a small online loan company through bank borrowing, shareholder borrowing, and other nonstandard financing shall not exceed the net assets of the company. The balance of funds received through standard financing forms, such as bond issuance and asset-backed securitization, shall not exceed four times the net assets of the company. In addition, for a single co-lending business, the proportion of the capital contribution of the credit facilitator shall not be less than 30 percent. The measures are expected to contribute to curbing the excessive leverage of loan facilitators, helping loan facilitators adjust the structure of their financing liabilities within the limit of the total amount and regulate their levels of operation and management, which will benefit the sound long-term development of the co-lending industry.

However, it should be noted that because of capital constraints, a credit facilitator may give priority to high-quality customers, which will likely act against the goal of directing inclusive finance toward clients who are not served by traditional commercial banks and small and micro-size enterprises facing financing constraints.

CRYPTOCURRENCY AND FRAUD REGULATION

Satoshi Nakamoto created the genesis block of bitcoin in 2009. The bitcoin price exceeded the US$50,000 mark in March 2021, and bitcoin and its underlying blockchain technology have been highly sought after by investors around the world. The global popularity of bitcoin has led to the rise of many other cryptocurrencies, such as Ether and USDT. However, cryptocurrency fraud is on the rise, and regulation faces unprecedented challenges.

The situation of cryptocurrency fraud is becoming increasingly severe, and such fraud is quickly emptying the wallets of victim investors. According to a survey conducted by the 360 Government & Enterprise Security Group, financial fraud was the most reported type of internet fraud in 2019.[2] Although cryptocurrency-related fraud accounted for only 2.9 percent of financial internet fraud by case number, the per capita loss of cryptocurrency fraud reached 13,522 yuan, ranking it the highest among all types of financial fraud. Among cases that have been filed or solved, BHB, HeroChain, PlusToken, and WoToken have been implicated in fraud exceeding a total of 100 million yuan and huge individual scams of up to 40 billion yuan. The number of cryptocurrency-related fraud cases has doubled year after year.

According to China Judgements Online, the number of judicial documents involving cryptocurrency has increased over the years, from 167 in 2015 to 1,480 in 2020 (as shown in figure 11-1). The massive amount of cryptocurrency fraud and the rapid growth of criminal cases have highlighted enormous risks that regulatory authorities cannot ignore.

FIGURE 11-1. **Number of Judicial Documents Involving Cryptocurrency in China, 2015–2020**

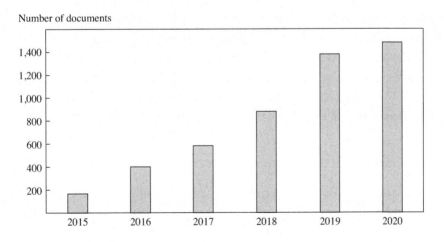

Source: China Judgements Online, https://wenshu.court.gov.cn.

Regulation 1.0: Cryptocurrencies Are Not Fiat Money

As early as 2013, regulatory authorities in China began keeping a close eye on criminal activities relating to bitcoin transactions. To protect the public's property rights, on December 5, 2013, the PBC, together with five ministries and departments, released a notice on guarding against bitcoin risks. The notice states that bitcoin does not have the legal attributes of a fiat currency and should not be used as fiat currency in the market.

The notice marks the beginning of China's cryptocurrency regulation. At present, the primary functions of the supervisory agency are to guide the public to properly understand the nonmonetary attributes of bitcoin and other cryptocurrencies and to prevent financial institutions and payment structures from conducting bitcoin-related business. Although the notice points out that it is necessary to strengthen the management of internet sites that provide services such as bitcoin registration and transactions, and that such sites should be registered with the telecommunications management agency, the overall regulatory attitude remains neutral, and only illegal bitcoin internet sites will be closed.

ICO activities are not forbidden. With the price of bitcoin continuing to hit record highs, every newly created cryptocurrency seems to be the next opportunity to get rich overnight. An ICO has quickly become a popular financing channel with flexible regulatory policy. Regulatory loopholes and the invisible nature of cryptocurrencies worsen the hidden hazard risks and information asymmetry between financiers and investors. A typical case is SpaceChain, an ICO project that claimed to apply blockchain technology to space, cloaking its claim in scientific terms such as *quantum* and *satellite*. SpaceChain quickly financed about 1 billion yuan in one day. Later, the media reported that SpaceChain had distorted its promotion and modified its ICO white paper, and the truth about its financial fraud emerged, leaving investors with significant losses.

Regulation 2.0: Ban on Domestic ICO Activities

In the face of the prevailing trend of financial fraud related to ICO activities, the PBC, together with six ministries and departments, released "Announcement on Preventing the Financing Risks of Initial Coin Offerings." The announcement states that no organization or individual in China may engage in ICO activities, and no financial institution or nonbank payment institution may conduct business related to an ICO. The announcement marks the second stage of China's cryptocurrency regulation.

Compared with Regulation 1.0, there are two critical differences in the second stage of supervision. First, the regulatory agency clearly defined the essential attributes of an ICO. An ICO is defined as unauthorized and illegal public financing behavior and is suspected of the illicit sale of tokens, illegal issuance of securities, illegal fundraising, financial fraud, pyramid schemes, and other criminal activities.

Second, all platforms that provide services such as cryptocurrency exchange and pricing and act as information intermediaries in China are ordered to shut down. It is worth noting that although this stage of regulation stops ICO activities in China, it does not prohibit the public from investing in cryptocurrency. Although regulators have warned the public of the potential risks, investors are responsible for investment losses.

Because of the ban on domestic ICO activities, some cryptocurrency-related platforms have moved overseas and continue to engage in fraud in a more deceptive manner. For example, PlusToken, a platform operating in China, South Korea, Japan, and other countries, claimed to offer arbitrage opportunities through different cryptocurrency exchange platforms. However, this was just a gimmick to attract users' funds; there was no such service on the platform. The platform promised to offer attractive rewards to users who recommended other users to join the platform. The more users they referred, the more compensation they would get. In this way, PlusToken developed multilevel marketing and illegally raised more than 40 billion yuan. PlusToken is not the only example; WoToken, BeeBank, Interesting Walking Chain, HeroChain, and other so-called blockchain-based programs are pyramid schemes in nature. In summary, although ICOs are now banned, there remains much cryptocurrency-related fraud owing to the public's inability to identify risk.

Regulation 3.0: Investor Education Has a Long Way to Go

In response to pyramid schemes (illegal fundraising under the guise of cryptocurrency), regulation not only stepped up law enforcement but also emphasized investor education and risk warning. In August 2018, the CBRC, together with five ministries and departments, released "Risk Warning on

Illegal Fundraising in the Guise of Cryptocurrency and Blockchain Technology."

Compared with the previous stages of regulation, the most important feature of Regulation 3.0 is the greatly strengthened guidance and education of investors, to guard against illegal fundraising, pyramid schemes, and fraud. Regulation 3.0 also clearly reminds investors that such fraudulent activities are networked, cross-border, and deceptive.

It should be noted that two new departments, the Ministry of Public Security and the General Administration of Market Supervision and Regulation, were added as issuing authorities for this regulation. This addition signals that as cryptocurrency fraud has become more violent in nature, relying solely on the supervision of administrative departments cannot effectively curb all kinds of illegal activity. It is imperative to strengthen the interventions and investigations of public security departments.

Summary and Outlook

China's supervision of cryptocurrency has gone through three main stages. Supervision has switched from the cryptocurrency business to the issuance and financing of tokens, and finally to investor education to prevent financial fraud under the guise of cryptocurrency. Although cryptocurrency is not a security recognized in China, suspected cryptocurrency-related activities may violate criminal law, such as illegal issuance of tokens, illegal issuance of securities, illegal fundraising, financial fraud, and other crimes. The Prevention and Disposal of Illegal Fund Raising act went into effect in May 2021, further strengthening the supervision of illegal fundraising activities related to cryptocurrency. Future regulations will put more effort into ex ante warnings and the investigation of cryptocurrency-related fraud and safeguarding the public's legitimate rights and interests.

BIG-DATA CREDIT AND PRIVACY PROTECTION

Digitized information and decisionmaking have had wide application in the financial era, driving the transformation and optimization of the operating logic and mode of financial businesses. The core strength of digital finance companies over traditional financial institutions is "know your customer"— that is, digital finance companies have a better understanding of consumer preferences and the underlying potential consumer pool. However, behind the digital information, there are great challenges in the protection of customer privacy.

Data Abuse and Infringement of Customers' Rights and Interests

Some digital finance enterprises purposely generate user portraits without the users' authorization and sell a product or service by conducting big-data analysis and inducing consumption using the customized user portraits. This behavior severely infringes on consumers' right to know, right to choose, and privacy. Some companies have multidomain businesses, relying on channel advantages and the accumulation of many users on e-commerce, social, and gaming platforms to control the flow entrance and develop a data monopoly. They also overharvest consumer information through hidden overlord terms. The Luohan Academy found that the longer customers used software applications, the more requests they received for permission to use their sensitive information; many users reported being forced to accept overlord terms.[3]

Data Theft under the Guise of Credit Investigation

Another challenge to privacy protection is data theft and the sale of these data on the black market under the guise of offering big-data credit. Digital finance companies overcollect consumer behavior trace data and associated derivative data. They even use crawler technology to illegally piece together sensitive information, such as phone numbers, addresses, photographs, and work information of users and their relatives and friends from various websites, and sell that information to multiple companies. Criminals use private information for telecom and internet fraud, swindling the elderly out of their pension money and pushing college students into the bottomless pit of student loans, leading to death by suicide of some students.

A Hot Potato: Privacy Protection

In 2015, the PBC issued "The Notice of Preparing for the Business of Personal Credit Investigation," commanding Sesame Credit, Tencent Credit,

Koala Credit, and five other institutions to prepare for individual credit investigations. One of the first credit management companies, Koala Credit divulged its users' credit ratings and specific information to cooperative online lending institutions for profit, shifting from being a state-approved credit management agency to being an online credit intermediary platform. What's more, Koala Credit's partners were of varying quality, including not only licensed institutions such as Beijing Bank Consumer Finance Co., Ltd.'s "Easy Loan" and Shanghai PPDAI Financial Information Services Co., Ltd.'s "Quick Loan" but also private P2P lending platforms that were without qualification. As of November 2019, the number of Koala Credit users exceeded 200 million. To improve their credit ratings (in the form of Koala Points), these users applied for loans and verified their ID cards, uploaded live identification videos, and provided real-name mobile phone numbers, call records, address books, real estate information, provident fund and social security information, credit card information, and much personal information. Using web crawlers, credit management agencies can further collect core privacy information, such as utility bill payments and personal tax payments.

Koala Credit used user information for credit management and provided "information reselling" and "ID card inquiry" services. The personal data of users who needed loans were resold to third-party online microloan companies, including Usury and Tricky Loan. Once a loan was overdue, the resold personal information was an essential resource for forcible debt collection. According to the police investigation, from March 2015 to November 2019, Koala Credit illegally provided results for 98 million "ID card inquiries," earning 38 million yuan, and illegally obtained and stored the names, ID card numbers, and photographs of nearly 100 million citizens. Behind credit management agencies like Koala Credit, dozens of data brokers buy and resell user information, ultimately eroding privacy. To avoid the severe consequences of the lax supervision of the "ID card inquiry" service, which led to the leakage of a large amount of user information, the National Citizen ID Card Number Inquiry service center closed down its "ID card inquiry" service, shifting to an "identity verification + facial recognition" service so that the credit platform no longer had the opportunity to cache the ID card information of citizens.

In addition to the case of Koala Credit, 51 Credit Card, an internet finance company listed in Hong Kong, was punished by the courts for the illegal crawling of its users' e-mail messages, obtaining users' card information through its cooperative bank, providing users' information held by other banks to its cooperative bank, and revealing the private information of users having overdue payments to debt collection companies. In 2018, when the supervision of big-data credit was not yet complete, the big-data risk management system of 51 Credit Card had mastered nearly 10,000 variables of more than twenty dimensions, working with more than one hundred institutions, including banks, consumer finance companies, and trust companies. Later in 2019, its immoral behavior of stealing and selling customer information was exposed: 460,000 credit card customer profiles were sold for less than US$1,000, and data on 900,000 financial users were sold at a low price of US$3,999. Although the chief executive officer of 51 Credit Card claimed that the company did not take information without the user's authorization, this exposure caused financial customers to worry about the security of their privacy and to distrust the new financial platform.

The situation is even worse when the stolen privacy data of customers become the source of financial fraud. After obtaining data from the black market, criminals take advantage of security loopholes at large banks, on shopping platforms, and on mobile payment applications to further grab user information, steal money, apply for online loans, and commit online fraud. Because fraudsters have access to detailed privacy information and the data of customers and can even synthesize voice and image data from live authenticated videos taken from various platforms, individuals often relax their vigilance and fall into traps. According to a report released by 360 DigiTech and 360 Group, 38 percent of the victims lost 10,000–50,000 yuan, and 11 percent lost more than 50,000 yuan in financial fraud resulting from information leaks.[4] There is an urgent need for relevant departments to pay attention to this new type of contactless financial fraud.

Overhaul of Privacy Protection and International Comparisons

The ebb and flow of big-data credit reflect the gradual improvement of relevant laws on the privacy protection of Chinese financial consumers. The Cybersecurity Law of the People's Republic of China was promulgated in November 2016. It stipulates that network operators shall not divulge, tamper with, or corrupt the personal information they collect, and personal information shall not be provided to others without the consent of the person. However, the difficulty in defining the ownership of derivative data unrelated to transactions in the Cybersecurity Law allows financial institutions and internet companies to overcollect and resell data. This limitation enabled cases such as Koala Credit and 51 Credit Card.

In June 2019, the PBC, in cooperation with the Ministry of Public Security, launched a campaign against the abuse and theft of data. More than 468 million personal information items and more than 94 million yuan were seized within six months. Managers and technical staff at 51 Credit Card, Koala Credit, and other big-data credit platforms were arrested and jailed. After the prosecution of these platforms, many investors anticipated that regulators would implement comprehensive and strict personal privacy protection. As a result, the stock prices of almost all digital finance companies, whose business focused on personal credit management services and loan intermediaries, fell sharply. This negative effect even spread to WEI and Hexindai, both listed in the United States.

In terms of privacy protection, China could learn much from the experiences of other countries. In May 2018, the European Consumer Protection Organization took Google, Facebook, Instagram, and WhatsApp to court, accusing them of violating the General Data Protection Regulation by forcing users to accept privacy data authorizations that invade consumer privacy. In July 2020, the European Court of Justice ruled that the European and American Privacy Shield signed in 2016 was not valid and banned all overseas transfers of European Union user data stored by digital finance companies, such as Google, Facebook, and Amazon.

Summary and Outlook

China has built the world's largest primary database of financial credit information.[5] Strengthening financial data protection is essential for ensuring customers' information security, safeguarding the rights and interests of users, and maintaining financial stability, as well as for governance and rectification of the financial sector. In recent years, incidents of large-scale personal information leaks from internet financial and credit industry giants have triggered user doubts about the security of digital finance. Therefore, regulatory authorities should clarify the supervision requirements of credit information protection, define ownership of data rights and interests, establish and improve the regulatory technology system, and strengthen coordination with other countries. Digital finance companies should be configured to "know you but not know who you are" by minimizing data collection, limiting unnecessary flows, encrypting or desensitizing data, and being alert to the security and stability of the internal system in guarding against the theft of customer information and fraud. Furthermore, financial fraud is common and results from the leakage and theft of private data, affecting even high-level knowledge groups, such as doctors and university professors, and causing tremendous losses. Therefore, regulatory authorities should conduct intensive education to protect the privacy of financial customers and draw public attention to the prevention of financial fraud.

REGULATORY INNOVATION IN CHINA'S DEVELOPMENT OF DIGITAL FINANCE

Developing an incentive-compatible regulatory framework that balances innovation in digital finance and risk prevention will help sustain development of digital finance. With the rapid development of digital finance, financial services have been promoted in the fields of operation and management, but new risks and supervisory challenges have emerged. Financial regulators thus need to strike a balance between encouraging innovation in digital finance and guarding against risks so that financial risks are controlled and there is enough room for innovation. These considerations place more stringent requirements for effectiveness and accuracy on the regulatory framework in the era of digital finance. Thus, the innovation of the regulatory model is the focus of the work of regulatory authorities. A regulatory sandbox framework, with an effective risk compensation and screening mechanism, not only screens and punishes unscrupulous enterprises that engage in fake innovation but also provides a trial-and-error evaluation tool for risky but real innovation. Regulatory sandbox frameworks have been increasingly adopted around the world for their remarkable ability to promote innovation and enhance market efficiency.

Function of a Regulatory Sandbox Framework

A regulatory sandbox framework was first put into practice by the UK Financial Conduct Authority. The agency defines a regulatory sandbox as "a 'safe space' in which businesses can test innovative products, services, business models, and delivery mechanisms without immediately incurring all the normal regulatory consequences of engaging in the activity in question"[6] The regulatory sandbox provides a scaled-down market with relaxed regulations and specific exemptions and allows regulators to rapidly respond to the problem that emerging financial products and services may not meet all regulatory requirements.

A regulatory sandbox framework addresses the ex ante regulation for entry, supervision during testing, and ex post regulation for evaluation. Compared with traditional regulation, the regulatory sandbox framework usually sets up a flexible entry barrier, which helps applicants implement their innovation program as soon as possible. Supervision during the test helps regulators understand, predict, and react quickly to potential risks. Companies offer new products and services to real consumers in the sandbox, and the test results can thus be used to assess the feasibility of innovative products and the integrated capabilities of the digital finance business. If the test fails, the promotion is terminated, thus avoiding the loss of more consumers in the overall market; if the test is successful, the innovative product may be allowed to launch.

Chinese Version of the Regulatory Sandbox Framework

At the stage of digital finance development, it is essential to implement the regulatory sandbox framework. We will discuss the current situation of the regulatory sandbox framework and the perspective of the situation in China, and then provide a comparison with the international situation.

Necessity of Implementing the Regulatory Sandbox Framework. With the rapid development of digital finance, China is already at the forefront of many digital finance fields. China has also experienced the complete collapse of the P2P lending industry, an event that has rarely happened in major economies. Suppose that the regulatory authorities take the wait-and-see approach to evolving digital finance; in this case, the advantages that China already has may become risks, which calls for immediate action to explore a proper regulatory framework that takes precautions against risks and facilitates the growth of the digital finance industry. Furthermore, China's current financial regulatory rules are mainly based on single and ex post supervision, and an effective ex ante regulatory mechanism has not yet been created to respond to digital finance innovation. This situation warrants a change to cope with new risks brought by the digital finance industry, such as cross-border, disintermediation, and decentralization risks.

Feasibility of Implementing a Regulatory Sandbox Framework. Sandbox supervision is a valuable supplement to the existing supervision system. It solves problems of financial technology development that the current supervision system cannot solve, such as the institutional mistakes of mixed operation and separate supervision. Sandbox supervision is being implemented in China as a pilot test rather than an overall break from the previous system, which is in line with the road map of China's reform and opening-up policies. The experience of managing the regulatory sandbox can be used to improve the design of the mechanism for subsequent regulation reform.

Current Situation of Regulatory Sandbox Practice. China has made progress in reforming its financial regulations. In July 2019, the deployment of China's regulatory sandbox in ten provinces and cities was formally proposed at the 4th Global Digital Finance (Beijing) Summit. As of December 2020, China's digital finance innovation regulatory pilot will take place in nine areas (Beijing, Shanghai, Chongqing, Shenzhen, the Xiong'an New Area, Hangzhou, Suzhou, Guangzhou, and Chengdu) and involve sixty innovation projects. Half of these programs relate to financial services and the other half to technology products, largely those of financial institutions and technology companies. Pilot programs include financing services for micro-size, small, and medium-size enterprises based on a multiparty security graph; intelligent supply chain financing services based on artificial intelligence; blockchain-based financial and government data fusion products; and digital risk management products of industrial finance.

Mechanism Design of the Chinese Version of a Regulatory Sandbox. Based on China's current situation and international experience, the design of its regulatory sandbox mechanism can be improved in five ways. First, the State Council Financial Stability and Development Committee should take the lead, and the PBC should be responsible for setting up a regulatory sandbox framework that can be implemented by the CBRC and the China Securities Regulatory Commission. Second, the five-step process of application, entry, midterm assessment, withdrawal decision, and out-of-sandbox evaluation should be adopted to achieve timely and dynamic regulation with interaction between the regulator and the innovator. Third, there should be clear guidelines and strict access at the sandbox access stage, but access should be granted to nonlicensed financial institutions. Fourth, the multilevel sandbox management tool should be put in place to give programs proper incentives during the sandbox testing period. Fifth, after testing, the program should be organized to get a license or exit the sandbox.

Moreover, regulatory sandboxes are encouraged to coordinate with the risk characteristics of programs. When the intensity of regulation is low, the sandbox cannot effectively screen real innovation from fake innovation, leading to many fake innovation programs entering the market and harming the interests of investors. When the intensity of regulation is too high, the profits of genuine innovations cannot cover the costs of compliance, which is not conducive to facilitating innovation activities. Therefore, regulatory technology (regtech) should be introduced into regulatory sandbox practice to adjust in a timely manner the optimal regulation intensity according to changes in the market environment.

International Comparison of Digital Finance Regulatory Sandboxes

Currently, the United Kingdom, Singapore, Australia, the United States, Canada, Japan, Hong Kong, and other countries and regions are actively promoting digital finance innovation and controlling innovation risk through the use of regulatory sandboxes. As of March 2021, about fifty countries and territories had explored regulatory sandboxes.

From the perspective of tolerating disruptive innovation, the United States has adopted a prudent strategy, whereas most countries, including the United Kingdom and Singapore, have adopted a proactive strategy. The United States believes that digital finance should be regulated at least as rigorously as formal finance. As both the United Kingdom and Singapore are regional financial centers with established financial systems and rich experience in financial development, their regulatory authorities have taken the initiative to create sandboxes for regulatory strategy and technology and to encourage financial start-ups to begin sandbox testing. The aim of these countries is to continue to maintain and uphold their positions as financial centers, leading a new era of digital finance development. In the United Kingdom, for example, most applications to use the first two sandboxes were submitted by start-ups younger than three years, and most of the start-ups were still in their financing stage. Some enterprises' products (such as those of Nimbla and Laka) are not yet officially available but are still filtered into the sandbox for experimentation. China's current regulatory sandbox design is not as radical as Britain's proactive strategy and is more tolerant of innovation than the United States' prudent strategy. China's sandbox is rapidly advancing the innovation of digital finance in pilot areas.

POSSIBLE APPROACHES TO FUTURE REGULATORY REFORM

The approach to regulatory reform will be discussed from the perspective of the professional functions of regulatory agencies, regulatory technology, and local governments' overall supervision.

Innovation Hubs

An innovation hub represents a regulator's professional function, in that it allows data sharing with innovative financial service providers and offers service providers an elaboration and explanation of the regulatory system to promote innovation. At the same time, regulators may use innovation hubs to develop appropriate regulatory policies. The United Kingdom has much experience with innovation hubs, with the Financial Conduct Authority encouraging industry experts to provide advice at hundreds of conferences, such as roundtable events and symposia, to obtain valuable information with which to establish relevant policy strategies and make systematic process changes. Additionally, national and regional financial regulators, including those of Singapore, Australia, Japan, and Hong Kong, have launched innovation hubs and digital finance contact points. Furthermore, in July 2019, the Bank for International Settlements announced the establishment of an innovation center that fosters cooperation among the central banks of member countries in the area of innovative financial technologies to improve the functioning of the global financial system.

Regtech

Regtech effectively solves regulatory compliance requirements and improves data collection and management capabilities, warning systems, supervision in an event, post-surveillance, and other aspects that have application value. For example, the Australian Securities and Investment Commission developed a market analysis and intelligence system to extract real-time data from stock and derivative transactions, monitor anomalies, and provide real-time early warnings. China's regulatory authorities should follow the pace of digital finance development and establish and improve the regulatory technology system to realize professionalism, unity, and the good penetration of financial regulation. Technically, regulatory departments can use the technologies of multiparty security computing, trusted blockchains, and tagging to ensure that data are recordable and usable but invisible, thus realizing dynamic and effective regulation, intelligent analysis, and sound decision-making while protecting the rights and interests of all parties.

Supervision Coordinated by Local Governments

With the rapid development of digital finance, many offline businesses have transferred to being online, offering P2P lending, crowdfunding, and other services. Online sales channels no longer depend on physical outlets. Thus, local digital finance companies can operate nationwide, which poses great challenges to territorial supervision. Moreover, regional financial offices usually lack financial talent. Meanwhile, the administrative functions of local financial offices should be strengthened, and the offices should be encouraged to cooperate with local public security departments to carry out anti–financial fraud tasks. In the case of imperfections in the legal system, consumers should be warned of the risks and their antifraud awareness should be strengthened in a timely manner through education to improve the coverage and efficiency of financial innovation regulation.

SUMMARY AND OUTLOOK

In November 2020, the Shanghai Stock Exchange announced the postponement of Ant Group's listing of A-shares and Hong Kong stocks. The suspension of the initial public offering of the world's largest digital finance company is undoubtedly a milestone in the development and regulation of digital finance in China and even the world. Although China is already at the forefront of many digital finance fields, its regulatory process is not always smooth. The difficulties range from frequent collapses of P2P lending companies and financial fraud under the guise of cryptocurrency to abuses of digital finance companies and the privacy crisis triggered by reselling data. This series of risks calls for the guidance of financial regulation to shoulder the development of digital finance in a healthy and orderly way.

This chapter focused on typical cases and regulations of online lending, cryptocurrency, and financial privacy protection in the development of digital finance in China. Furthermore, there is concern about the industrial monopolies of large digital finance companies in terms of data, traffic, and markets. In the second quarter of 2020, Alipay and WeChat Pay (TenPay) accounted for 55.39 and 38.47 percent, respectively, of China's third-party mobile payment market and for about 94 percent of the industry combined. The two digital finance giants have been in dispute for a long time. During the Spring Festival of 2015, WeChat blocked red envelopes, links, and requests associated with Alipay. These behaviors have sparked a debate on whether large digital finance companies have abused their dominant market positions. To maintain a fair market competition order, regulators have started to pay close attention to issues such as winner-takes-all and restrictive competition among digital finance giants and have put antimonopoly supervision measures in place. This has led to a more competitive industry pattern. As new participants emerging in third-party payment, Duoduo Wallet and Douyin Payment have been launched, and large internet companies such as ByteDance and Kuaishou have cooperated with third-party institutions. These new entrants might improve competitiveness and boost the development of digital finance in China.

The essence of future digital finance regulation is to fully unleash innovation in digital finance while preventing and defusing risks quickly and effectively. Innovative regulatory tools represented by the sandbox can provide a reasonably relaxed environment for the development of digital finance and guard against risks relating to the uncertainty of digital finance as part of ex ante, in-process, and ex post supervision. A number of cities in China have carried out pilot regulatory work on digital finance innovation, and an increasing number of projects are applying to participate in the Chinese regulatory sandbox. At the same time, regulators are actively embracing regulatory tools empowered by advanced digital technologies to balance development promotion and risk management and facilitate the development of digital finance.

NOTES

1. Guo Shuqing, "Fintech Development, Challenges and Regulation." Speech at the Singapore Fintech Festival, December 8, 2020, http://www.pbc.gov.cn/goutong jiaoliu/113456/113469/4140486/index.html.

2. 360 Government & Enterprise Security Group, *Research Report on Internet Fraud Trends in 2019*, January 7, 2020, https://110.360.cn/index/newsInfo?id=141 &src=warn.

3. "A Data Trade-Off Derby: Consumers vs. Sellers - Spoiler Alert, It's a Tie." Luohan Academy, January 3, 2020, https://www.luohanacademy.com/frontiers/A -Data-Trade-Off-Derby:-Consumers-vs.-Sellers---Spoiler-Alert,-It%E2%80%99s-a -Tie.

4. 360 Government & Enterprise Security Group, *Research Report on Internet Fraud Trends in 2019*.

5. The Credit Reference Center, the People's Bank of China, "Overview," http://www.pbccrc.org.cn/crc/zxgk/index_list_list.shtml (accessed December 2021).

6. "Regulatory Sandbox." Financial Conduct Authority, November 2015, https://www.fca.org.uk/publication/research/regulatory-sandbox.pdf.

12

The Implications of New Financial Technologies for the International Monetary System

ESWAR PRASAD

The international monetary system is the conglomeration of individual countries' financial markets and currencies, and the connections—exchange rates between currencies and capital flows among countries—that bind them, along with various rules of the game that countries have agreed to and that are refereed by international institutions such as the International Monetary Fund and the Bank for International Settlements.

There are a number of concerns about the existing state of this system. International commerce is hindered by costly and inefficient payment systems. Some types of financial flows across national borders often generate far more problems than benefits for the recipient countries. Emerging market economies (EMEs) feel that the rules of the game are rigged in favor of the advanced economies, which dominate international rulemaking bodies and the major multilateral institutions.

The US dollar is by far the dominant international currency in all respects—as a unit of account, medium of exchange, and store of value. The dollar's overwhelming dominance, and the absence of any serious competition to this dominance, gives the United States outsize influence. In 1960, the United States accounted for about 40 percent of global GDP (at market exchange rates). By 2000, this share was down to 30 percent. In the two decades since then, as China, India, and other emerging markets have made enormous strides, this share has fallen farther, to 24 percent. The dollar's role in global finance, and with it US influence on global financial markets, is far greater than its weight in the global economy.

Much of the world sees this as an undesirable situation, with good reason. The fact that so much of international trade and finance is intermediated through the dollar leaves other countries, especially smaller and developing ones, at the mercy of the dollar and the policies of the United States. It means, for instance, that fluctuations in the dollar's value and actions taken by the Federal Reserve affect other economies, sometimes in undesirable ways. For instance, when the Fed cuts interest rates, money often flows out of US financial markets and into EMEs in search of better returns, which may fuel undesirable booms in their stock markets and other asset markets. When the dollar appreciates against other currencies, either because of the Fed raising rates or because of other reasons, capital tends to flow out of those economies and into dollar assets, often putting downward pressure on those countries' stock markets and currencies. To the chagrin of policymakers around the world, the Fed considers only domestic factors when making its policy decisions. For the most part, it ignores the effects of its policies on other countries, as this is not part of its official mandate.

This is just a sampling of the many distortions and imbalances in the workings of the international monetary system. Will fintech (short for *financial technology*), central bank digital currencies (CBDCs), and other new financial technologies pave the way to improvements or, perhaps, even more fundamental changes?

New financial technologies are engendering changes to the forms and uses of national monies, as well as to different aspects of financial markets and institutions. This has led to some speculation that such forces will foster a reshaping of the international monetary system, particularly the balance of power among currencies.

INTERNATIONAL PAYMENTS

Fintech innovations and digital currencies offer the promise of faster, cheaper, and more secure international payments. This would mark a substantial improvement for settlement of trade-related transactions as well as remittances. Even cross-border settlement of other types of financial transactions could benefit from these developments. Distributed ledger technologies (DLTs) offer the potential for reliable tracking of different stages of trade and financial transactions, reducing one of the frictions associated with such transactions. Will all of these innovations displace traditional financial institutions or simply lead to better ways of doing business? There are some elements of the international payment system that are ripe for disruptive change.

The transfer of funds across institutions in different countries is now intermediated through SWIFT, the Society for Worldwide Interbank Financial Telecommunication. SWIFT does not actually transfer funds; rather, it provides a financial messaging service that connects more than 11,000 financial institutions in virtually every country in the world through a common messaging protocol. SWIFT faces competition from alternative international payment messaging systems that offer similar services at a lower cost. SWIFT's major advantage over potential competitors is that it has become a widely accepted and trusted protocol, but this might not be sufficient for a durable business model. Indeed, many countries such as China and Russia are setting up their own payment systems to reduce their reliance on foreign ones and to serve as a gateway to a new international payment system. In other words, such countries could conceivably link their individual payment systems, routing bilateral international transactions through these systems rather than relying on SWIFT and the institutions that use it for messaging.

SWIFT faces technical challenges as well. The system passes payments through a number of nodes, slowing down the transaction process. Cryptocurrencies and other payment systems that use DLTs might bypass the need for routing through multiple nodes. Moreover, vexed by the system's vulnerability to US pressure, many central banks, including the European Central Bank, have been studying the potential for expanding the interoperability of digital currencies for cross-border trade. The central banks of Canada, Singapore, Hong Kong, and Thailand are also exploring new initiatives to process cross-border transactions without SWIFT.

A number of countries have begun developing alternatives to SWIFT and international payment systems that rely on its messaging services. In some cases, this ties in with broader national interests. China's Cross-Border Interbank Payment System (CIPS), which commenced operations in 2015, offers clearing and settlement services for cross-border payments in renminbi. CIPS has the capacity to easily integrate with other national payment systems, which could help in promoting international use of the renminbi by making it easier to use the currency for cross-border payments. CIPS currently uses SWIFT as its main messaging channel, but it could eventually serve as a more comprehensive system that includes messaging services using an alternative protocol. CIPS has adopted the latest internationally accepted message standard (ISO 20022) and also allows for messages to be transmitted in either Chinese or English, with a standardization system that allows for easy translations between the two.

New financial technologies are likely to speed up the disruption of existing international messaging and payment systems. The days of SWIFT's uncontested dominance of international payment messaging are numbered, which could have knock-on effects on the dollar's dominance of international payments. Admittedly, the ability of new payment messaging systems to ensure security and to be scaled up to handle large volumes, while staying on the right side of domestic and international regulations, is not yet assured and could take some years to come to fruition. Still, the confluence between the rapidity with which payment technologies are evolving and the desire of much of the world to break free of the dollar-dominated financial system could hasten these changes.

Given the extensive frictions that beset international payments, it is certainly a plausible proposition that stablecoins such as Libra (recently renamed as Diem) could gain traction as media of exchange that supplement, but do not supplant, existing payment currencies. However, it is unlikely that such stablecoins would represent alternative stores of value. Indeed, the allure of stablecoins is precisely that their value is tightly linked to existing reserve currencies in which savers and investors around the world are willing to place their trust. In short, the emergence of stablecoins linked to existing reserve currencies will reduce direct demand for those currencies for international payments but will not in any fundamental way transform the relative balance of power among the major reserve currencies.

Mark Carney, the former governor of the Bank of England, has proposed the creation of a synthetic hegemonic currency that would be "provided by the public sector, perhaps through a network of central bank digital currencies" (2019). He depicted this currency as taking the form of an invoicing and payment currency whose widespread use could eventually lead central banks, investors, and financial market participants to perceive the currencies that compose its basket as reliable reserve assets, thereby displacing the dollar's dominance in international trade and finance, including in credit markets. However, it seems unlikely that there is enough of a consensus at the global level on the desirability of such a currency, which could make it harder to get it off the ground.

VEHICLE CURRENCIES

Will the proliferation of new payment systems affect the role that major international currencies play in intermediating international trade? Such "vehicle currencies" as the US dollar play an important role in international trade as they serve as widely accepted units of account (for denominating trade and financial transactions) and as media of exchange (for making payments to settle those transactions). The US dollar is the dominant vehicle currency, with a few others, such as the euro, the British pound sterling, and the Japanese yen, also playing this role.

As EMEs grow larger and as their financial markets develop, the costs of trading their currencies for other emerging market currencies is likely to decline. New financial technologies that make international payments quicker and easier to track will also play a role. Risks arising from exchange rate volatility are mitigated if a payment for a trade transaction can be settled instantaneously rather than over a matter of days, which is typically the case now. A longer-term and perhaps less likely outcome is the emergence of cryptocurrencies, or at least decentralized payment systems, that function as media of exchange in international transactions. These forces, to varying extents, will diminish reliance on vehicle currencies.

Changes in international payment systems that allow for faster payment and settlement will shorten the periods over which exchange rate movements need to be hedged. For financial transactions that have short horizons, there could be material decreases in hedging requirements and the associated costs. In some cases, instantaneous payment and settlement of transactions can remove the risks to revenues from short-term exchange rate volatility even without involving the costs of hedging.

For the foreseeable future, exchange rates of each country's currency relative to those of their trading partners as well as major currencies that serve as units of account and media of exchange will remain important in the functioning of the international monetary system. In short, while new financial technologies could over time influence the relative importance of different currencies in the denomination and settlement of cross-border transactions, the basic mechanics of foreign exchange markets are unlikely to be significantly altered.

A GLOBAL MARKET FOR FINANCIAL CAPITAL

The great promise of financial globalization was that it would allow capital to be allocated to its most productive uses worldwide. This would benefit firms looking to finance their investments and working capital requirements as they would no longer be constrained by domestic savings. It would also give savers the ability to invest in financial markets around the world.

Fintech firms could in principle help foreign investors assess risk better and also create channels for directly investing in productive firms, bypassing creaky domestic financial systems. Fintech is unlikely to change the fundamental drivers of global capital flows, but by reducing explicit and covert barriers to such flows, it could influence the allocation of global capital. This could eventually set off a new wave of financial globalization that could generate a number of benefits—even if it did not mean a return to the same scale of cross-border flows as in their recent heyday.

Significant changes are in store for retail investors as well. Fintech firms might eventually make it possible for retail investors to allocate part of their portfolios to stock markets around the world at a low cost. In many advanced countries, one can already do this simply by buying shares in a mutual fund that invests abroad. Such funds typically charge higher fees than funds that invest in domestic stocks and bonds. New investment platforms are likely to lead to lower costs, forcing even existing investment management firms to reduce their fees.

Fintech firms are reducing the costs of both getting information about foreign markets and investing in those markets. Moreover, new investment opportunities are also being opened up by technologies that allow for more efficient pooling of small savings amounts of individual households into larger pools that can be deployed more effectively.

One of the next frontiers in the fintech evolution is likely to be the intermediation of capital flows at the retail level, enabling less wealthy households and smaller firms in both rich and poor economies to gain access to global financial markets more easily. Diversifying one's portfolio should become easier as stock markets around the world open up to foreign investors and as the costs of transacting across national boundaries fall. Fintech firms that help overcome information barriers, reduce costs and other frictions in international capital movements, and create new savings and financial products are likely to experience significant demand for their services. Of course, as with any financial innovation, there will be risks and stumbles in this process, and financial regulators will face the usual trade-offs between facilitating innovations and managing those risks. In fact, the capital flows themselves pose risks not just to individual investors but also at the country level.

While greater financial integration has numerous potential benefits, these come at a price, especially for smaller and less developed economies. This group is particularly vulnerable to whiplash effects from volatile capital flows, with this volatility caused in part by monetary policy actions of the major advanced economies. New and relatively friction-free channels for cross-border financial flows could exacerbate these "spillover" effects across economies. These new channels could not only amplify financial market volatility but also transmit it more rapidly across countries. In other words, the availability of more efficient conduits for cross-border capital flows could intensify global financial cycles and all the domestic policy complications that result from them.

Developments in financial markets and new technologies threaten to undermine whatever capital controls are still in place. While governments around the world try to limit the use of cryptocurrencies for purposes such as avoiding capital controls or more nefarious aims, it is unclear if and how long such measures will remain in effect in the face of strong economic incentives for capital flows. For instance, despite China's crackdown on bitcoin trading, one research firm estimated that nearly US$50 billion worth of cryptocurrency moved from China-based digital addresses to overseas addresses between July 2019 and June 2020, with at least part of these flows representing capital flight.[1] And it is not just private cryptocurrencies that provide conduits for evasion of capital controls.

It is clear that both official and private channels for cross-border capital flows are expanding. Official channels—such as the cross-border payment system that the central banks of Canada, Singapore, and the United Kingdom have been collaborating on—will make such flows easier while allowing governments to modulate these flows and reduce the risk of illegitimate financial activity. Private channels, on the other hand, could become increasingly difficult to monitor and manage, especially if they are created and used by informal financial institutions that will be harder to regulate.

The existence of a privately issued currency that is recognized and accepted worldwide, such as Diem, would also affect the ability of governments to control capital flows across their borders. If money can be moved electronically, without going through any financial institutions run by a nation's regulatory agencies, it becomes difficult for that government to control inflows and outflows of financial capital in any meaningful way.

CURRENCY COMPETITION

The dollar's dominance in the global financial system has given the United States enormous financial and geopolitical power that hurts its rivals and rankles even its allies. The uncomfortable reality that other countries face is that the preeminence of the dollar makes it difficult for them to avoid the dollar-based financial system.

The demand for bitcoin as a store of value rather than a medium of exchange has stoked discussion about whether such cryptocurrencies could challenge that role of traditional reserve currencies. It is more likely that, as the underlying technologies become more stable and better verification mechanisms are developed, such decentralized cryptocurrencies will start playing a bigger role as media of exchange. Even that proposition is a tenuous one given the high levels of price volatility experienced by such currencies recently. Nevertheless, this shift could occur over time as the payment functions of cryptocurrencies take precedence over speculative interest in them, especially if private stablecoins gain more traction.

The decline in transaction costs and easier settlement of transactions across currency pairs could have a more direct and immediate impact: a decline in the role of the US dollar as a vehicle currency. The dollar's role as a unit of account is also subject to erosion. It is hardly a stretch to conceive of the denomination and settlement of contracts for oil and other commodities in other currencies, perhaps even emerging market currencies such as the renminbi. Indeed, China's purchases of oil from Saudi Arabia are reportedly now increasingly being contracted for and settled in renminbi. China has started issuing yuan-denominated oil futures as a way of shifting more of the financial transactions related to oil purchases and sales, including in derivatives markets, away from the dollar. Such developments are important but should be kept in proper perspective. While the very existence of yuan-denominated oil derivative contracts is a noteworthy development, this is a far cry from such contracts playing a major role in global markets.

Notwithstanding any such changes, the role of reserve currencies as stores of value is not likely to be affected. Safe financial assets—assets that are perceived as maintaining most of their principal value even in terms of extreme national or global financial stress—have many attributes that cannot be matched by nonofficial cryptocurrencies.

One important characteristic of a store of value currency is *depth*. That is, there should be a large quantity of financial assets denominated in that currency so that both official investors (such as central banks) and private investors can easily acquire those assets. There is a vast amount of US Treasury securities, not to mention other dollar-denominated assets, that foreign investors can easily acquire. Another characteristic that is important for a store of value is its *liquidity*. That is, it should be possible to easily trade the asset even in large quantities. An investor should be able to count on there being enough buyers and sellers reliably on both sides of the market to facilitate such trading, even in difficult circumstances.

For an aspiring safe-haven currency, depth and liquidity of the relevant financial instruments denominated in that currency are indispensable. More important, both domestic and foreign investors tend to place their trust in such currencies during times of financial crisis since they are backed by a powerful institutional framework. The elements of such a framework include an institutionalized system of checks and balances, the rule of law, and a trusted central bank. These elements provide a security blanket to investors that the value of those investments will be largely protected and that investors, both domestic and foreign, will be treated fairly.

While reserve currencies might not be challenged as stores of value, digital versions of extant reserve currencies and improved cross-border transaction channels could intensify competition among reserve currencies themselves. In short, the finance-related technological developments that are on the horizon portend some changes to domestic and international financial markets, but a revolution in the international monetary system is not quite in the cards for the foreseeable future.

Given the extensive frictions in international payments, it is certainly plausible that stablecoins could gain traction as media of exchange that supplement, but do not supplant, existing payment currencies. However, it is unlikely that such stablecoins would present alternative stores of value. Indeed, the allure of stablecoins is precisely that their value is tightly linked to existing reserve currencies that savers and investors around the world are willing to place their trust in. In short, the emergence of stablecoins linked to existing reserve currencies will reduce the direct demand for those currencies for international payments but will not in any fundamental way transform the relative balance of power among the major reserve currencies.

WILL CHINA'S e-CNY PROMOTE THE RENMINBI'S INTERNATIONAL ROLE?

The renminbi made a dramatic move onto the global financial stage after 2010, when the Chinese government started opening up China's capital account and promoting its currency through a variety of policy measures. In 2016, the International Monetary Fund gave the renminbi its official seal of approval as a reserve currency by including it in the Special Drawing Rights basket of currencies, potentially adding momentum to the renminbi's progress toward becoming an international payment currency.

The renminbi has since come to be a modest player in international finance, now accounting for about 1.9 percent of global payments intermediated through the SWIFT network (as of July 2020). As with other measures of the renminbi's role as an international currency, this represents a decline after a rapid rise from just 0.3 percent in 2010 to 2.8 percent in 2015. Other indicators such as renminbi deposits in Hong Kong and the offshore issuance of renminbi-denominated bonds (dim sum bonds), both of which were on a rapidly rising trajectory in the first half of this decade, have fallen off sharply since 2015.

The renminbi now accounts for 2 percent of global foreign exchange reserves, an important but still modest fraction. Nevertheless, even these modest shares rank the renminbi fifth worldwide as an international payment currency and as a reserve currency. The currencies ahead of the renminbi are the dollar, the euro, the Japanese yen, and the British pound sterling. The renminbi and the Canadian dollar share the fifth rank in both respects.

Is China's CBDC—the e-CNY—likely to be a game changer in the renminbi's putative rivalry with the dollar or, more generally, in its status as a reserve currency?[2] In some respects, especially in the technological sophistication of its retail payment systems, China has managed to leapfrog the United States. And since China's CBDC is likely to be in operation before those of other major economies, it is plausible that the e-CNY will give the renminbi a boost in the tussle for global financial market dominance.

In the short run, the e-CNY will only be usable for payments within China, as the People's Bank of China has restricted its use abroad. This restriction is likely to be eased over time as the government becomes more comfortable with controlling its digital currency. The e-CNY, in tandem with China's cross-border payment system, will eventually make it easier to use the currency for international transactions. Russia—or for that matter, Iran and Venezuela—may find it easier to get paid in renminbi for its oil exports to China. This means it can avoid US financial sanctions, a tempting prospect for many such governments. As the renminbi becomes more widely used, other smaller and developing countries that have strong trade and financial links with China may find it advantageous to invoice and settle their trade transactions directly in that currency.

However, the e-CNY by itself will make little or no difference as to whether foreign investors see the renminbi as a reserve currency. That will depend more on the Chinese government's policies related to capital account liberalization and exchange rate flexibility. For reserve managers and other foreign investors, the breadth, depth, and liquidity of China's financial markets, especially fixed-income markets, will be a key factor.

In short, the e-CNY is likely to help promote the role of the renminbi as an international payment currency. But it will hardly put a dent in the dollar's status as the dominant global reserve currency.

MONETARY POLICY TRANSMISSION

The effective transmission of monetary policy to economic activity might seem to be of more relevance for domestic monetary management. But effective monetary management also has cross-border implications. New financial technologies could affect monetary policy transmission in both direct and indirect ways.

Consider, for instance, that a number of banks and consortiums of banks are exploring the use of DLTs for bilateral settlement of clearing balances without going through a trusted intermediary such as the central bank. DLTs in principle make it easier to track and verify transactions. If all participants in a closed pool can monitor such activities and if there is a permanent indelible transaction record that is tamper-proof, they may be able to use group monitoring as an alternative for a trusted central counterparty.

Will such developments dilute the ability of the central bank to affect interest rates in the economy through its control of very short-term policy interest rates (such as the discount rate and the Fed funds rate in the United States)? This gets to the crux of the question about whether central banks can maintain their influence over aggregate demand and inflation even if they are sidelined from some of their traditional roles—issuing (outside) money and providing payment and settlement services for major financial institutions.

If banks and other major financial institutions do create such payment and settlement mechanisms among themselves (both bilaterally and across members of the group) and are also able to more effectively manage their liquidity positions and overnight balances, then settlement and liquidity management through the central bank might play a less important role. Of course, the ability to observe such transactions (or even to observe that such transactions are taking place between certain participants in the system) conveys important information that banks might not want to reveal to their competitors. Thus, competitive forces might limit the use of DLTs as an alternative for a trusted third party such as a central bank to provide settlement services while maintaining the confidentiality of those transactions. In short, significant technological as well as conceptual hurdles will need to be overcome before commercial banks sideline the central bank.

If these challenges are overcome, one possibility is that the central bank eventually becomes a liquidity provider of last resort in times of crisis; otherwise, commercial banks will route their settlement and liquidity management operations through direct channels among themselves. Of course, through other tools such as open market operations, a central bank can still implement monetary policy.

A related issue is whether nonbank and informal financial institutions are less sensitive to policy interest rate changes than traditional commercial banks. If these institutions do not rely on wholesale funding and have other ways of intermediating between savers and borrowers, then the central bank might face significant challenges to the effectiveness of monetary policy transmission. This might prove to be a long-term challenge for advanced economies if and when the relative importance of traditional commercial banks declines, although in developing economies informal financial institutions already play a significant role. Despite the proliferation of nonbank financial institutions and more direct intermediation channels, it is far from obvious that these can be scaled up such that they displace (rather than erode the prominence of) commercial banks. The relative sensitivity of the nonbank financial sector to changes in policy interest rates and other operational tools of monetary policy needs further study as the structures of financial systems undergo changes that could significantly affect the implementation and transmission of monetary policy.

CONCLUSION

New and evolving financial technologies, including the advent of cryptocurrencies and CBDC, will have implications for certain aspects of the international monetary system, but these are not likely to be revolutionary and will be realized only over a number of years. Some changes could occur earlier, although their effects on global finance will mostly be limited to the structures of financial markets themselves rather than any fundamental reordering of the international monetary system.

More efficient payment systems will bring a host of benefits. For example, economic migrants will be able to send remittances back to their home countries more easily, and it will be easier for investors with modest savings to diversify their portfolios and seek higher returns through better access to international investment opportunities. In principle, financial capital will be able to flow more smoothly within and across countries to the most productive investment opportunities, raising global economic welfare—at least as measured by GDP and consumption possibilities. But with capital flows across national borders becoming easier, many countries will also face risks related to the volatility of those flows and the complications that it creates for managing their exchange rates and economies. New channels for transmitting payments across borders more quickly and cheaply will likely make it more difficult to regulate and control capital flows. The resulting challenges will be especially thorny for EMEs and other small, open economies.

The landscape of global reserve currencies may seem to be at the threshold of disruption as cryptocurrencies gain traction as media of exchange and stores of value. In reality, the proliferation of cryptocurrencies will not have a substantial disruptive effect on the major reserve currencies, especially the

US dollar. Unbacked cryptocurrencies are much too volatile to be considered stable sources of value or reliable media of exchange. On the other hand, stablecoins backed by major corporations such as Amazon and Facebook are likely to gain traction as means of payment. But since their stable values are on account of their being backed by fiat currencies, stablecoins are unlikely to become independent stores of value.

Smaller and less developed economies could face greater challenges. National currencies issued by their central banks could lose ground to private stablecoins and perhaps also to CBDCs issued by the major economies.

A digital renminbi will help the currency gain traction as a payment currency, but the digitization of the currency by itself will do little to boost its status as a reserve currency. The renminbi's further rise, even if gradual and modest, and the advent of more stablecoins could reduce the importance of the second-tier reserve currencies, including the euro, British pound sterling, Japanese yen, and Swiss franc. But the dollar's dominance among global fiat currencies will remain unchallenged, especially because other major currencies could see even greater erosion in their prominence as media of exchange and safe havens.

NOTES

1. "East Asia: Pro Traders and Stablecoins Drive World's Biggest Cryptocurrency Market," *Chainalysis* (blog), August 20, 2020, https://blog.chainalysis.com /reports/east-asia-cryptocurrency-market-2020. The report notes that the stablecoin Tether, whose value is pegged to the US dollar, has become a popular cryptocurrency in China and other parts of East Asia.

2. The e-CNY is the payment component of a larger project called Digital Currency/Electronic Payment, which was initiated a few years ago.

BIBLIOGRAPHY

Bank of Canada, European Central Bank, Bank of Japan, Sveriges Riksbank, Swiss National Bank, Bank of England, Board of Governors of the Federal Reserve, and Bank for International Settlements. 2020. *Central Bank Digital Currencies: Foundational Principles and Core Features.* Basel, Switzerland: Bank for International Settlements. BIS, www.bis.org/publ/othp33.pdf.

Bank of England. 2020. "Central Bank Digital Currency: Opportunities, Challenges and Design." Discussion Paper, www.bankofengland.co.uk/-/media/boe/files /paper/2020/central-bank-digital-currency-opportunities-challenges-and -design.pdf.

Carney, Mark. 2019. "The Growing Challenges for Monetary Policy in the Current International Monetary and Financial System." Speech at the Jackson Hole Symposium, Federal Reserve Bank of Kansas City, August 23.

Li, Shiyun, and Yiping Huang. 2021. "The Genesis, Design, and Implications of China's Central Bank Digital Currency." *China Economic Journal* 14 (1): 67–77.

Libra Association Members. 2019. "An Introduction to Libra." White Paper, https://libra.org/en-US/white-paper/.

Mancini-Griffoli, Tommaso, Maria Soledad Martinez Peria, Itai Agur, John Kiff, Adina Popescu, and Celine Rochon. 2018. "Casting Light on Central Bank Digital Currency." IMF Staff Discussion Note, SDN 18/08, November. Washington: International Monetary Fund.

Prasad, Eswar S. 2014. *The Dollar Trap: How the U.S. Dollar Tightened Its Grip on Global Finance.* Princeton, NJ: Princeton University Press.

———. 2016. *Gaining Currency: The Rise of the Renminbi.* New York: Oxford University Press.

———. 2021. *The Future of Money: How the Digital Revolution Is Transforming Currencies and Finance.* Cambridge, MA: Harvard University Press.

Wong, Paul, and Jesse Leigh Maniff. 2020. "Comparing Means of Payment: What Role for a Central Bank Digital Currency?" FEDS Notes, August 13. Washington: Board of Governors of the Federal Reserve System.

13

International Cooperation in and Regulation of Fintech Development

DAVID DOLLAR

Fintech (short for *financial technology*) is defined as the use of computer programs and internet technology to support or enable banking and financial services, including payments. It is particularly associated with the development of mobile payments in China. In the last ten years, China has leapfrogged magnetic cards and moved to a payments system based on smartphones and Quick Response (QR) codes. Network externalities have facilitated the explosive growth of two private companies: Alipay, working via Alibaba, and WeChat Pay, linked with Tencent. China accounts for 40 percent of global e-commerce transactions, larger than the combined value of France, Germany, Japan, the United Kingdom, and the United States (Woetzel and others 2017). The value of China's mobile payments in 2016 totaled $790 billion, eleven times that of the United States, the next largest market.

The rapid expansion of fintech, particularly in a few countries but more generally around the world, raises various issues of international cooperation and regulation. This chapter focuses on three issues in particular. First, there is the relatively straightforward sharing of information and experiences across countries, facilitated by the International Monetary Fund (IMF), the Bank for International Settlements (BIS), and other groupings. Given the explosive growth of mobile payments and digital currencies, central banks are trying to get out ahead of this issue with their own digital currencies.

Numerous different experiments are occurring, particularly with the issuance of central bank digital currencies (CBDCs), and it is valuable for these agencies to share information as they proceed. This aspect of cooperation, which is working well, is discussed in the first section of the chapter.

Second, there is the more contentious area of regulating aspects of fintech, especially cross-border data flows. China, the United States, and the European Union are each developing different approaches to regulation of trade in digital services, which risks creating a bifurcated (or trifurcated) landscape. The second section of the chapter examines the three different approaches and the potential for compromise leading to a unified system. The third issue is the use of fintech to make cross-border payments. This is the holy grail of fintech—a world of easy transfer of payments globally to facilitate trade, travel, remittances, and investment. However, the obstacles to widespread use of fintech in cross-border payments are large, and resolution of these problems is probably far off. For the moment, payments generally go through the traditional banking routes with the associated delays and costs.

SHARING OF INTERNATIONAL EXPERIENCES

The rapid development of fintech in China has caught the eye of central banks and regulators around the world. Payment clearance through commercial companies, sidestepping the banking system, has proved cost-effective and inclusive, as households without bank accounts are able to move away from unwieldy cash to electronic payments using smartphones and QR codes. (Strictly speaking, one does not need a smartphone to participate: even homeless individuals in China have QR code printouts that they can use to receive donations and then use at virtually all merchants.)

Another motivating factor for central banks is the emergence of cryptocurrencies and stablecoins issued by private firms. Cryptocurrencies are created through distributed ledger blockchain technology. Initially bitcoin and its imitators held out hope for a currency outside official manipulation and control. However, in practice the prices of cryptocurrencies have been extremely volatile, making them unsuitable for traditional currency functions and more akin to a highly speculative investment. During 2021 the price of bitcoin soared above $60,000, then fell by one-half (figure 13-1). Such a volatile instrument is clearly not suited as a means of payment for ordinary transactions.

FIGURE 13-1. **Price of Bitcoin, 2013–2021**

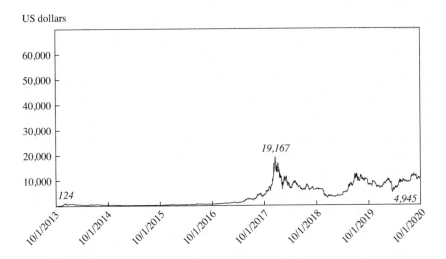

US dollars

Source: coindesk.com.

The idea of stablecoins, as the name suggests, was to avoid this volatility and to tie the value of a crypto instrument to an anchor such as the US dollar or gold. While the prices of the main stablecoins have been relatively stable, they have nevertheless not been truly stable (for example, the price of one popular coin fell to 50 cents). The underlying problem is that market participants cannot easily verify whether a stablecoin is in fact fully backed by gold or dollars or some other type of anchor. Hence, the drive to develop CBDC aims to meet the demand for digital currency while addressing the weaknesses of these other approaches.

One of the first proposed stablecoins was Libra, introduced by Facebook and supported by an association registered in Switzerland. The evolution of the concept of Libra over time illustrates the problems with stablecoins. The initial idea of Libra was to create a kind of money tied to the value of a basket of currencies that could be used for payments globally. It would be a digital asset built by Facebook and powered by a new Facebook-created version of blockchain, the encrypted technology used by bitcoin and other cryptocurrencies. The Libra Association was described by Facebook as an independent, not-for-profit organization based in Switzerland. It would serve three main functions: validate transactions on the Libra blockchain, manage the reserve that Libra is tied to, and allocate funds to social causes. Libra would be used in conjunction with Calibra, a digital wallet that would allow users to send Libra to anyone with a smartphone. It would be available in Messenger and WhatsApp and as a standalone app (Paul 2019).

Mark Carney, former Bank of England governor, said that if Facebook succeeded in its aims, Libra would instantly become systemic and would have to be subject to the highest standards of regulation. The Libra concept brings with it a range of financial-crime concerns, from hacking to tax evasion. But at the top of the list is money laundering. (Before traditional lenders open accounts for customers, they must undertake rigorous background checks to ensure funds are not ill-gotten gains. By comparison, Facebook's original plan allowed for "pseudonymous" users able to create multiple accounts not based on their real-life identity.) In response to pushback from regulators, the Libra Association came out with a new white paper in April 2020 with four key changes: Libra would (1) introduce single-currency coins, in addition to the multicurrency version; (2) operate within a robust compliance system (i.e., it would not operate outside the existing financial regulatory framework); (3) forgo the transition to a permissionless system; and (4) build strong protections into the design of the Libra Reserve (Helms 2020b).

Regulators' concerns were crystallized in an October 2020 G-7 statement affirming that "no global stablecoin project should begin operation until it adequately addresses relevant legal, regulatory, and oversight requirements through appropriate design and by adhering to applicable standards." While the G-7's statement refers to "global stablecoin projects," in this case it was aimed in particular at Facebook's Libra project. The implication of the G-7 statement is that regulators would be open to stablecoins that can fit within one regulatory and monetary policy regime. In this regard, the statement is a positive development for CBDCs (and for well-crafted single-currency stablecoins) that can launch via regulated entities. Libra's biggest barrier to launching has been its underestimation of the multijurisdiction regulatory challenge and its lack of collaboration with the global regulatory community in general (McDonald 2020).

In December 2020, the Libra concept was rebranded as Diem. Along with the change in the name of the stablecoin comes the downgrading of the entire project: Diem is shifting its operations to the United States and will partner with Silvergate, a San Francisco–based bank, to focus on launching a single coin backed one for one by the dollar instead of a basket of mainstream currencies, as originally proposed. The project has dropped its application to the Swiss Financial Market Supervisory Authority to operate as a payments service and will instead apply to register as a money services business with the US Treasury, scaling back its global vision. The project is supported by twenty-six businesses and nonprofits, but a number of its founding members—including PayPal, Mastercard, Vodafone, and eBay—quit in late 2019 and early 2020 over fears of monetary stability and reputational concerns. The newly renamed Diem Association issued a white paper outlining its plan to develop a blockchain-based payment system that facilitates the real-time transfer of Diem stablecoins among approved network participants, called the Diem Payment Network (Diem Association, 2020).

In this context, it seems clear that the main reason central banks are looking into the possibility of issuing their own digital currencies is because they are afraid that the private sector will get out ahead of them and drive sovereign currencies out of the market. While exploring CBDC, central banks have so far been cautious about introducing digital currency because the banking system has a vested interest in remaining an intermediary for payments clearance. The central bank could lose control of the money supply and monetary policy, and financial risks could develop in a poorly regulated part of the nonbank system. These concerns have spurred central banks to consider how the issuance of CBDC could potentially provide the benefits of rapid clearance while addressing its issues and risks.

According to the IMF, nearly fifty jurisdictions were considering introducing retail CBDC as of mid-2020 (table 13-1). CBDC is a digital representation of a sovereign currency issued by a central bank and appearing as a liability on its balance sheet. Some of the experiments with CBDC are in fairly advanced stages of implementation. The same study indicates a variety of objectives for these programs and is worth quoting at length:

1. CBDC could enhance payment system competition, efficiency, and resilience in the face of increasing concentration in the hands of a few very large companies.

2. CBDC may be a means to support financial digitization, reduce costs associated with issuing and managing physical cash, and improve financial inclusion, especially in countries with underdeveloped financial systems and many unbanked citizens.

TABLE 13-1. Countries Where Retail CBDC Is Being Explored (as of May 27, 2020)

Countries where central banks are in the advanced stages of retail CBDC exploration	
Bahamas (pilot launched)	Sweden (proof of concept started)
China (pilot launched)	Ukraine (pilot completed)
Eastern Caribbean (pilot launched)	Uruguay (pilot completed)
South Africa	

Countries where central banks are exploring issuing retail CBDC	
Australia	Jamaica
Brazil	Japan
Canada	Korea
Chile	Mauritius
Curacao and St. Maarten	Morocco
Denmark	New Zealand
Ecuador	Norway
Euro Area	Russia
Finland	Switzerland
Ghana	Trinidad and Tobago
Hong Kong SAR	Tunisia
Iceland	Turkey
India	United Kingdom
Indonesia	United States
Israel	

Countries where central banks are exploring issuing CBDC (according to media, unconfirmed by central banks)	
Bahrain	Lebanon
Egypt	Pakistan
Haiti	Palestine
Iran	Philippines
Kazakhstan	Rwanda

Source: IMF (2020).

3. CBDC could improve monetary policy effectiveness to implement targeted policy, or to tap more granular payment flow data to enhance macroeconomic projections.

4. An interest-bearing CBDC could enhance the transmission of monetary policy, by increasing the economy's response to changes in the policy rate. Such a CBDC could be used to break the "zero lower bound" on policy rates to the extent cash were made costly.

5. CBDC would also help reduce or prevent the adoption of privately issued currencies, which may threaten monetary sovereignty and financial stability, and be difficult to supervise and regulate.

6. CBDC could help improve traction of local currency as means of payments in jurisdictions attempting to reduce dollarization.

7. CBDC could play a role in distributing fiscal stimulus to unbanked and other recipients. (Kiff and others 2020)

Central banks that are exploring CBDC issuance are struggling with a common set of fundamental design choices. These include determining the operating model, whether to use a centralized or decentralized platform, whether to pay interest, and privacy considerations. These design decisions are influenced by country-specific characteristics and must balance CBDC policy objectives with the imperative that CBDC be attractive to consumers and merchants. CBDC demand will ultimately be shaped by the level and trend of cash usage in a specific country, and incentives for stakeholders, including end users and merchants. While access to CBDC might become more convenient than withdrawing cash from an ATM, that would only make CBDC another type of bank debit card (Khiaonarong and Humphrey 2019). If CBDC is not interest-bearing, the only incentive to use it is the convenience of access and ease of use compared with cash. Cost sharing and interoperability arrangements for point-of sale terminals could incentivize merchants to accept CBDC for the purchase of their products or services. Hence, CBDC demand may be weak in countries where cash usage is already very low, owing to a preference for cash substitutes (cards, electronic money, mobile phone payments). Where cash usage is high, demand for CBDC could be stronger, owing to a lack of cash substitutes. In other words, in a country like China, where cash usage is low and mobile phone payments via Alipay

and WeChat Pay are common, getting users to shift to CBDC may be difficult. The same may be true of advanced economies like the United States,
where credit card usage is widespread. When China piloted its CBDC, the
central bank did not allow nonbank payment providers like Alipay and
WeChat Pay to use CBDC. Instead, the currency had to be held at a commercial bank. It remains to be seen whether there will be much take-up of the
instrument.

While China's CBDC pilot is at an early stage, it has already demonstrated
one of the potential benefits. One district in Shenzhen, a city in Guangdong
Province, piloted the CBDC by giving out 200 yuan "red envelopes" through
a random draw. Winners of the lottery can download an app and use the
200 yuan for purchases at merchants in the district (Xinhua Net 2020). Aside
from piloting the digital currency, this experiment is a way to encourage consumption in the wake of the COVID-19 recession, a novel kind of fiscal
stimulus. At the same time as the pilot test, the People's Bank of China is
lobbying the National People's Congress to make legal changes necessitated
by the new instrument, such as legislation to make the digital yuan a legal
form of money and to make any other issuance of digital yuan illegal (Helms
2020a).

The European Central Bank is exploring issuance of a digital euro and
recently called for comments from the public and financial institutions (Benjamin 2020). The call makes it clear that the bank's effort is defensive in
nature, in response to the possibility that some private entities will create a
digital euro and drive out central bank money.

As these and other pilots progress, the design concept may have to take
into account situations in which CBDC and other retail digital payment
platforms drive cash out of common usage. There may be some people who
cannot afford the necessary hardware, and others may have limited internet connectivity. For example, a survey found that 17 percent of the UK population, composed mostly of the poor and elderly, would struggle to cope in
a cashless society (Access to Cash Review 2019). Sweden dealt with this issue
by enacting legislation on January 1, 2020, requiring banks to provide adequate cash services, although it did not require merchants to accept cash
(Sveriges Riksbank 2020).

Central banks that are seriously exploring CBDC are using various techniques to bring user perspectives into the design process. Optimal user satisfaction and usability can also be achieved through product design processes

such as user-centered design and user experience analysis. For the Bank of Canada, this has included the use of surveys and focus groups of potential users (BoC 2020; Huynh and others 2020). According to Sun (2020) and Huynh and others (2020), the most important features to users, in descending order of importance, are low transaction costs, ease of use, affordability, and security perceptions. Engaging users (including merchants) throughout the design process can produce highly usable and accessible products, enhance robustness, promote adoption, and instill trust (Interaction Design Foundation 2019).

According to the Bank of England (BoE 2020), a number of attributes are key to CBDC success. The CBDC system should provide 24/7 payments, including offline payments under certain conditions, with no planned downtime, and should be able to recover quickly from operational disruption. It should be able to handle increased volume if demand for CBDC payments increases significantly. The payment process should finish quickly, and clearly confirm completion. Users should be able to make real-time peer-to-peer payments, and the process should be intuitive, requiring little technical literacy and using the fewest steps possible. The CBDC payment system should minimize barriers experienced by people with disabilities, as well as hardware or mobile data network access barriers. In addition, users should expect privacy and security in lawful transactions, and the system should conform with all relevant privacy laws and regulations. Any privacy costs of making payments in CBDC should be clear to all users.

More broadly, the design decisionmaking process starts with a comprehensive review of the financial integrity, cybersecurity, and privacy risks. Key issues like mitigation of the financial integrity and cybersecurity risks are not afterthoughts. Instead, they are drivers of architecture design decisions. The effective implementation of financial integrity measures is important in all cases. This entails ensuring compliance with the Financial Action Task Force standards and taking effective action to mitigate money laundering and terrorist financing risks. Cybersecurity across different product layers forms the basis for a reliable and resilient CBDC payment system that is resistant to fraud and cyberattacks. Incorporating flexibility into the architecture can support future-proofing the CBDC to account for changing user needs, regulations, and technology. A flexible design could reduce costs associated with required rework or upgrades of the operating model or design features the central bank chooses or needs to adopt. This type of architecture could allow a controlled open architecture enabling third parties, such as payment system providers, to integrate or build their own services on top of the CBDC platform. Such an open architecture could facilitate a competitive market for CBDC-related payment services, although its design should ensure that there are no structural factors that could lead to winner-take-all market dynamics for such provision (BoE 2020). It would also be useful if such payment systems were interoperable with each other and enabled prospective cross-border CBDC payments (more on this below).

REGULATION OF CROSS-BORDER DATA FLOWS

There is currently a lack of coordination and depth to the regulation of cross-border data flows. *Cross-border data flows* refers to the movement or transfer of information between computer servers across national borders. Such data flows are increasingly fundamental to the operation of a modern economy. They enable people to transmit information for online communication, track and manage global supply chains, share research, provide cross-border services including financial services, and support technological innovation. Cross-border data flows go well beyond fintech, but such flows are the foundation for the global development of fintech.

The three biggest economies in the world—the United States, the European Union, and China—are taking different approaches to cross-border data flows (Meltzer 2020). For the United States, ensuring open cross-border data flows has been an objective in recent trade agreements and in broader US international trade policy. The free flow of personal data, however, has raised security and privacy concerns. US trade policy has traditionally sought to balance the need for cross-border data flows, which often include personal data, with online privacy and security. There have been a number of efforts in the US Congress to legislate better protection of personal data privacy, but so far no consensus has emerged.

Recent incidents of private information being shared or exposed have heightened public awareness of the risks posed to personal data stored online. Organizations value consumers' personal online data for a variety of reasons, such as analyzing marketing information and increasing the efficiency of transactions. In the realm of fintech, consumers' personal data can be used to analyze financial solvency and likelihood of repayment, enabling fintech companies that make loans to reduce the risk of default. Concerns are likely to grow as the amount of online data that companies collect and the level of global data flows expand. At the moment, there is no globally accepted standard or definition of data privacy in the online world, and there are no comprehensive binding multilateral rules specifically about cross-border data flows and privacy. Several international organizations, including the Organization for Economic Cooperation and Development (OECD), G-20, and the Asia Pacific Economic Cooperation forum have sought to develop guidelines and principles on data privacy and cross-border data flows, although they are not legally binding. Recent trade agreements such as the US-Mexico-Canada Agreement and the Trans-Pacific Partnership are establishing new enforceable trade rules and disciplines with a focus on allowing freer cross-border flows. Key provisions of these agreements include prohibitions on requirements for data localization and for sharing companies' proprietary source codes with regulators.

Countries vary in their data policies and laws; some focus on limiting access to online information by restricting the flow of data beyond a country's borders, aiming to protect domestic interests (e.g., constituents' privacy). However, these policies can also serve as protectionist measures. The European Union and China have established prescriptive rules on cross-border data flows and personal data from different perspectives. The EU General Data Protection Regulation is driven by privacy concerns; China is focused on security. While the United States and other countries work to define their respective national privacy strategies, many stakeholders seek a more global approach that would allow interoperability between differing national regimes to facilitate and remove discriminatory trade barriers to cross-border data flows. China's perspective on governing digital services and data is informed by its relatively closed domestic market for digital services, its data flow regulations (the most restrictive in the world), and Beijing's effort to shape the international environment to support its vision of data governance and digital services exports.

China maintains a relatively restricted market for digital services. The OECD digital services trade index (figure 13-2) shows barriers affecting trade in digitally enabled services categorized into five policy areas: infrastructure and connectivity, electronic transactions, payment systems, intellectual property rights, and other barriers. The higher the score, the greater the

FIGURE 13-2.   OECD Digital Services Trade Restrictiveness Index, 2020

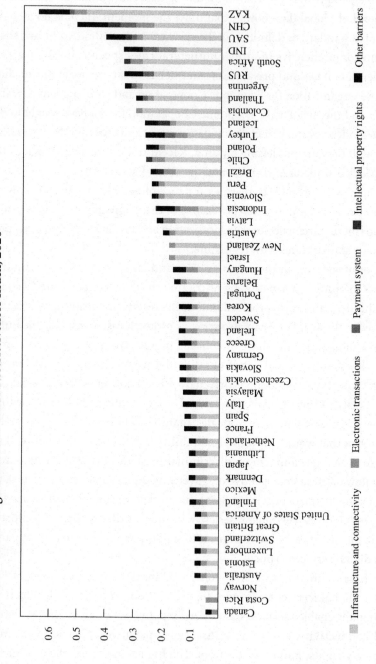

Source: OECD (2020).

restrictions. Among the listed countries, China is the second most restrictive (after Kazakhstan) when it comes to digital services across all metrics. For telecommunications services, China is the most restrictive (OECD 2020).

These restrictions are paired with domestic policy aimed at dominating emerging technologies, including industrial policies such as the National Medium and Long-Term Science and Technology Development Plan Outline (2006–2020) (MLP). The policy calls for China to become an innovation-oriented society by 2020 and a world leader in science and technology by 2050, based on developing capabilities for indigenous innovation. The Made in China 2025 initiative, launched in 2015, is a ten-year plan for China to achieve 70 percent self-sufficiency in strategic technologies such as advanced information technology, robotics, aircraft, new energy vehicles, new materials, and biotechnology. Similar industrial policies are also being implemented by subnational governments (Naughton 2021). The Made in China 2025 industrial policy was one factor leading to the US-China trade war. The plan is protectionist on the face of it and aimed at keeping foreign firms and foreign technology out of key sectors in China. Subsequently, in response to criticism from different partners and from within China itself, the government has moved away from the explicit targets in the blueprint in favor of a more general objective to become a leading R&D and innovation economy. The details of the 14th Five-Year Plan (2021–2025) will be important in determining whether China continues to open its economy and partner with foreign firms or strengthens inward-oriented tendencies.

China also employs extensive restrictions on access to and use of data, including data localization requirements and restrictions on movement of data across borders. It has the most restrictive regime for cross-border data flows among Asia Pacific Economic Cooperation countries. China's most restrictive cross-border data flow regulations govern security, internet access and control, and financial information. Such restrictions include a requirement for banks and insurers to localize data according to standards in China's cybersecurity law. In addition to restricting data flows, which affects access for digital services, these regulations could be used to access foreign companies' source codes and intellectual property under the guise of national security, which could then be appropriated by Chinese companies in order to compete against US and other foreign companies.[1] This is the most important area for negotiation and coordination between the United States and China. If the two can work out an acceptable compromise, then fintech firms will be able to work on both sides of the Pacific. If compromise is impossible, then separate systems will continue to develop.

Hence, going forward, a key question is whether China, the United States, and the European Union can work out a compromise to harmonize their different approaches to cross-border data flows. If they can, the global benefits are likely to be large, as it would open up new opportunities for cross-border trade, investment, and R&D. But if each governing body develops its own regulations and these prove incompatible, then we are likely to see increasingly compartmentalized cyberspace and fintech development.

THE CHALLENGE OF CROSS-BORDER PAYMENTS

While domestic payment systems face many challenges, they pale in comparison with the difficulties of cross-border payments. Under the 2020 Saudi Arabian presidency of the G-20, an important issue added to the global agenda was improving cross-border payments. Within the BIS, the Committee of Payments and Market Infrastructures was tasked with coming up with recommendations for improving cross-border payments (BIS, CPMI 2020). The slow speed and high cost of cross-border payments are a serious impediment to international trade and financial flows. Merchants involved in international trade face delays in receiving payments. Remittances from migrants have become an important source of finance for poor countries. The high cost and slow speed of transmitting remittances are a serious burden for the world's relatively poor population. The average transaction cost for a person-to-person transfer is 6 percent, about twice the level that the G-20 sees as a reasonable long-run aspiration (figure 13-3). Cross-border payments is an area with clear economies of scale. Costs drop from consumer-to-consumer (C2C) (6%) to consumer-to-business (C2B) (3.5%), business-to-consumer (B2C) (1.5%), and business-to-business (B2B) (0.1%). Large businesses bundle many transactions and send funds to a local affiliate or partner, options not available to people sending relatively small amounts.

The task force identified seven challenges and frictions concerning cross-border payments, which affect both retail and wholesale payments (BIS, CPMI 2020, p. 4):

1. Long transaction chains involving multiple players and often multiple currencies

FIGURE 13-3. **Revenue Margin, 2017**

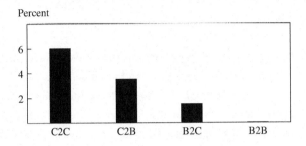

Source: McKinsey (2018).

2. Outdated technology platforms resulting in slow, batch processing and a lack of real-time monitoring

3. Limited operating hours resulting in processing delays, particularly in corridors with large time-zone differences

4. Complexities in meeting compliance requirements around anti–money laundering/counterterrorist financing

5. Fragmented data processing resulting in a low rate of straight-through processing and automated reconciliation

6. Significant barriers to entry for intermediaries, resulting in a lack of competition and high margins

7. Requirements to pre-position funding, often across multiple currencies

Most of the recommendations of the task force apply to improving the existing bank-based international payments system. These recommendations fall into four broad categories: (1) develop common cross-border vision and targets: What are reasonable expectations in terms of time and costs for cross-border settlement? (2) coordinate regulatory, oversight, and supervisory frameworks across countries in order to reduce the costs of meeting multiple frameworks; (3) improve the existing payments infrastructure, including extending operating hours and pursuing interlinking of payments systems; and (4) increase data quality and harmonize data format across jurisdictions. The task force report also acknowledged the potential for fintech to make a contribution to enhanced cross-border payments, but viewed this as a long-term proposition:

> Recent advances in technology and innovation have created the potential for new payment infrastructures and arrangements that could be applied to cross-border payments. So far, these have not been implemented broadly; some are still in their design phase and others remain theoretical. Hence their potential to enhance cross-border payments cannot yet be fully assessed. The building blocks in this focus area are aimed at exploring the potential that new multilateral cross-border payment platforms and arrangements, central bank digital currencies (CBDCs) and so called global "stablecoins" could offer for enhancing cross-border payments. This focus area is more exploratory than the others and is likely to be on a longer trajectory. (BIS 2020, p. 4)

Some progress has been made in the use of fintech for international payments as Chinese travelers go abroad and foreigners visit China. Initially, foreign visitors were not eligible to use Alipay and WeChat Pay because they required a link to a local bank account and a local phone number. Recently, however, these mobile payments services have developed international versions in which a foreigner can register for ninety days of use with an international phone and an international credit card. This is a convenience, given that many retail establishments no longer take cash and never took international credit cards directly. But this system is not efficient, as foreigners are essentially using international credit cards with all the associated fees and then adding on an additional mobile transaction fee. Some progress has also been made in the other direction: as Chinese travelers increasingly go abroad, Royal Caribbean cruise lines and many retail establishments in Las Vegas and Los Angeles have begun using Chinese mobile payments services. But the transaction still goes through the international banking system, as the Chinese purchaser draws down a yuan account and the merchant receives dollars. As long as multiple currencies are involved, it is hard to sidestep the traditional slow, expensive bank-based payments system.

The same problem exists with the CBDC experiments. Although today's CBDC projects and pilots are primarily focused on domestic payments (Auer, Haene, and Holden 2020), some bilateral experiments have been started in an effort to demonstrate the feasibility of using CBDCs for cross-border payments (e.g., ECB and BoJ 2019; BoC and MAS 2019; BoT and HKMA 2020). CBDC could be used for cross-border payments in several ways. To avoid the expensive step of currency transformation, a domestic CBDC could be used for payments from, to, and perhaps even within another currency area. This might lower transaction costs and facilitate efficiency, but it would also create risks for the foreign jurisdiction. Fundamental issues are whether the holding of CBDC is anonymous or in accounts with real names, and whether foreign entities can hold CBDC. The two questions are interlinked: if CBDCs are anonymous, then it would be impossible to prevent foreign entities from ownership. If the holdings are linked to real identities, there would still be pros and cons to foreign ownership. If existing reserve currency countries like the United States issue CBDC that can be held by foreigners, then that currency is likely to drive out domestic currency in many developing countries with weak institutions and at best short records of macroeconomic stability. Many countries around the world already struggle with problems of dollarization, even though the use of cash is costly and cumbersome. Imagine a world in which agents could almost costlessly shift into dollars and use them for trade and investment. Problems of dollarization would only accelerate.

With this kind of CBDC, capital flight and contagion at the macroeconomic level and bank runs at the microeconomic level would be much more common. Authorities would have a difficult time imposing capital controls if the payments system avoided the banking system completely. For all of these reasons, it is unlikely that major currencies would have CBDC that could be owned by foreigners. This means that cross-border payments via CBDC would have to go through two or more currencies, as is the case now. Thus, it seems inevitable that any widely used CBDC will be tied to the existing bank-based system and not bring about radical change.

Even if CBDCs are held domestically, CBDC systems could still be designed with an eye toward interoperability—that is, the ability to facilitate cross-border and cross-currency payments. *Interoperability* is a broad term and potentially covers a range of ways that payments systems or arrangements can interact with one another. At a basic technical level, interoperability would reduce the barriers to membership of both systems—for example, through common messaging standards and overlapping working hours. Moving beyond this, coordination between the systems can extend to common business arrangements, such as a designated settlement agent between the systems for certain payments. Another means is integration of the systems through an interoperable link where the infrastructures combine their functions (e.g., arrangements involving multiple CBDCs [Auer, Haene, and Holden 2020]). A future challenge with interoperability may be the number and diversity of payments systems domestically and internationally. CBDC systems will enter a crowded field of domestic payments systems, and interoperability can enable complementarity and coexistence.

For cross-border payments, closed-loop systems (e.g., global stablecoins) can potentially offer some efficiencies but only if they interoperate with others (CPMI 2018). Common international standards (such as ISO 20022) can help. Yet for CBDC systems, their additional functionalities and future designs may require enhancement of these standards and collaboration among central banks to develop them. Similarly, if CBDC systems are linked with supplementary systems and data services (e.g., digital identity repositories), then common international standards will be required for seamless cross-border payments. New systems based on different technologies (e.g., token based) may also present challenges. Interoperability between domestic CBDCs is, however, not just a question of technical design and work on common standards and interfaces. BIS (2020) describes five "focus areas" to improve cross-border payments, of which only one involves exploring new payment infrastructure. Different legal and regulatory frameworks present a significant obstacle to cross-border payments. Harmonizing these frameworks would be a challenge. Finally, monetary policy and financial stability implications related to cross-border CBDC arrangements need thorough analysis.

A CBDC that is convenient for cross-border payments could facilitate broad adoption. Giving tourists and foreign travelers easy access to such a platform could incentivize merchant acceptance. But it would require a special arrangement of temporary holdings for travelers. Otherwise, significant foreign holdings of a CBDC could result in stronger unintended international spillovers, as discussed earlier (Ferrari, Mehl, and Stracca 2020). Specifically, large-scale foreign holdings of CBDC could result in undesirable volatility in foreign exchange rates, "digital dollarization" for other countries, and, if laws and regulations are not equivalent, facilitation of tax avoidance and loss of oversight by domestic authorities. More research on the potential spillover risks and challenges of a cross-border CBDC is needed to better understand how to safely realize efficiencies.

CONCLUSION

The world is far from a seamless system of international payments via fintech. The current collaboration among the IMF, BIS, and other international bodies is working well. Countries are learning from each other about developing and regulating domestic payments via fintech companies that sidestep the banking system. Sharing data from experiments with CBDCs is particularly common. This aspect of international cooperation is relatively costless for each participant and of mutual benefit. It will be more difficult to move from this type of sharing to collaborative development of international fintech, including global use of CBDCs.

The fundamental problem is that each country (or bloc, in the case of the eurozone) has its own currency, and all countries have some type of capital control. Even countries that we think of as having open capital accounts, such as the United States, have controls in the form of financial sanctions aimed at particular countries. The banking system is well set up to deal with currency exchange and compliance with financial rules and sanctions. It is hard to see how a global fintech company or group of companies could replicate what the banking system does for international payments.

That said, there is much potential for better coordination of the laws and regulations around fintech in order to make different domestic systems more compatible. Here the critical issue is cross-border data flows. The United States, European Union, and China are each developing different approaches, which will make international coordination more difficult. If, alternatively, the three could compromise and find a common way forward, that would create a better foundation for making international payments more efficient.

NOTE

1. A. Viswanatha, K. O'Keeffe, and D. Volz, "U.S. Accuses Chinese Firm, Partner of Stealing Trade Secrets from Micron," *Wall Street Journal*, November 1, 2018, www.wsj.com/articles/u-s-accuses-two-firms-of-stealing-trade-secrets-from-micron -technology-1541093537?mod=article_inline.

REFERENCES

Access to Cash Review. 2019. *Access to Cash Review: Final Report*, https://www .accesstocash.org.uk/media/1087/final-report-final-web.pdf.

Auer, R., P. Haene, and H. Holden. 2020. "Multi CBDC Arrangements and the Future of Cross-Border Payments." BIS Paper 115. Basel, Switzerland: Bank for International Settlements.

Benjamin, G. 2020. "European Central Bank Is Consulting the Public on CBDC." Blockchain.News, October 13, 2020, https://blockchain.news/news/european -central-bank-consulting-the-public-on-cbdc.

BIS (Bank for International Settlements). 2020. *Central Bank Digital Currencies: Foundational Principles and Core Features.* Basel, Switzerland.

BIS, CPMI (Bank for International Settlements, Committee on Payments and Market Infrastructures). 2020. *Enhancing Cross-Border Payments.* Stage 3 Report to the G20. Basel, Switzerland.

BoC (Bank of Canada). 2020. "Contingency Planning for a Central Bank Digital Currency," February 25, https://www.bankofcanada.ca/2020/02/contingency -planning-central-bank-digital-currency/.

BoC and MAS (Bank of Canada and Monetary Authority of Singapore). 2019. *Enabling Cross-Border High Value Transfer Using Distributed Ledger Technologies,* May, https://www.mas.gov.sg/-/media/Jasper-Ubin-Design-Paper.pdf?la=en &hash=EF5857437C4857373A9287CD86F56D0E7C46E7FF.

BoE (Bank of England). 2020. "Central Bank Digital Currency: Opportunities, Challenges and Design." Discussion Paper. London, March.

BoT and HKMA (Bank of Thailand and Hong Kong Monetary Authority). 2020. *Inthanon-LionRock: Leveraging Distributed Ledger Technology to Increase Efficiency in Cross-Border Payments,* January, https://www.hkma.gov.hk/media /eng/doc/key-functions/financial-infrastructure/Report_on_Project_Inthanon -LionRock.pdf.

CPMI (Committee on Payments and Market Infrastructures). 2018. *Cross-Border Retail Payments,* February, https://www.bis.org/cpmi/publ/d173.pdf.

Diem Association. 2020. "White Paper," https://www.diem.com/en-us/white-paper/.

ECB and BoJ (European Central Bank and Bank of Japan). 2019. *Synchronised Cross-Border Payments,* June, https://www.ecb.europa.eu/paym/intro/publications /pdf/ecb.miptopical190604.en.pdf.

Ferrari, M., A. Mehl, and L. Stracca. 2020. "Central Bank Digital Currency in an Open Economy." Working Paper 2488. Frankfurt: European Central Bank, forthcoming.

Helms, K. 2020a. "China Drafts Law to Legalize Digital Yuan, Outlawing Competitors." Bitcoin.com, October 24, 2020, https://news.bitcoin.com/china-law-legalize -digital-yuan/.

———. 2020b. "Facebook Libra Redesigned: New System and Cryptocurrency to Comply with Regulations." Bitcoin.com, April 17, 2020, https://news.bitcoin.com /facebook-libra-new-cryptocurrency/.

Huynh, K., J. Molnar, O. Shcherbakov, and Q. Yu. 2020. "Demand for Payment Services and Consumer Welfare: The Introduction of a Central Bank Digital Currency." Bank of Canada Staff Working Paper 2020-7. Ottawa: Bank of Canada.

Interaction Design Foundation. 2019. "User Centered Design," https://www.interaction
-design.org/literature/topics/user-centered-design (accessed October 14, 2021).

Khiaonarong, T., and D. Humphrey. 2019. "Cash Use across Countries and the Demand for Central Bank Digital Currency." IMF Working Paper WP/19/46.
Washington: International Monetary Fund.

Kiff, J., J. Alwazir, S. Davidovic, G. Huertas, A. Khan, T. Khiaonarong, M. Malaika,
H. Monroe, N. Sugimoto, H. Tourpe, and P. Zhou. 2020. "A Survey of Research
on Retail Central Bank Digital Currency." Working Paper 20-104. Washington:
International Monetary Fund.

McDonald, T. 2020. "Why G7 Ban on Facebook's Libra Is a Good Thing for Digital
Cash in the Long Run." *Financial News*, October 20, 2020, www.fnlondon.com
/articles/why-g7-ban-on-facebooks-libra-is-a-good-thing-for-digital-cash-in
-the-long-run-20201020.

McKinsey Global Institute. 2018. *A Vision for the Future of Cross-Border Payments*.

Meltzer, Joshua. 2020. "China's Digital Services Trade and Data Governance: How
Should the U.S. Respond?" Brookings China Global working paper, https://www
.brookings.edu/articles/chinas-digital-services-trade-and-data-governance
-how-should-the-united-states-respond/.

Naughton, Barry. 2021. *The Rise of China's Industrial Policy, 1978–2020*. Boulder,
CO: Lynne Rienner.

OECD (Organization for Economic Cooperation and Development). 2020. *OECD
Services Trade Restrictiveness Index: Policy Trends up to 2020*. January 2020,
www.oecd.org/trade/topics/services-trade/documents/oecd-stri-policy-trends
-up-to-2020.pdf.

Paul, K. 2019. "What Is Libra? All You Need to Know about Facebook's New Cryptocurrency." *The Guardian*, June 18, 2019, www.theguardian.com/technology
/2019/jun/18/what-is-libra-facebook-new-cryptocurrency.

Sun, T. 2020. "Preconditions for Digital Money Adoption—What Can We Learn
from Alipay?" IMF Working Paper, forthcoming.

Sveriges Riksbank. 2020. "Do We Have the Right to Pay in Cash?" In *Payments in
Sweden 2019*, https://www.riksbank.se/en-gb/payments--cash/payments-in
-sweden/payments-in-sweden-2019/the-payment-market-is-being-digitalised
/cash-use-in-constant-decline/do-we-have-the-right-to-pay-in-cash/.

Woetzel, J., J. Seong, K. Wang, J. Manyika, M. Chui, and W. Wong. 2017. "China's
Digital Economy: A Leading Global Force." Discussion Paper, August. McKinsey
Global Institute.

Xinhua Net. 2020. "China's Shenzhen to Issue 10 mln Digital Yuan in Pilot Program,"
October 10, 2020, www.xinhuanet.com/english/2020-10/10/c_139430180.htm.

Contributors

DAVID DOLLAR is a senior fellow in the John L. Thornton China Center at the Brookings Institution and host of the *Dollar & Sense* podcast on international trade. His most recent book is *China 2049*, coauthored with economists from Peking University. From 2009 to 2013 he was the US Treasury's economic and financial emissary to China, based in Beijing. Before his time at the Treasury, Dollar worked at the World Bank for twenty years, including five years as country director for China and Mongolia. During his time in the World Bank's research department, Dollar published articles and books on trade and growth, economic reform in the developing world, and aid effectiveness. He has a PhD in economics from NYU and a BA in Asian studies from Dartmouth College.

QIANG GONG is dean and professor of economics at Wenlan School of Business, Zhongnan University of Economics and Law, and a senior researcher at the Institution of Digital Finance of Peking University. He also serves as the vice chairman of China Information Economics Society. He received his PhD from Kellogg School of Business, Northwestern University. His research fields include digital economics and finance, and industrial organization, and his research has been published in leading academic journals including *Marketing*

Science and the *Journal of Banking & Finance.* He has won many awards, including the CFA Institute Asian Pacific Capital Market Research Award.

FENG GUO is an associate professor at the School of Public Economics and Administration, Shanghai University of Finance and Economics, and a guest research fellow at the Institute of Digital Finance, Peking University. Before this, he spent six years as a research fellow at the Shanghai Finance Institute, a nongovernment nonprofit think tank. Guo received his PhD in economics from Fudan University in 2015, his MA in economics from Shanghai University of Finance and Economics in 2010, and his BS in mathematics and finance from Sichuan University in 2007. His academic interests lie broadly in the digital economy and digital finance of China.

YIPING HUANG serves as deputy dean and Sinar Mas Chair Professor of Finance and Economics in the National School of Development, and director of the Institute of Digital Finance of Peking University, focusing on macroeconomic policy and financial reforms. Between June 2015 and 2018, Huang was a member of the Monetary Policy Committee of the People's Bank of China. Currently, he performs multiple roles as vice chairman of council at the Public Policy Research Center and research fellow at the Financial Research Center, both of which are affiliated with the Counsellors' Office of the State Council. As a director-level member of the Special Committee on Fintech Development and Research of the National Internet Finance Association of China and member of the Chinese Economists 50 Forum, he also chaired the academic committee of the China Finance 40 Forum. Huang also serves as editor in chief of the English journal *China Economic Journal* and vice editor of *Asian Economic Policy Review.*

ZHUO HUANG is assistant dean and associate professor of economics in the National School of Development at Peking University. He is also a deputy director and senior research fellow at the Institute of Digital Finance of Peking University. He graduated from Stanford University in 2011 with a PhD in economics. His primary research fields include financial economics, digital finance, and big-data finance.

AARON KLEIN is a senior fellow in economic studies at the Brookings Institution, where he focuses on financial regulation and technology. He coauthored *Understanding FinTech and Banking Law: A Practical Guide* and was coeditor of Thompson Reuters *FinTech Law Review*. Klein served as deputy assistant secretary of the US Treasury Department from 2009 through 2012 for economic policy. Before his appointment he was chief economist for the US Senate Banking, Housing, and Urban Affairs Committee for chairmen Chris Dodd and Paul Sarbanes.

ESWAR PRASAD is the Tolani Senior Professor of Trade Policy and professor of economics at Cornell University. He is also a senior fellow at the Brookings Institution, where he holds the New Century Chair in International Economics, and is a research associate at the National Bureau of Economic Research. He is a former head of the International Monetary Fund's China Division. Prasad is the author of *The Future of Money: How the Digital Revolution Is Transforming Currencies and Finance* (Harvard University Press, 2021), *Gaining Currency: The Rise of the Renminbi* (Oxford University Press, 2016), and *The Dollar Trap: How the U.S. Dollar Tightened Its Grip on Global Finance* (Princeton University Press, 2014).

YAN SHEN is deputy director of the Institute of Digital Finance and professor of economics at the National School of Development at Peking University. She obtained her PhD in economics from the University of Southern California in 2003 and is a member of the Econometric Society and the American Economic Association. She is the deputy director of the Ministry of Education–Peking University Human Capital and National Policy Research Center, and a member of the Standing Committee of the Chinese Institute of Quantitative Economics. She is also an anonymous reviewer for the *Journal of Econometrics*, *China Economic Review*, and *Economic Development and Cultural Change*. Her research areas include big data and internet finance, theoretical and empirical econometrics, microfinance, and socioeconomic status.

JINGYI WANG is a specialist at Alibaba and research fellow at the Institute of Digital Finance, Peking University. He received his bachelor's degree from the School of Electronic Engineering and Computer Science at Peking University and received his PhD from the National School of Development at Peking University in 2019. Before joining Alibaba, he was an assistant professor in the School of Finance at Central University of Finance and

Economics. His academic interests include the digital economy and fintech. He has published several papers in *China Economic Review* and distinguished Chinese journals.

XUN WANG currently serves as associate research professor at the National School of Development and senior research fellow at the Institute of Digital Finance of Peking University. He served as a postdoctoral research fellow at the Stockholm China Economic Research Institute of Stockholm School of Economics from September 2011 to July 2013. He received his PhD in economics from the China Center for Economic Research, Peking University, in 2011. His research focuses on financial liberalization, financial regulation, and digital finance. He has published academic papers in *China Economic Review, Journal of the Asia Pacific Economy, Oxford Bulletin of Economic & Statistics*, and *Asian Economic Papers*.

XUANLI XIE is associate professor of strategic management at the National School of Development at Peking University. She received her PhD in strategic management from the University of North Carolina at Chapel Hill, and her MA and BA from Peking University. Her research interests include innovation, entrepreneurship, corporate governance, and international business.

YUAN XU is an associate professor at the National School of Development, Peking University. He is also a senior fellow at the Institute of Digital Finance of Peking University. Before joining Peking University, he taught at the University of Hong Kong and McGill University. He received his PhD in economics from Duke University. Xu's research interests include macroeconomic evolution and economic reform in China, and Chinese financial markets. Xu conducts in-depth research into China's macroeconomy, urbanization, real estate market, exchange rate, and digital currency. His research has appeared in the *Journal of Finance, Review of Finance*, and *Journal of Empirical Finance*, among others.

XUN ZHANG is an associate professor in the Department of Financial Statistics, Beijing Normal University, and senior research fellow at the Institute of Digital Finance, Peking University. His research interests cover development economics and digital finance. He has published several papers in

China Economic Review, Contemporary Economic Policy, and *World Economy.* Most of his papers written in Chinese have been published in distinguished Chinese journals, namely, *Economic Research Journal, Management World, China Economic Quarterly,* and *Journal of World Economy.* He also has cooperated with the Asian Development Bank, People's Bank of China, and United Nations ESCAP regarding sustainable economic development.

Index